Applied Linguistics and Knowledge Transfer

Linguistic Insights

Studies in Language and Communication

Edited by Maurizio Gotti,
University of Bergamo

Volume 268

PETER LANG
Bern · Berlin · Bruxelles · New York · Oxford

Ana Bocanegra-Valle (ed.)

Applied Linguistics and Knowledge Transfer

Employability, Internationalisation and Social Challenges

PETER LANG
Bern · Berlin · Bruxelles · New York · Oxford

Bibliographic information published by die Deutsche Nationalbibliothek
Die Deutsche Nationalbibliothek lists this publication in the Deutsche Nationalbibliografie; detailed bibliographic data is available on the Internet at ‹http://dnb.d-nb.de›.

Library of Congress Cataloging-in-Publication Data
A CPI catalog record for this book has been applied for at the Library of Congress.

ISSN 1424-8689
E-ISBN 978-3-0343-3718-2 (E-PDF)
E-ISBN 978-3-0343-3720-5 (MOBI)
ISBN 978-3-0343-3714-4 (Print)
E-ISBN 978-3-0343-3719-9 (EPUB)
DOI 10.3726/b16992

Wabernstrasse 40, CH-3007 Bern, Switzerland
bern@peterlang.com, www.peterlang.com

Acknowledgements

I am grateful to all the contributing authors for their commitment and hard work and to the reviewers of the initial proposals for their thoughtful comments. These are, in alphabetic order:

Isabel Alonso Belmonte
Irina Argüelles Álvarez
Raquel Criado Sánchez
Juan Antonio Cutillas Espinosa
Belén Díez Bedmar
Francisco Gallardo del Puerto
Honesto Herrera Soler
Ana Llinares García
Carmen Pérez-Llantada Auría
Inmaculada Pineda Hernández
Lourdes Pomposo Yanes
Hanna Skorczynska

I am also grateful for the guidance and efficient work of the editorial and production team at Peter Lang.

Finally, I would also like to thank the Spanish Association of Applied Linguistics (AESLA) for their support in this project and for making this publication opportunity possible.

Contents

Ana Bocanegra-Valle

Applied Linguistics at the Interface between Scholarly Research and Society[1]

1 Introduction

As a well-established area of study and research, Applied Linguistics can contribute to enhancing economic growth and societal well-being by facing today's social challenges and integrating employability, internationalisation[2] initiatives and knowledge transfer issues across higher education and elsewhere. This volume aims to first raise awareness of the significant contribution of Applied Linguistics to these key issues and then explore the challenges which scholars, researchers and students need to address when trying to build successful and sustainable collaboration between universities, industry and the public sector in national, transnational and international contexts.

The different approaches undertaken throughout the chapters (theoretical, quantitative and qualitative) make the book potentially interesting for a diverse group of readers. First, it will appeal to graduate (masters' and PhD) students working in the field of Applied Linguistics, and then, to novice and established scholars in need of new research themes or in need of connecting the key areas of enquiry addressed in this volume with their current work. It also provides clear pointers

1 The introduction and edition of this volume is a contribution to project "Ecologies of genres and ecologies of languages: an analysis of the dynamics of local, cross-border and international scientific communication" (FFI2015-68638-R MINECO/FEDER, EU) funded by the Spanish Ministry of Economy and Competitiveness and the European Social Fund.

2 In this volume, I will be using the British English spelling for the term "internationalisation"; however, authors' choice for either the British or the American English spellings (that is, "internationalization") has been respected for both original chapters and references.

for policy makers, education providers and curriculum developers in charge of implementing content in higher education programmes and endorsing university degrees with skills and competences in line with today's job market and social demands.

2 Key areas of enquiry in Applied Linguistics today

This volume provides an overview of themes that connect the work of applied linguists with learning, living and working today. The themes of knowledge transfer, internationalisation, employability and social challenges cut across the chapters in this book to show the significant contribution of Applied Linguistics to these emergent areas of enquiry. These areas intertwine and relate to each other in many ways (see Fig. 1-1); thereby, building complex connections that, as the chapters in this volume attest, are of benefit to the advancement of Applied Linguistics research. These connections are explained below following the organisation of the parts and chapters in the book.

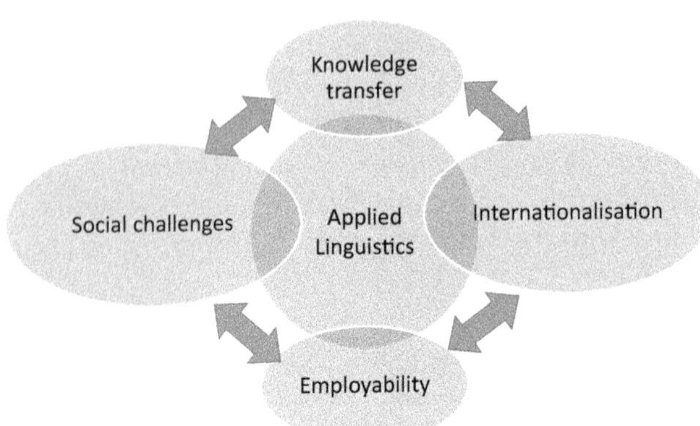

Fig. 1-1: Key areas of enquiry in current Applied Linguistics research.

The first area of enquiry that is discussed in this volume con-rns *knowledge transfer*. Following the University of Cambridge's nition:

> Knowledge transfer (KT) is a term used to encompass a very broad range of activities to support mutually beneficial collaborations between universities, business and the public sector. It's all about the transfer of tangible and intellectual property, expertise, learning and skills between academia and the non-academic community. (University of Cambridge 2009: n.p.)

Thus, knowledge transfer encompasses a two-way exchange process, thanks to which researchers can gain new perspectives on possible directions and approaches for research, and the non-academic community can get an important return that is converted into economic growth and societal well-being (University of Cambridge 2009).

The notion of knowledge transfer is often associated with other terms like knowledge management, knowledge sharing, innovation and entrepreneurship, probably because (i) they all show ways for academic and non-academic communities' mutual acquaintance and collaboration; and (ii) they all entail a wide variety of channels through which knowledge and technology are shared and transferred from research institutions to industry and vice versa.

Knowledge transfer can be attained at the local, regional, national, transnational and international level, and particularly universities and research institutions endeavour to build collaborative networks that enhance the outcomes of such transfer. Knowledge transfer has been identified as a key strategy in universities' mission and, more recently, as an indicator of the internationality of the institution (Kuenssberg 2011; Arias-Coello/Simon-Martin/Sanchez-Molero 2018; Bocanegra-Valle 2018, 2019).

The processes, origins and outcomes of *internationalisation* have become a key area of enquiry often associated in educational contexts with teaching and learning processes. In this volume, however, internationalisation is viewed as a more overarching driver for higher education institutions; in particular, as what Hudzik has defined as *comprehensive internationalization*:

> Comprehensive internationalization is the means by which higher education institutions respond to widening and more complex expectations to connect globally across all missions to better serve students, clientele, and society in a twenty-first century context. In brief, comprehensive internationalization seeks to mainstream access of all institutional clientele to international, global, and comparative content and perspective. (Hudzik 2015: 1)

The international dimension of higher education has lately grown in scope, scale and value with its benefits, risks and unintended consequences (Knight 2012). As a process, internationalisation evolves by adapting its approaches to the priorities of national and local educational contexts. In this volume, the contribution of internationalisation to achieving priorities such as knowledge transfer and social goals is discussed.

The connection between knowledge transfer and internationalisation has been noted by scholars like Teichler (2004), who contends that knowledge transfer is one of the three areas of learning and research related to internationalisation; the impact of internationalisation, however, will vary substantially by academic discipline:

> Knowledge in normal disciplines (i.e., not specialised on international issues) is more frequently, more intensively and more rapidly transferred from one country to the other. This is undertaken […] through various means, notably through media (books, electronic media and similar means), physical mobility (conferences, study abroad, academic staff exchange, etc.), joint curricula and research projects as well as trans-national education. (Teichler 2004: 10–11)

The third area of enquiry discussed in this book is *social challenges*, among which *employability* stand out. Employability means "having a set of skills, knowledge, understanding and personal attributes that make a person more likely to choose and secure occupations in which they can be satisfied and successful" (Dacre Pool/Sewell 2007: 280). A person's employability very much depends on what that person knows (i.e., his/her knowledge), and on what that person is able to do with such knowledge (i.e., his/her skills). Applied Linguistics can positively contribute to the development of the knowledge and skills required in employment-related contexts.

Current reports emphasize that the unacceptably high rates of youth unemployment across the European Union are mainly due to employers' dissatisfaction with applicants' skills, rather than to the lack of availability of jobs in the continent. By way of example, 27 % of vacancies were left open in 2014 because employers could not find employees with the right skills and more than half of employers were dissatisfied by their workforce's skill levels (Mourshed/Patel/Suder 2014). For the European Union, this percentage rises to 40 % (European Commission 2016). However, and interestingly enough, 74 % of education providers "were confident that their graduates were prepared for work" (Mourshed/Patel/Suder 2014: 2). This not only shows the disparities between job market needs and the training offered, but is a clear indicator for education providers and policy makers to provide solutions that allow graduates to build the core and transversal (also, transferable) skills that are expected and required to grow in the labour market – in this book some of them are: foreign language skills, pronunciation skills, literacy skills, intercultural skills, knowledge transfer skills or entrepreneurial skills.

The connection between internationalisation and employability has attracted the attention of current literature (e.g., Jones 2013, 2016; Brandenburg 2014; Ripmeester 2016; Coelen/Gribble 2020) and is also put forward in this volume. There are many factors that make a student globally employable, and thanks to the so-called *international experience* (Jones 2013) many graduates have the possibility of becoming equipped with the transferable skills required in today's job market. As recently reported in different contexts around the world (see Coelen/Gribble 2020), international experiences of all kinds (i.e., transnational education, internationalisation at home, intra-degree mobility or learning abroad, and full degree mobility) contribute to aligning graduates' transversal skills with those skills sought and valued by employers. The internationalisation of higher education is, thus, partly viewed as "a response to work environments which are increasingly globally integrated" (Gribble/Coelen 2020: 1).

Very probably, the possibility of students spending a time period of study abroad (via mobility programmes) has been at the centre of most discussions regarding higher education internationalisation and employability. The European Commission (see Brandenburg 2014) investigated the effects of Erasmus mobility programmes upon students' skills and employability, and gathered 78,891 responses to a number of surveys distributed among higher education institutions and employers across 34 countries. The Commission's main findings revealed that "Erasmus students are in better position to find their first job and to enhance their career development" (Brandenburg 2014: 14), and data showed that:

- on average, mobility students have better employability skills after a stay abroad than 70 % of all students;

- 81 % of Erasmus students perceive an improvement in their transversal skills upon return; and
- 64 % of employers consider an international experience as important for recruitment, and 92 % are looking for transversal skills that are developed thanks to the international experience.

Nevertheless, as already noted, internationalisation is viewed in this volume as comprehensive; therefore, it extends the scope of internationalisation beyond mobility programmes to embrace other activities, some of them developed at a local level, that show the thrust and the many facets of this area of enquiry. Part two in this book also shows that internationalisation is not just a students' issue, but also concerns staff and academics.

Besides increasing employability rates and enhancing labour quality, today's society has many other social challenges that need to be addressed: climate change, precarity and poverty, government transparency and corruption, religious and large scale conflicts, aging and discrimination, birth rate, fake information, to name a few. Applied Linguistics does also have to add to the investigation of these social changes. In this volume, migration mobility and gender inequality are two challenges covered from the viewpoint of how discourse is constructed (by young people and experts) to either boost or reduce its impact on public opinion and society in general.

3 Structure, themes and contents of this volume

This volume brings together research on current key areas within Applied Linguistics: knowledge transfer, internationalisation and social challenges (including employability as, very probably, one of the most important challenges today). As noted in the introduction, these are not independent, but overlapping areas, and the twelve chapters in this volume have been organised according to the intention that prevails or features most prominently in each study.

3.1 Knowledge transfer

The first part contains four chapters that show the very diverse opportunities that knowledge transfer dynamics can offer to Applied Linguistics researchers. Chapter one aims to demonstrate that linguistics currently offers promising avenues of research, with application in a variety of disciplines ranging from computational science to biomedicine. Ricardo Mairal-Usón and Pamela Faber examine the ways Applied Linguistics can contribute to the new social challenges of this 21st century as defined in two relevant documents (the 2030 Agenda for Sustainable Development and the Development of Sustainable Goals) adopted in 2015 by Heads of State and Government at a special United Nations summit. In particular, four key areas are discussed in depth: (i) the impact of the digital and information revolution upon discourse analysis, sociolinguistics, lexical semantics and pragmatics research as supported by Internet data and computation analysis tools; (ii) human-machine interaction as applied to text mining, speech recognition systems, intelligent search engines or sentiment analysis; (iii) the human brain and neurodegenerative diseases that cause major mental and linguistic deficits; (iv) biolinguistics and the evolution of language and biolinguistics.

A good example of how applied linguists and industry can develop their activities in view of mutually beneficial collaborations is found in chapter two. Here, Sven Tarp explores the application of information technologies to the writing and editing of texts either in a mother tongue or a foreign language. He focuses on digital integrated writing assistants as tools that are integrated into text-processing programmes and provide assistance to users when engaged in writing texts, speed up the process or support the learning of a new language. As detailed in this chapter, writing assistants work on digital devices (smartphones, tablets, etc.) and have several important functionalities. The work carried out and the usefulness of this tool are presented in Sections 5–7 of this chapter. Here, *Write Assistant*, a tool developed by the Danish high-tech company Ordbogen A/S (a provider of language services and online dictionaries), is presented and explained in detail. I truly believe that both lexicographers and dictionary users will find this chapter most illuminating given that, in Tarp's words, "[w]riting assistants are here to stay" (page 71).

Following on from this, Jonás Fouz-González looks into the relationship between Applied Linguistics and technology capabilities – this time, technology as implemented in language classrooms. By focusing on the mobile-assisted language learning offered by software applications, this chapter analyses the potential of a commercial smartphone app to first explore how technology can enhance pronunciation training in foreign language contexts. Then, Fouz-González explores learners' views about the usability and suitability of this particular app for autonomous foreign language learning, and gathers a number of recommendations on how to improve app-based training that can be useful to both teachers and app developers alike.

In the last chapter of this part, Carmen Sancho Guinda digs into entrepreneurship as one of the key lifelong learning competencies fostered in Europe by the Bologna Process and very often linked to notions like innovation and knowledge transfer. This chapter analyses student output at the very first stage of the ACTÚA-UPM contest (a competition of business ideas among schools and promoted by the Technical University of Madrid) so as to detect communicative needs and establish the bases for a permanent collaboration between language and content teachers. Sancho Guinda discusses the type of communication that is required and the register and tone that are expected in the contest forms, and takes three persuasive strategies from Classical Rhetoric (namely *logos*, *ethos*, *pathos*) as a baseline for her analysis of discursive features. Her main conclusion points at the stylistic hybridity of entrepreneurial discourse with features of *promotional interlanguage* – that is, "features of engineering writing (restrained persuasion and nominalisation), academic writing (little explicit evaluation, low emotivity, and formality) and computer-mediated communication (author foregrounding and emotional marketing)" (page 127).

3.2 *Internationalisation*

The second part brings together four chapters that make internationalisation the core of the discussions. This is appropriately opened by

Elspeth Jones, who builds on her extensive previous work on this topic to address the real and potential outcomes of a transformational form of internationalisation for higher education students living and working in multicultural societies in today's interconnected globalised world. Jones encourages us "to reflect on previous practice and to broaden internationalisation efforts from what may have been a rather narrow focus" (page 136) which extends beyond students' mobility programmes and includes all stakeholders. Thus, this chapter is an excellent example of how the key areas in this volume intersect. It explores the ways in which international experience developed through study, work placement or volunteering can develop the kinds of transversal skills that are highly sought and valued by employers. This idea is further developed with the examination of the role of languages in internationalisation and the window of opportunity offered by *interculturalisation at home* initiatives, which suggest that "language study is not the only route to intercultural communicative competence, nor is a period of study abroad a prerequisite" (page 151).

The next two chapters focus on internationalisation and mobility and address the current challenges posed by study abroad programmes for successful foreign language development. Carmen Carracelas-Juncal contends in her chapter that undergraduates can also learn outside formal education and, therefore, she brings to the fore the possibilities of service-learning as a complement to a study abroad curriculum. She analyses student gains after integrating service-learning into a host institution study abroad programme, a learning experience that often goes unrecognised. This service-learning course titled "Sociocultural immersion in Pamplona: Service learning and communication in Spanish" was initially organised as a conventional culture-related course and involved a small cohort of undergraduates. Students were allowed to choose between two services sites in the Spanish city of Pamplona that offer after-school support and include adult immigrants learning Spanish. Findings reveal that this internationalisation initiative is a welcome addition to the curriculum. As the author herself puts it, "engaging study abroad students in the host communities is crucial to their success" and, therefore, "service-learning should be added to host country institutions course offerings for international students" (page 177).

In line with Carracelas-Juncal's chapter and study abroad, Vasi Mocanu and Enric Llurda examine how European students involved in a study abroad programme construct and reconstruct their attitudes towards languages and language learning. They report on quantitative data from questionnaires administered among 155 international students enrolled in study abroad programmes in three different countries. The main themes under study are: imagined identities and European citizenship; multilingualism and language learning attitudes to languages; investment, expectations and perceived outcomes of the stay at personal, academic and professional levels; and, language use, linguistic practices, and perceived language-related outcomes. As these authors report, at the end of their stay, expectations and reality are different across the three student groups, particularly as far as social aspects are concerned and the role given to local languages vis-à-vis English language mastery and use.

A different focus of internationalisation, this time in connection with knowledge transfer, is the one presented in the last chapter of this second part. By adopting a qualitative approach, and with the aid of computer-assisted qualitative data analysis software, Oana Maria Carciu and Laura-Mihaela Muresan investigate the views of academics about the internationalisation of teaching, learning and research. Based on the connection between knowledge transfer, social changes and higher education internationalisation policies, this chapter aims to contribute to the understanding of how scholars perceive the impact (in particular, the opportunities and challenges) of internationalisation on their academic activities. The study data was gathered from ten interviews conducted among Romanian scholars, and the findings reveal the complex and multi-dimensional nature of internationalisation in academia.

3.3 Employability and social challenges

The third and last part of this volume comprises four chapters which cover some of the current challenges faced by today's society and to which Applied Linguistics can contribute positively.

Departing from the claim that "pronunciation communicates many types of information tied to utterance meaning and speaker identity" (page 225), Martha C. Pennington discusses on the importance of pronunciation as a factor in employability in international contexts. She illustrates how pronunciation can negatively affect intelligibility and fluency and, hence, communication and listener perceptions. Particularly interesting are sections 3 and 4 dealing with the ways pronunciation can impede intelligibility and performance in international and second-language communication. The examples given clearly illustrate how pronunciation-related features like pitch, intonation, voice quality, speed and pacing can cause communication difficulties and decrease comprehensibility with a negative impact upon job-related performance. Considering today's discussions that support English as a lingua franca for international communication purposes, particularly within the framework of multilingual educational policies in Europe, Pennington's discussion on accent and linguistic stereotyping may appear controversial as, so she claims, "[a]n accent which is accepted in one setting or for certain kinds of work can make a person unemployable in another setting or for other kinds of work, even if the person is understandable and highly qualified, for the fact that the accent is unfamiliar or is negatively valued, stereotyped or stigmatized" (page 234).

Following on from this, Troy B. Wiwczaroski and Mária Czellér explore the disparities between foreign language skills and job market needs and how they impact on employability rates. Even though the context of this study is the Hungarian city of Debrecen, readers might find some similarities with their own country, particularly if this is located in the European Higher Education Area. The authors make a case for large and small businesses in their context, and urge universities and policy makers to forge connections with local and regional employers, encourage dialogue, conduct needs assessments and match those skills offered by university degrees with those expected by employers.

On a different note, the next two chapters deal with migration and the role of women in the professions, two social challenges that are gaining momentum in the literature (Holmes/Meyerhoff 2008; Canagarajah 2017). First, Penny MacDonald and Llum Bracho investigate university students' attitudes towards immigration when writing in English. Together with unemployment, migration has been found to be a relevant concern among European citizens, and these authors have set to explore how attitudes towards migration are expressed by young people when using a second or foreign language. One hundred and fifty compositions written by both Spanish and incoming Erasmus exchange students were qualitatively analysed. Positive, negative and neutral positionings regarding migration were identified from the students' compositions; however, negative quotes were found to be greater in frequency and discourse strength. Moreover, disparities between Erasmus and Spanish students and gender differences across groups were also found.

Finally, in the last chapter of this volume, Silvia Molina-Plaza and Samira Allani adopt a multimodal text-based approach to reflect on the barriers women face in the professions in a predominantly male-supportive environment. This chapter explores the multimodal communicative strategies employed by The Women's Engineering Society (WES) to present women engineers as competent professionals and construct their professional identity. It begins by analysing how information is structured on the WES webpage; next, it examines the most salient elements which act as macro-Themes; after that, it focuses on the role models section – a part of the text which encourages other women to find out what it is like to be a woman in engineering, science and technology; lastly, on the basis of such multimodal approach and with the aim of illustrating the authors' claims, it discusses the cases of two woman engineers, Julia Yeomans and Abbie Hutty, a leading physicist and a mechanical engineer, respectively.

4 Concluding remarks

The studies developed across the twelve chapters in this volume reveal that Applied Linguistics is at the intersection of today's society needs, demands and challenges, and that it is the role of universities and higher education programmes to keep up with such challenges. As Mairal-Usón and Faber claim in the introduction to their chapter:

> [...] the humanities (particularly linguistics), is not in crisis, but can envisage an optimistic horizon of professional development, with new job profiles, which are clear indicators of employability and entrepreneurship. Quite another issue is whether universities currently provide students with academic programs that respond to the demands of the modern world. (Page 28)

This compilation of studies tries to foreground the potential that Applied Linguistics research holds for non-academic communities. For this purpose, it has placed centre-stage promising areas of enquiry which emerge as intersecting broad themes to connect the work developed in the field of Applied Linguistics research with today's society.

References

Arias-Coello, Alicia/Simon-Martin, Jose/Sanchez-Molero, Luis Gonzalo 2018. Mission Statements in Spanish Universities. *Studies in Higher Education*. DOI: 10.1080/03075079.2018.1512569

Bocanegra-Valle, Ana 2018. Promotional Discourse at Internationalised Universities: A Critical Discourse Analysis Approach. In Díaz Pérez, Francisco Javier/Moreno Moreno María Águeda (eds.) *Languages at the Crossroads: Training, Accreditation and Context of Use*. Jaén: Publicaciones de la Universidad de Jaén, 175–188.

Bocanegra-Valle, Ana 2019. University Mission Statements and the Projection of Internationalisation in the European Higher Education Area. Paper presented at the 37th International Conference of the Spanish Association of Applied Linguistics. University of Valladolid (Spain), March 27–29.

Brandenburg, Uwe (coord.) 2014. *The Erasmus Impact Study. Effects of Mobility on the Skills and Employability of Students and the Internationalisation of Higher Education Institutions*. Luxembourg: Publications of the European Union. <https://ec.europa.eu/programmes/erasmus-plus/sites/erasmusplus2/files/erasmus-impact_en.pdf>.

Canagarajah, Suresh (ed.) 2017. *The Routledge Handbook of Migration and Language*. New York: Routledge.

Coelen, Robert/Gribble, Cate (eds.) 2020. *Internationalization and Employability in Higher Education*. New York: Routledge.

Dacre Pool, Lorraine/Sewell, Peter 2007. The Key to Employability: Developing a Practical Model of Graduate Employability. *Education + Training* 49/4, 277–289.

European Commission 2016. *A New Skills Agenda for Europe. Working Together to Strengthen Human Capital, Employability and Competitiveness*. Report COM(2016) 381 final. <https://ec.europa.eu/social/BlobServlet?docId=15621&langId=en>.

Gribble, Cate/Coelen, Robert 2020. Introduction. In Coelen, Robert/Gribble, Cate (eds.) *Internationalization and Employability in Higher Education*. New York: Routledge, 1–7.

Holmes, Janet/Meyerhoff, Miriam (eds.) 2008. *The Handbook of Language and Gender*. Malden, MA: Blackwell Publishing.

Hudzik, John K. (ed.) 2015. *Comprehensive Internationalization. Institutional Pathways to Success*. London: Routledge.

Jones, Elspeth 2013. Internationalization and Employability: The Role of Intercultural Experiences in the Development of Transferable Skills. *Public Money & Management* 33/2, 95–104.

Jones, Elspeth 2016. Mobility, Graduate Employability and Local Internationalisation. In Jones, Elspeth/Coelen, Robert/Beelen, Jos/de Wit, Hans (eds.) *Global and Local Internationalization*. Rotterdam: Sense Publishers, 107–116.

Knight, Jane 2012. Five Truths about Internationalization. *International Higher Education* 69, 4–5.

Kuenssberg, Sally 2011. The Discourse of Self-Presentation in Scottish University Mission Statements. *Quality in Higher Education* 17/3, 279–298.

Mourshed, Mona/Patel, Jigar/Suder, Katrin 2014. *Education to Employment: Getting Europe's Youth into Work*. McKinsey Center for Government. <http://egdcfoundation.org/work/assets/McKinsey-Education-to-Employment-Europe.pdf>.

Ripmeester, Nannette 2016. Internationalisation and Employability. Making the Connection between Degree and the World of Work. In Jones, Elspeth/Coelen, Robert/Beelen, Jos/de Wit, Hans (eds.) *Global and Local Internationalization*. Rotterdam: Sense Publishers, 121–127.

Teichler, Ulrich 2004. The Changing Debate on Internationalisation of Higher Education. *Higher Education* 48/1: 5–26.

University of Cambridge 2009. *What is Knowledge Transfer?* < https://www.cam.ac.uk/research/news/what-is-knowledge-transfer>.

Part 1: Knowledge Transfer

Ricardo Mairal-Usón/Pamela Faber

Linguistic Research in the 21st Century: Looking Beyond[1]

1 Introduction

The 20th century witnessed a proliferation of linguistic theories that endeavored to explain the diversity of language and language structure in the world. Each theoretical approach had a different perspective. Some approaches were formal (e.g. Generative Grammar, Lexical Functional Grammar, Categorial Grammar, Head-Driven Phrase Structure Grammar); others were more functional (e.g. Van Dijk's Functional Grammar, Systemic Functional Grammar, Functional Typological Grammar, Emergent Grammar, and Role and Reference Grammar); and still other theories were cognitive (e.g. Cognitive Semantics, Frame Semantics, Conceptual Semantics – see Dirven/Ruiz de Mendoza 2010 for an overview). This intense research activity led to significant advances in the academic and linguistic world though its impact on the professional world was minimal, as reflected in the absence of linguistic initiatives in competitive knowledge transfer programs.

This lack of social projection is paradoxical given that language is an integral part of so many different knowledge areas. Evidently, linguistics should have a more central position in research agendas that target the social challenges defined in the following two documents: (i) Agenda 2030 (<https://www.agenda2030.gob.es/>); (ii) Development of Sustainable Goals (<https://sustainabledevelopment.un.org/>). Interestingly, some of

1 Financial support for this research has been provided by the Spanish Ministry of Economy, Competitiveness and Science, grants FFI2014-53788-C3-1-P and FFI2017-89127-P. We would also like to thank professors Mendívil Giro, Balari and Lorenzo and Benitez-Burraco for their valuable contributions and comments regarding Section 4. Of course, any errors or oversights still remaining are our responsibility.

the goals defined in these documents are directly related to spheres in which language has a prominent role. This is the case of human-machine interaction and artificial intelligence (AI), data mining and text mining, health, security, ageing and gender, as well as many others.

This chapter examines ways in which linguists can make important contributions to this new social setting and become key players in cutting-edge research scenarios. The following sections highlight the need for linguists to collaborate with researchers from other disciplines and vice versa. Since linguistic research in the 21st century covers a wide range of fields, multidisciplinary teams have become a necessity.

This chapter focuses on the following areas:

1) The digital and information revolution has produced a veritable social upheaval. It has given our society new prospects that far outweigh other potentially negative aspects. It has also provided people with new ways to interact and communicate, access to huge quantities of information that can be mined and processed, data collection and analytics, and finally the capabilities of machine learning with all that they entail. Within this new scenario, research into discourse analysis, sociolinguistics, lexical semantics, and pragmatics acquires a new dimension. The scope of analysis provided by the huge amounts of Internet data in combination with effective computational tools can offer innovative research possibilities and exciting new professional roles for students in the field of linguistics
2) Human-machine interaction came into the spotlight with the advent of artificial intelligence. The dramatic increase of computational power is most evident in data storage and availability, which are now over a thousand times greater than before. Thanks to more efficient algorithms, processing speed is also at least a hundred times faster. As observed by MIT's Tomaso Poggio (<www.youtube.com/watch?v=_svW8NV1A6k>), these improvements combine to endow computing with infinite power as reflected in applications such as the pedestrian detection vision systems in self-driving cars, speech recognition systems, intelligent search engines, text mining, sentiment analysis, etc. Since all of these projects involve language processing, the participation of linguists in this type of research is necessary and thus should be a non-issue.

3) Research into the human brain and the neurodegenerative diseases that cause major mental and linguistic deficits should also be a priority. Research in the 21st century increasingly targets the human brain. According to the Carnegie Melon Neuroscience Institute (<http://carnegieprize.ni.cmu.edu/>):

> […] understanding how the brain works is one of the biggest puzzles left for science to solve. Answers to critical questions in neuroscience lie at a pivotal intersection between biology, cognitive psychology, computer science, statistics, and engineering.

In our opinion, linguistics should also be included in this list of disciplines. Linguistic deficits are at the core of an array of neurodegenerative diseases (i.e. Alzheimer's, Parkinson's, Huntington's, dementia with Lewy body, corticobasal syndrome amyotrophic lateral sclerosis – see Boschi et al. 2017). Consequently, linguists are needed to participate in the creation of analytical tools to measure and evaluate the linguistic deficits associated with these diseases.

4) Linguistics can also converge with biological research. For example, biolinguistics is "the study of the biology of language" (Jenkins 2018: 4), and deals with how language has evolved over time (e.g. Berwick/Chomsky 2017; Boeckx/Grohmann 2018). Although the evolution of language has always been present since the work of Lennenberg in 1967, biolinguistics first came to the forefront as an orientation for generative grammar, which would more clearly differentiate it from linguistic theories that minimize the weight of biology in the design of human language and which mostly focus on the sociocultural dimension of language. Therefore, in the beginning, biolinguistics was simply an alternative denomination for a Chomskyan type of linguistic theory, which targeted the study of language from an internal perspective, in other words, language as perceived and understood in the individual rather than as transmitted and shared in the world or community. However, as time passed, biolinguistics diversified to become a highly interdisciplinary field.

In all of its various flavors (see Mendívil Giró 2014), biolinguistics now targets the biological foundations of language with the

> objective of characterizing the narrower phenotype. The strategy consists in trying to establish systematic relations between what we know about language (its structure and function) and what we know about the brain (its structure and function, evolution in the species, and childhood development). In this type of research, rules and constraints should be as few as possible, and they should be motivated by principles of efficiency and optimal computation.

These considerations indicate that the humanities (particularly linguistics) is not in crisis, but can envisage an optimistic horizon of professional development, with new job profiles, which are clear indicators of employability and entrepreneurship. Quite another issue is whether universities currently provide students with academic programs that respond to the demands of the modern world.

2 Linguistics and artificial intelligence

The information and telecommunications revolution is expected to continue for various decades. Deep learning and big data provide mechanisms to mine data in an intelligent way so as to provide accurate descriptions and predictions. In today's world, data storage and its intelligent data management is at the core of almost any aspect of society. This includes travel safety, medical records, public and private administration, architectural design, engineering, and the video game industry, among others.

2.1 Text mining

Over the years, the web has amassed huge quantities of digitally coded information, though recently this information has increased exponentially. Social media, smartphone sensors, digital channels, etc. now allow users to enter a new virtual landscape of shared data, where they are linked to each other in complex networks of relationships. This has given rise to social sensors and sentiment analysis, which are based on research in lexical semantics, discourse analysis, pragmatics, and sociolinguistics.

Sentiment analysis is an umbrella term for analyzing a piece of text. It initially referred to the analysis of large quantities of textual data based on meaning, as well as the positivity and negativity of these data. Large companies use sentiment analysis to measure the popularity of their products. This type of analysis is currently used to study meronymy discrimination, agreement detection, polarity classification, feature extraction, and subjectivity detection. It implements the principles of evaluation and axiology within the framework of natural language processing (NLP).

A sentiment analysis computer program is capable of reading large chunks of textual data and analyzing them based on a preset algorithm. A sentiment analyzer takes a page of text and generates an output by grading the entirety of the text's content. The output of the machine can be set to show percentages of positivity or negativity, and can underline opinion words to illustrate their degree of subjectivity.

Cambria et al. (2013) summarize the four most common methods used in opinion mining solutions: (i) keyword spotting; (ii) lexical affinity; (iii) statistical method; (iv) concept-based method. As shall be seen, all of these methods rely on some degree of linguistic and lexical analysis.

In keyword spotting, sentiment analysis systems use universal adjective and adverb lists. These lists contain the keywords that determine the affinity of a sentence. The affinities within these lists are marked as positive or negative. Positive and negative sentences are marked and then compared, and this gives the text-level polarity results.

The lexical affinity method uses affinity lists as keywords. Included in these lists are verbs, nouns, adjectives, and adverbs, which are then categorized. Each word in the list has a percentage of positivity, and the system calculates the occurrence count and percentage values of each word to obtain a result.

The third method is statistical. It relies on sentiment analysis data previously reviewed by a human. It assumes that these data sets are correct decisions and handles new input based on these data.

The concept-based method uses tailor-made keywords of a given genre and concept to extract the required sentiment data from the text. This keyword set also focuses on nouns. These nouns may include frequent terms of the subject. Concept-based methods also have rule sets, which permit certain words to be ignored, whereas others may have stronger effects.

In Spain, for example, the Technolengua (<http://tecnolengua.uma.es>) research group focuses on aspect-based sentiment analysis, which goes beyond the classification of documents, depending on their degree of polarity.[2] In their view, a theory-independent, application-oriented, data-driven approach is more flexible and does not impose unnecessary restrictions or limitations. The tools developed identify the polarity of the sentiment, emotions expressed in a message, identification of lexical features, and iconographic conditions by means of algorithms that categorize the documents (Moreno Ortiz 2016, 2017).

Social sensors are also valuable for the real-time detection of problems, and have a strong impact on the management of decision-making processes. For example, the automatic detection of hazards and disasters can be useful not only for citizens but also for companies and emergency responders.

This concern led to the design and development of CASPER (CAtegory- and Sentiment-based Problem FindER) by the LexiCom Research Group. This application analyzes English micro-texts (e.g. tweets) for the automatic detection of user-defined multi-domain problems. CASPER is able to detect hazardous and critical situations that could help guide emergency managers in decision-making (Periñán-Pascual/Arcas-Tunez 2019). For this purpose, it adopts a knowledge-based approach that requires no training, thus facilitating the portability of the system to new topic domains. An added value is that it classifies micro-texts with respect to a variety of problems and assesses each micro-text with a score that determines the reliability that a given micro-text actually deals with a certain problem.

This line of research can also be applied to discourse analysis, pragmatics, and sociolinguistics because it is capable of measuring feelings and attitudes of people based on the texts that they write. It thus opens up new horizons for linguists since it provides them with an almost

---

2 Another example of the positive result of a research transfer program, is a technology-based company <http://www.auduckcity.com>.

infinite number of texts to analyze as well as a wide range of computational tools that they can use to mine data and obtain objective evidence that verifies their assertions.

2.2 Intelligent systems and intelligent resources

The incorporation of world knowledge into AI/NLP systems is also an important research topic. Linguists are crucial here since many information-processing applications deal with natural language texts. Applications for intelligent information access or machine translation must be capable of going beneath the surface structure and processing the meaning of the texts. In this sense, knowledge-based NLP systems should not only have grammatical and semantic knowledge, but also domain or world knowledge (Mahesh/Nirenburg 1996). One way to do this is to take advantage of the knowledge in dictionaries or lexical databases. Not surprisingly, computer scientists are always seeking lexical resources (e.g. WordNet or formal ontologies) to make NLP systems more intelligent.

Precisely for this reason, electronic dictionaries are in great demand since they can be used to map word meaning systematically onto word use. However, digital lexical resources (at least in their current form) are not as yet up to the task. According to Hanks (2010), algorithms using electronic versions of current dictionaries designed for human users are still not sufficiently intelligent to enhance NLP systems (see Ide/Wilks 2006). Hierarchical lexical ontologies such as WordNet also have problems (Nirenburg 2007) and are not the panacea for NLP systems. According to Hanks (2010), such resources fail to meet the challenges of mapping meaning onto words, He suggests that meanings should be associated with both words and patterns in the sense of Hunston and Francis (2000) or with words and constructions in the sense of Goldberg (2006). This is still another area where computer scientists need the collaboration of linguists.

Conversely, NLP techniques are also valuable for linguists since they can be used to construct, maintain, and enrich lexical resources. This affects modeling linguistic phenomena such as terminology, definitions, phraseological units, or clustering techniques for subject areas. NLP techniques are also applicable to corpus compilation, corpus pattern analysis, and the extraction of semantic relations.

Evidently, the availability of large electronic corpora has dramatically changed the work of lexicographers. Modern monolingual and bilingual dictionaries are now created, thanks to the application of corpus-driven and corpus-based approaches (see Tognini-Bonelli 2001). This signifies that dictionary compilation can now be accelerated and certain processes performed automatically (Klosa 2010).

Thanks to the digital age, dictionaries have been liberated from the prison of space constraints. In fact, there is currently no limit on the range of information that a lexicographic resource can offer. Nevertheless, the vast potential of the electronic medium has not as yet been fully explored. According to Fuertes-Olivera (2016), only a few online dictionaries are substantially different from their printed counterparts. The majority are clones of their respective paper versions and only include the traditional inventory of grammatical, morphological, semantic and pragmatic information in their entries.

However, multimedia content can now be incorporated in dictionary entries. This allows users to view graphical resources, obtain contextual examples, visualize semantic networks, and access as many information modules as developers wish to create. Lexicographers need to *think outside the box* and take advantage of the innovative new capacities of e-dictionaries and lexical resources in general. This means presenting data in non-traditional ways, which are still another connection between computational science and linguistics. Linguists and computer scientists are thus obliged to work together in order to do the following: (i) use lexical resources for improving NLP; (ii) construct, maintain, and enrich lexical resources.

2.2.1 Intelligent lexical resources

Since approximately 2004, a popular trending topic is eLexicography. In fact, much has been published on the subject (Granger/Paquot 2010; Lew 2014; Kosem et al. 2015). However, there is still a certain lack of concrete results throughout the world.

In Spain, *Diccionarios Valladolid-UVa* is a project whose objective is the production of 28 dictionaries for Spanish and English (Fuertes-Olivera/Tarp/Sepstrup 2018). This project envisages an integrated dictionary portal composed of various three-component devices: (a) editors; (b) search engines; (c) dictionary interfaces. When these products are finished and made available, they will target both humans and machines. The assumption is that these resources will be of use for text decoding and text production. Accordingly, they should be the basis for interactive applications since information will also provide the algorithms used in a *Writing Assistant* (see Chapter "Integrated Writing Assistants and Their Possible Consequences for Foreign-Language Writing and Learning" by Tarp, this volume) and *Translation Assistant*. The project is based on the Function Theory of Lexicography (Bergenholz/Tarp 1995, 2003) and premises of computational science. The objectives of this project are evidently ambitious, and since the project is ongoing, it is still too early to evaluate the results.

2.2.2 Intelligent terminological resources

Still another interesting area of professional development lies in specialized language. Terminology work comprises the practices, activities, methods, and techniques related to collecting and describing terms, compiling terminological lexicons, establishing concept systems or ontologies, etc. (Kageura 2015). As such, terminology is a dynamic area of professional development since governments, international organizations, and private companies require high-quality terminology management in order to enhance their efficiency and cost-effectiveness.

The purpose of terminology work is not only to compile monolingual or multilingual dictionaries and databases in special subject domains. According to Steurs, De Wachter, and De Malsche (2015), terminology work plays a key role both in monolingual knowledge management processes, and in multilingual document management and translation work. As such, its role is crucial in information management and knowledge engineering. Knowledge management includes actions, such as creating information, using and re-using knowledge, and disseminating information (Van Heghe 2011).

There is, thus, a clear need for specialized language resources that involve considerably more than a list of terms belonging to a specialized domain. More specifically, an intelligent terminological resource should be based on an ontology that can be optimally used for knowledge acquisition, text understanding, and text generation.

EcoLexicon (<ecolexicon.ugr.es>) is a freely available multilingual terminological knowledge base (TKB) on the environment created by the LexiCon research group at the University of Granada (see Faber/León Aráuz/Reimerink 2014). Based on Frame-Based Terminology (Faber 2012, 2015), this resource provides an internally coherent information system covering a wide range of specialized linguistic and conceptual needs. The dynamic user-friendly interface combines conceptual, linguistic, and graphical information and is hosted in a relational database, linked to an ontology.

The knowledge base was initially implemented in Spanish, English, and German though some terms are now available in Modern Greek, Russian, French, and Dutch. So far it has 4,471 concepts and 23,529 terms. It is now widely used by translators, technical writers, environmental experts, etc., who wish to expand their knowledge of the environment for the purpose of text comprehension or generation

The research that produced EcoLexicon also led to EcoLexiCAT, a terminology-enhanced computer-assisted translation (CAT) tool that provides easy access to domain-specific terminological knowledge in context (León-Araúz/Reimerink/Faber 2017). EcoLexiCAT (temporarily hosted at <manila.ugr.es:9966>) is also freely available for any user interested in translating English or Spanish environmental texts. This application integrates all features of the professional translation workflow in a stand-alone interface where a source text is interactively enriched with terminological information (i.e. definitions, translations, images, compound terms, corpus access, etc.) from different external resources: (i) EcoLexicon, a multimodal and multilingual terminological knowledge base on the environment (Faber et al. 2016); (ii) BabelNet, an automatically constructed multilingual encyclopedic dictionary and semantic network (Navigli/Ponzetto 2012); (iii) the EcoLexicon English Corpus (EEC), powered by Sketch Engine, the well-known corpus query system (Kilgarriff et al. 2014); (iv) IATE, the multilingual glossary of the European Commission; and (v) other external resources that can be customized by users (i.e. Wikipedia, Wordreference, Linguee, etc.).

The Frame-based methodology for creating intelligent resources has been applied to spheres other than environmental science, namely military science as reflected in MiliMarco (<http://ecolexicon.ugr.es/milimarco/index.html>), an interactive knowledge base of military operations, doctrine, and principles.

2.2.3 The Semantic Web, ontology localization, and linked data

Well-structured lexical and terminological resources can provide valuable information for the Semantic Web, an extension of the current web in which information is given well-defined meaning, better enabling computers and people to work in cooperation (Berners-Lee/Hendler/Lassila 2001). As emphasized by Fu, Brennan and O'Sullivan (2010), the promise of the Semantic Web is that of a new way to organize, present and search information that is based on meaning and not just text. Ideally, language-independent knowledge could be accessible across different natural languages, which is how the Multilingual Semantic Web (MSW) is envisioned.

However, the Semantic Web is still essentially monolingual, and there is a growing need for multilingual resources that can help overcome communication barriers. This entails creating more high-quality multilingual resources and providing ways to link and share them (León-Araúz/Faber 2014).

Ontology localization has been identified as one of the main challenges of the MSW (Espinoza/Montiel-Ponsoda/Gómez-Pérez 2009; Gracia/Montiel-Ponsoda/Gómez-Pérez 2012). It has been defined as "the process of adapting a given ontology to the needs of a certain community, which can be characterized by a common language, a common culture". In this sense, terminology work encompasses the development of certain standard vocabularies and formats for data interoperability in combination with ontologies. Thus, the link between Terminology and knowledge representation is clear. In fact, its relevance in the field is now widely acknowledged (Buitelaar et al. 2011) because of the advent of multilingual ontologies.

Ontology indexes and repositories are key factors in the realization of the Semantic Web. As observed by Berners-Lee (2006), the Semantic Web is not just about putting data on the web. It is about making links so that a person or machine can explore the web of data. Linked Data is a method for publishing structured data using vocabularies that can be connected and interpreted by machines. By using Linked Data, statements encoded in triples can be spread across different websites. For example, Website A can present the entity *tsunami* and the fact that it can be generated by underwater earthquakes. Website B can provide all the information about the characteristics of tsunamis and their warning signs, and then Website C can show where tsunamis have recently occurred and the effects that they have produced.

Linked Data extends standard Web technologies to share information in a way that can be read automatically by computers. This enables data from different sources to be connected and queried to allow users to retrieve and manipulate data. Datasets such as DBpedia, Wikidata, and Geonames are all interlinked to form the Linked Open Data Cloud. Evidently, multilingual lexicographic resources can also benefit from Semantic Web technologies (Bosque-Gil et al. (2018).

Initiatives that permit semantic data-sharing include Simple Knowledge Organization System (SKOS) – see León-Araúz/Faber (2014) – and the Lexical Model for Ontologies (*lemon*) developed with the collaboration of researchers from the Technical University of Madrid (Aguado de Cea/Montiel-Ponsoda 2012; Montiel-Ponsoda et al. 2013).

3 Linguistics and health sciences

The study of the brain is one of the top research priorities in the 21st century. As is well known, language is one of its major functions. There are a number of different diseases and disorders (asperger, autism, dyslexia, epilepsy, etc.) that are directly linked to language deficits, each with different manifestations such as agrammatism, anomia, syntactic and morphological deficits, semantic paraphrasias, etc.

Clinical linguistics is a new discipline that targets these phenomena. Since its scope is so wide, this chapter focuses on the role that linguists and linguistics can play in the study of neurodegenerative diseases and the resection of low-grade gliomas (see Mairal-Usón 2020).

In the case of neurodegenerative diseases, the prevalence of dementia is expected to double between 2001 and 2040. In fact, dementia has been described as the greatest medical challenge of the 21st century with Alzheimer's disease accounting for up to 70 % of all dementia. Although Alzheimer's is regarded as a memory disorder, it also produces a severe deficit of language abilities which, according to Boschi et al. (2017), includes language impairment in the early stages of the disease (episodic memory), a decline in lexical semantic abilities, with anomias and semantic paraphasias, word comprehension, and verbal fluency impairment (semantic memory), and disorders at the pragmatic level of language processing, namely alteration in discourse planning. Moreover, as the disease progresses, severe language impairment becomes pervasive with speech restricted to echolalia and verbal stereotypes (Boschi et al. 2017).

Given that semantic memory loss is perhaps its most evident manifestation, the issue is whether this type of memory loss can actually be quantified, in other words, whether it can be analyzed, detailed, and scientifically measured. In this case, the challenge lies in identifying regular patterns that define this semantic deficit. According to Mortamais et al. (2017: 487), semantic memory is a fertile line of research:

> Compared to episodic memory, there has been little exploration of semantic memory, this being restricted principally to tasks of category fluency and naming.

This signifies finding answers for the following:

- How is semantic memory structured?
- Are verbs, nouns, adjectives, and adverbs stored in the same brain area, and how are they stored?
- When semantic memory deteriorates, what type of histological manifestations appears in a functional magnetic resonance imaging (fMRI)?

- What types of brain lesions (if any) are produced? Are the lesions different in patients that cannot retrieve nouns from those who cannot retrieve verbs?
- If one part of the brain is damaged, can the patient activate another route to find the answer?
- Do deficits in semantic memory stem from damage in the frontal and temporal lobes?

As for the methodology, neurolinguistic tests are the analytical tools that provide measures in relation to semantic memory loss. The most popular tests include the following: Boston Test (The Cookie Theft), Hayling test, CAMDEX-R, Alzheimer Disease Assessment Scale (ADAS), Abbreviated Barcelona Test, Mini Mental State Examination, Buscke's test, Vallecas Project, etc. All involve tasks based on single word or isolated sentence processing. However, more recent research has opted for connected speech tests. The analysis of connected speech provides data about all linguistic levels: phonetic, phonological, lexicosemantic, morpho-syntactic, syntactic, and discourse-pragmatic (Boschi et al. 2017).

More recently, in a more qualitative approach to semantic memory loss, the responses of Parkinson patients to the Hayling test were analyzed using text-mining techniques. Patterns accounting for the gradual loss of semantic memory and impairment of the executive function were identified, and new methodological procedures based on computational techniques were developed to improve the data analysis derived from the performance of patients during fluency and executive function tests (Mairal-Usón 2017). The results showed that it was possible to automatically assign and classify the patients' responses to the Hayling test, and thus use a scientific procedure that guaranteed that the score assigned to each question responded to a uniform analysis without human intervention.

Still another issue to explore is whether there is any correlation between this gradual semantic decline and the activity reported in an fMRI. A new methodology was thus proposed that combines linguistic findings with fMRI indicators plus biological markers.

> An increasing number of studies are combining biological, neuroimaging, and cognitive biomarkers in large cohorts to determine whether sequentially cognitive changes follow on from biomarker changes or whether they may be detected at an earlier and parallel stage using conventional testing. (Mortamais et al. 2017: 469).

This new methodology favors an interpretation of linguistic data in the light of the results obtained in biology and resonance images. This provides a unified picture of how the different factors involved in Alzheimer or Parkinson converge. In this new line of research, linguists work in close collaboration with neurologists, biologists, and radiologists.

Hence, the analysis of semantic memory loss in the sphere of neurodegenerative diseases opens up new venues of research for linguists. This means examining issues regarding the automation of tests by applying computational text-mining techniques, and also using a new methodology that combines fMRI results, biological markers, and linguistic traits.

The second area of research is related to oncological brain tumor resection in speech areas of the brain (Barcia et al. 2012; Rivera-Rivera et al. 2016; Duffau 2017). According to Barcia et al. (2012), intrinsic brain tumors are a pathology that generally has an extremely poor prognosis. The average survival of patients with a high-grade glioma (HGG) is about 12 months whereas average survival is even lower for patients with a low-grade glioma (Barcia, 2018). Not surprisingly, both groups have high levels of morbility from the disease as well as its treatments. Barcia et al. (2012) affirm that a residual volume of over 30 ml means a high risk of malignancy over time. This evidently worsens the prognosis, which means that radical resection is an important factor in its treatment.

The speech functions in the cerebral cortex near or within intrinsic brain tumors limit their complete resection since this would severely damage language comprehension and production. Nevertheless, a possible solution lies in the inhibition of the functions of these areas by means of cortical stimulation, and the simultaneous rehabilitation of the same functions so that other areas of the brain can take over and perform these functions (brain plasticity).[3] This would permit a more

3 In relation to brain plasticity, Pascual Leone at the Harvard Medical School and Andrés Lozano at the University of Toronto have conducted cutting-edge research into this topic though from a neurosurgical perspective.

radical resection of these tumors, minimize the functional deficits, and favor the patient's quality of life (see Barcia et al. 2012; Rivera-Rivera et al. 2016; Duffau 2017).

Within this context, there are many linguistic issues. For this reason, we began to collaborate with medical professionals in order to analyze the degree of linguistic recovery experienced by patients after this type of prehabilitation (Mairal-Usón 2017, 2020). In this regard, we focused on the following questions:

a) In the area of the brain tumor resection, if it is possible to replicate linguistic capacities in the right hemisphere of the brain to facilitate speech after surgery, what is the format of this new linguistic module?
b) What type of compensatory mechanisms can we provide so that patients do not lose their linguistic capacity after tumor resection?
c) In this replication of language functions in the right hemisphere, are there any differences between a monolingual and a bilingual brain or a child and an adult brain?
d) Is this change of function permanent or does language eventually return to the left hemisphere?
e) Is it possible to replicate 100 % of linguistic capacity or does one or more of the language components (i.e. syntax, semantics, phonetics, or pragmatics) experience loss?
f) Can resected patients still understand ambiguity, sarcasm, and/or irony?
g) Is this replication more successful when the patient speaks more than one language?

The answers to these research questions are the first step towards a more ambitious research program in neuroscience using the linguistic and computational tools developed in previous projects (Mairal-Usón 2020).

Finally, there are various research groups in Spain that are working on the application of linguistics to the health sciences, such as the *Instituto de Lingüística Aplicada* at the University of Cadiz directed by Casas Gómez (www.ila.uca.es) and the Basque Center on Cognition Brain and Language directed by Manuel Carreiras (<www.bcbl.eu/2017/10/master-in-cognitive-neuroscience-of-language>). In addition, Benítez-Burraco at the University of Seville is in the process of identifying the genes responsible for language deficits and disorders (Benítez-Burraco 2018; Murphy/Benítez-Burraco 2018: Niego/ Benítez-Burraco 2019). Other research groups in this area include the Seconds group (<www.seconds.edu.es>) and the FunGramKB (<www. fungramkb.com>) group as well as the research group headed by López García (2013) at the University of Valencia, which includes the work on aphasia by Hernández Sacristán and Serra. In this same line, Gallardo Paúls has compiled the Corpus PerLA (Perception, Language, and Aphasia) (<www.uv.es/perla/CorpusPerla.htm>), and Fernández Pérez and the Koine research group at the University of Santiago de Compostela are carrying out research on language deficits.

4 Linguistics and biology

Even though the evolution of language has always been a topic of interest, it came into limelight during the development of generative grammar. In this theoretical approach, linguistic models composed of complex rule systems gradually receded into the background. In fact, there are now good reasons to believe that the central component of human language is far simpler than was previously thought. According to Berwick and Chomsky (2017: 2), this is good news for both evolutionary biology and linguistics since:

> [....] the more narrowly defined the 'phenotype', literally the outward 'form that shows', the better our biological grip on how the phenotype would have evolved-and equally, the narrower the gap between us and the species that lack language.

For this reason, many scholars believe that the minimalist program is one of the driving forces behind the development of biolinguistics. The reason for this belief clearly lies in the fact that previous models (i.e. those in Aspects and Principles and Parameters), despite their high degree of descriptive adequacy, envisaged a language faculty that had myriad properties and an extremely complex structure. However, this does not coincide with how language is acquired. Berwick and Chomsky (2017: 6) affirm that the effortless acquisition of language by children, regardless of the language involved, is still a mystery.

The advantage of the minimalist program is that it simplifies previous premises in order to provide a total account of language (insofar as its nature, acquisition, usage, evolution, etc.) without reducing the empirical adequacy of the approach. This is far from simple because it means admitting that certain components of the language faculty are neither specifically human nor linguistic. Instead, they would be shared by other organisms and by other human cognitive capacities. The foundational proposal is that of Hauser, Chomsky, and Fitch (2002), and is based on the factorization in Chomsky (2005).

In the biolinguistic perspective of language, the genetic endowment (language-dependent principles) is reduced as much as possible by placing much of the theoretical burden on principles of economy and efficient computation. Both pertain to Chomsky's (2005) third factor, which involves the conditions that apply to the general cognitive system, and which are thus independent of the faculty of language. Evidently, if what is specific to human language can be reduced to simpler mechanisms or principles, it is more plausible to focus on the study of how these principles are implemented in the brain and how they arose during evolution (see Mendívil-Giró 2019).

According to Mendívil-Giró (personal communication), the most promising (though controversial) proposal is that of Berwick and Chomsky (2017), who state that the evolution of human language is a relatively recent and even sudden event that took place approximately 80,000 years ago. To a certain extent, it involved the innovation or new connection of a recursive computational system (known as the Merge operation) to a pre-existing intentional-conceptual system. In their opinion, this system was shared with our pre-linguistic ancestors and possibly other organisms as well. This gave rise to an internal language that connects with the sensory-motor system, also pre-existing and shared with other organisms, so that this internal language could be used for communication with other entities. This process is the externalization of language, and the subsequent model has been positively evaluated by researchers such as Tattersall (2019).

Within this framework, an interesting line of research is *the homological program* of Balari and Lorenzo (2017),[4] which targets the origin of evolutionary novelties (or new homologs). It is usually the case that *language* is (uncritically) taken to be an evolutionary novelty without actually defining precisely what is meant by this. The homological program provides the tools needed to do exactly this, and Balari and Lorenzo show that language has homologs in the natural world, where *homolog* is understood in the classical sense: "the same character in two animals under any variety of form and function" (Owen 1843: 379, cited in Balari/Lorenzo 2017).

Generally speaking, determining homolog relations involves the discovery of shared ontogenetic resources, which have been referred to in the literature as *Character Identity Networks* (ChINs). These networks participate in the construction of the character or organ in question. This is not only the case of the extremities of vertebrates (including fish) that share a ChIN, but also of the feathers, scales, and fur of different animals.

Accordingly, when Balari and Lorenzo state that language can have homologs, we can also affirm that the organ or nature X in species A can have homologs in species B, C, and D, which are present though perhaps with different functions and forms (e.g. feathers in birds, scales in fish and reptiles, and fur in mammals). The issue is whether it is possible to find a relevant ChIN. Consequently, if language is assumed to be an organ of our brain, that same organ, though perhaps with non-linguistic functions, may be present in the brains of other animals. It is a question of finding empirical evidence of homolog organs of language. Quite possibly, the answer lies in the genes that revolve around the *FOXP2* in humans and the corresponding ones in other species as well as their spatiotemporal expression. Their research seems to indicate that this is where the ChIN resides.

A second line of research is concerned with tracing the origins of language. Benítez Burraco (2018) uses published data on genetic differences between modern humans and Neanderthals to propose a model

4 Proyecto DALiV (Desarrollo, adquisición y mecanismos de variación lingüística), <http://pagines.uab.cat/daliv/ca>.

of human biology and culture that explains the appearance of language and human cultures (Murphy/Benítez Burraco 2018). Furthermore, this research has been applied to the treatment of language disorders from the perspective of evolutionary developmental biology (informally, *evodevo*), a field of biological research that compares the developmental processes of different organisms to infer the ancestral relationships between them and how developmental processes evolved. Hopefully, this will result in better diagnoses and more effective treatments.

Finally, though in a different line from the minimalist program and the biolinguistic perspective, it is necessary to mention the Department of Evolutionary Otoacoustics and Paleoanthropology, recently created by the HM Hospital Group and the University of Alcalá (UAH). The research conducted at the archeological site in Atapuerca on the anatomy and physiology of the inner and middle ear and its relation to the origin of human language may very well provide valuable insights into modern hearing pathologies such as deafness, which can be applied in modern medicine.

This new research institute will study the results obtained from this archeological research, which shows the evolution of the human ear and its direct relations with the appearance of language. The first objective is to continue investigating the Atapuerca site to ascertain the relation between language and hearing, and thus discover the evolutionary process that modified the human ear in order to adapt it to oral language. The second objective focuses on the evolution of the anatomy and physiology of the ear, and its applications in the field of otolaryngology to help patients who are deaf or hard of hearing or who suffer from other hearing pathologies.

5 Conclusions

This chapter has given an overview of the wide range of possibilities now open to linguists who wish to engage in multidisciplinary projects. Language is evidently a topic that overlaps with many different areas, and has far-reaching implications in the digital and information revolution, human and machine interaction, the human brain and neurodegenerative diseases, and evolutionary developmental biology, to mention a few. In our opinion, linguistic research in the 21st century should have a social vocation and play a leading role in a wide variety of projects that would foment progress and help to create a better world. Accordingly, the focus should be on interdisciplinary work that would involve collaboration with researchers from other fields.

Not surprisingly, linguistics has become a prominent area of research, which has applications in many disciplines ranging from computational science to biomedicine. Computer scientists, biologists, and medical researchers require the collaboration of linguists, who possess the knowledge of language necessary to explore phenomena such as semantic memory, knowledge representation, language deficits, and the evolution of the language faculty.

This chapter has also highlighted a selection of pioneering work currently being carried out in Spain. However, there are still far more questions than answers; the results obtained have barely scratched the surface. Precisely for this reason, more researchers are required. This means creating programs and fomenting awareness of the new horizons open to those with the right training. The key to the future thus lies in creating a context in which linguists are aware of the vast range of possibilities open to them. It is for universities to provide students with academic programs that respond to the demands of the modern world.

References

Aguado de Cea, Guadalupe/Montiel-Ponsoda, Elena 2012. Term Variants in Ontologies. In *Proceedings of the 30th Conference of AESLA*. Lleida: University of Lleida. <http://oa.upm.es/19602/1/INVE_MEM_2012_137765.pdf>

Balari, Sergio/Lorenzo, Guillermo 2017. What Lenneberg Got Right. A Homological Program for the Study of Language Evolution. *Biolinguistics* 11, 139–170.

Barcia, Juan A. 2018. *Brain Plasticity Applied to Subcortical Cerebral Tumors*. Unpublished lecture.

Barcia, Juan A./Sanz Cortés, Ana/Balugo, Paloma/Alonso-Lera, Pedro/Brin, Juan R./Yus, Miguel/González-Hidalgo, Mercedes/Acedo, Victoria M./Oliviero, Antonio 2012. High-Frequency Cortical Subdural Stimulation Enhanced Plasticity in Surgery of a Tumor in Brocas Area. *Neuroreport* 23/5, 304–309.

Benítez-Burraco, Antonio 2018. Genetics of Language: Roots of Specific Language Deficits. In Boecx, Cedric/Grohmann, Kelanthes K. (eds.) *Biolinguistics*. Cambridge: Cambridge University Press, 375–412.

Bergenholtz, Henning/Tarp, Sven (eds.) 1995. *Manual of Specialised Lexicography*. Amsterdam/Philadelphia: John Benjamins.

Bergenholtz, Henning/Tarp, Sven 2003. Two Opposing Theories: On H.E. Wiegand's Recent Discovery of Lexicographic Functions. *Hermes. Journal of Linguistics* 31, 171–196.

Berners-Lee, Tim. 2006. *Linked Data – Design Issues*. <http://www.w3.org/DesignIssues/LinkedData.html>.

Berners-Lee, Tim/Hendler, James/Lassila, Ora 2001. The Semantic Web. *Scientific American*, 17 May, 29–37.

Berwick, Robert C./Chomsky, Noam 2017. *Why Only Us. Language and Evolution*. Cambridge: MIT Press.

Boecx, Cedric/Grohmann, Kelanthes K. (eds.) 2018. *Biolinguistics*. Cambridge: Cambridge University Press.

Boschi, Veronica/Catricalà, Eleonora/Consonni, Monica/Chesi, Cristiano/Moro, Andrea/Cappa, Stefano F. 2017. Connected Speech in Neurodegenerative Language Disorders: A Review. *Frontiers in Psychology* 8, Article 269.

Bosque-Gil, Julia/Gracia, Jorge/Montiel-Ponsoda, Elena/Gómez-Pérez, Asunción 2018. Models to Represent Linguistic Linked Data. *Natural Language Engineering* 24/6, 811–859.

Buitelaar, Paul/Cimiano, Philipp/McCrae, John/Montiel-Ponsoda, Elena/Declerck, Thierry. 2011. Ontology Lexicalisation: The Lemon Perspective. In *Proceedings of the 9th International Conference on Terminology and Artificial Intelligence*, 33–36. <http://oa.upm.es/9772/1/Ontology_Lexicalisation.pdf>.

Cambria, Erik/Schuller, Björn/Xia Yunqing/Havasi, Catherine 2013. New Avenues in Opinion Mining and Sentiment Analysis. *IEEE Intelligent Systems* 28/2, 15–21.

Chomsky, Noam 2005. Three Factors in Language Design. *Linguistic Inquiry* 36/1, 1–22.

Dirven, René/Ruiz de Mendoza, Francisco J. 2010. Looking Back at 30 Years of Cognitive Linguistics. In Tabakowska, Elzbieta/Choinski, Michal/Wiraszka, Lukasz (eds.) *Cognitive Linguistics in Action: From Theory to Application and Back*. Berlin: De Gruyter, 13–70.

Duffau, Hugues. 2017. The Error of Broca: From the Traditional Localizationist Concept to a Connectomal Anatomy of Human Brain. *Journal of Chemical Neuroanatomy* 89, 73–81.

Espinoza, Mauricio/Montiel-Ponsoda, Elena/Gómez-Pérez, Asunción 2009. Ontology Localization. In *Proceedings of the Fifth International Conference on Knowledge Capture*, 33–40. <https://dl.acm.org/citation.cfm?id=1597735&picked=prox>

Faber, Pamela (ed.) 2012. *A Cognitive Linguistics View of Terminology and Specialized Language*. Berlin/New York: De Gruyter.

Faber, Pamela 2015. Frames as a Framework for Terminology. In Kockaert, Hendrik J./Steurs, Frieda (eds.) *Handbook of Terminology*, vol. 1. Amsterdam/Philadelphia: John Benjamins, 14–33.

Faber, Pamela/León-Araúz, Pilar/Reimerink, Arianne 2014. Representing Environmental Knowledge in EcoLexicon. In Bárcena, Elena/Read, Timothy/Arús, Jorge (eds.) *Languages for Specific Purposes in the Digital Era*. Berlin: Springer, 267–301.

Faber, Pamela/León-Araúz, Pilar/Reimerink, Arianne 2016. EcoLexicon: New Features and Challenges. In Kernerman, Ilan/Kosem, Iztok/Krek, Simon/Trap-Jensen, Lars (eds.) *GLOBALEX 2016: Lexicographic Resources for Human Language Technology*, 73–80. <http://www.lrec-conf.org/proceedings/lrec2016/workshops/LREC2016Workshop-GLOBALEX_Proceedings-v2.pdf>.

Fu, Bo/Brennan, Rob/O'Sullivan, Declan 2010. Cross-Lingual Ontology Mapping and Its Use on the Multilingual Semantic Web. In the *2nd Workshop on the Multilingual Semantic Web*, 13–20. <http://ceur-ws.org/Vol-571/paper3.pdf>.

Fuertes-Olivera, Pedro A. 2016. A Cambrian Explosion in Lexicography: Some Reflections for Designing and Constructing Specialised Online Dictionaries. *International Journal of Lexicography* 29/2, 226–247.

Fuertes-Olivera, Pedro/Tarp, Sven/Sepstrup, Peter 2018. New Insights in the Design and Compilation of Digital Bilingual Lexicographical Products: The Case of the *Diccionarios Valladolid–UVa*. *Lexikos* 28, 152–176.

Goldberg, Adele E. 2006. *Constructions at Work. The Nature of Generalization in Language*. Oxford: Oxford University Press.

Gracia, Jorge/Montiel-Ponsoda, Elena/Gómez-Pérez, Asunción 2012. Cross-Lingual Linking on the Multilingual Web of Data. In *Proceedings of the 3rd Workshop on the Multilingual Semantic Web*. <http://ceur-ws.org/Vol-936/paper6.pdf>.

Granger, Sylviane/Paquot, Magali (eds.) 2010. *eLexicography in the 21st Century: New Challenges, New Applications*. Louvain: UCL Presses Universitaires de Louvain.

Hanks, Patrick 2010. Elliptical Arguments: A Problem in Relating Meaning to Use. In Granger, Sylviane/Paquot, Magali (eds.) *eLexicography in the 21st Century: New Challenges, New Applications*. Louvain: UCL Presses Universitaires de Louvain, 109–124.

Hauser, Marc D./Chomsky, Noam/Fitch, W. Tecumseh 2002. The Faculty of Language: What Is It, Who Has It, and How Did It Evolve? *Science* 298, 1569–1579.

Hunston, Susan/Francis, Gill 2000. *Pattern Grammar*. Amsterdam/Philadelphia: John Benjamins.

Ide, Nancy/Wilks, Yorick 2006. Making Sense about Sense. In Agirre, Eneko/Edmonds, Philip (eds.) *Word Sense Disambiguation. Algorithms and Applications*. Berlin: Springer, 47–74.

Jenkins, Lyle 2018. Biolinguistics: A Historical Perspective. In Boecx, Cedric/Grohmann, Kelanthes K. (eds.) *Biolinguistics*. Cambridge: Cambridge University Press, 4–11.

Kageura, Kyo 2015. Terminology and Lexicography. In Kockaert, Hendrik J./Steurs, Frieda (eds.) *Handbook of Terminology*, vol. 1. Amsterdam/Philadelphia: John Benjamins, 45–59.

Kilgarriff, Adam/Baisa, Vít/Bušta, Jan/Jakubíček, Miloš/Kovář, Vojtech/Michelfeit, Jan/Rychlý, Pavel/Suchomel, Vít 2014. The Sketch Engine: Ten Years On. *Lexicography* 1/1, 7–36.

Klosa, Annette 2010. On the Combination of Automated Information and Lexicographically Interpreted Information in Two German Online Dictionaries. In Granger, Sylviane/Paquot, Magali (eds.) *eLexicography in the 21st Century: New Challenges, New Applications*. Louvain: UCL Presses Universitaires de Louvain, 157–164.

Kosem, Iztok/Jakubíček, Miloš/Kallas, Jelena/Krek, Simon (eds.) 2015. *Electronic Lexicography in the 21st Century: Linking Lexical Data in the Digital Age*. In *Proceedings of the eLex 2015 Conference, 11–13 August 2015, Herstmonceux Castle, United Kingdom*. Ljubljana/Brighton: Trojina, Institute for Applied Slovene Studies/Lexical Computing Ltd. <https://elex.link/elex2015/conference-proceedings/>.

Lennenberg, Eric H. 1967. *Biological Foundations of Language*. New York: Wiley and Sons.

León-Araúz, Pilar/Faber, Pamela 2014. Context and Terminology in the Multilingual Semantic Web. In Buitelaar, Paul/Cimiano, Philipp (eds.) *Towards the Multilingual Semantic Web*. Berlin/Heidelberg: Springer, 31–47.

León-Araúz, Pilar/Reimerink, Arianne/Faber, Pamela 2017. EcoLexiCAT: A Terminology-enhanced Translation Tool for Texts on the Environment. In Kosem, Iztok/Kallas, Jelena/Tiberius, C./Krek, Simon/Jakubíček, Miloš/Baisa, Vít (eds.) *Electronic Lexicography in the 21st Century. Proceedings of eLex 2017 Conference*, 321–341. <https://elex.link/elex2017/wp-content/uploads/2017/09/paper20.pdf>.

Lew, Robert 2014. How Can We Make Electronic Dictionaries More Effective? In Granger, Sylviane/Paquot, Magali (eds.) *Electronic Lexicography*. Oxford: Oxford University Press, 343–361.

López García, Ángel. 2013. *Los Mecanismos Neuronales del Lenguaje*. Valencia: Tirant Universidades.

Mahesh, Kavi/Nirenburg, Sergei 1996. *Knowledge-Based Systems for Natural Language Processing*. Las Cruces, NM: New Mexico State University, Computing Research Laboratory.

Mairal-Usón, Ricardo 2017. Constructing Meaning for Clinical and Computational Purposes. Paper presented at the *6th International Conference on Meaning and Knowledge Representation*. St. Petersburg, Russia.
Mairal-Usón, Ricardo. 2020. La lingüística clínica. *Revista Española de Lingüística* 49.
Mendívil Giró, José L. 2014. Biolingüística: Breve Biografía de una Disciplina Emergente. *ConCIENCIAS* 13, 34–46.
Mendívil-Giró, José L. 2019. How Much Data Does Linguistic Theory Need? On the Tolerance Principle of Linguistic Theorizing. *Frontiers in Communication/Language Sciences* 3, 62.
Montiel-Ponsoda, Elena/McCrae, John/Aguado-de-Cea, Guadalupe/Gracia, Jorge 2013. Multilingual Variation in the Context of Linked Data. In *10th International Conference on Terminology and Artificial Intelligence* (TIA'13), 19–26. <http://oa.upm.es/21494/1/MontielPonsodaEtAl2013.pdf>.
Moreno-Ortiz, Antonio. 2016. *Lingmotif 1.0 [Computer Software]*. Málaga: University of Málaga. <http://tecnolengua.uma.es/lingmotif>.
Moreno-Ortiz, Antonio. 2017. Lingmotif: A User-Focused Sentiment Analysis Tool. *Procesamiento del Lenguaje Natural* 58, 133–140.
Mortamais, Marion/Ash, Jessica A./Harrison, John/Kaye, Jeffrey/Kramer, Joel/Randolph, Christopher/Pose, Carine/Albala, Bruce/Ropacki, Michael/Ritchie, Craig W./Ritchie, Karen 2017. Detecting Cognitive Changes in Preclinical Alzheimer's Disease: A Review of its Feasibility. *Alzheimer's & Dementia* 13/4, 468–492.
Murphy, Elliot/Benítez-Burraco, Antonio 2018. Towards the Language Oscillogenome. *Frontiers in Psychology* 9, Article 1999.
Navigli, Roberto/Ponzetto, Simone P. 2012. BabelNet: The Automatic Construction, Evaluation and Application of a Wide-Coverage Multilingual Semantic Network. *Artificial Intelligence* 193, 217–250.
Niego, Amy/Benítez-Burraco, Antonio 2019. Williams Syndrome, Human Self-Domestication, and Language Evolution. *Frontiers in Psychology* 10, Article 521.

Nirenburg, Sergei 2007. Homer, the Author of the Iliad, and the Computational-Linguistic Turn. In Ahmad, Khurshid/Brewster, Christopher/Stevenson, Mark (eds.) *Words and Intelligence II. Essays in Honour of Yorick Wilks*. Dordrecht: Springer, 159–193.

Periñán-Pascual, Carlos/Arcas-Túnez, Francisco 2019. Detecting Environmentally-Related Problems on Twitter. *Biosystems Engineering* 177, 31–48.

Rivera-Rivera, Paola/Rios-Lago, Marcos/Sánchez-Casarrubios, Sandra/Salazar, Osman/Yus, Miguel/González-Hidalgo, Mercedes/Sanz, Ana/Avecillas-Chasin, Josué/Álvarez-Linera, Juan/Pascual-Leone, Álvaro/Oliviero, Antonio/Barcia, Juan A. 2016. Cortical Plasticity Catalyzed by Prehabilitation Enables Extensive Resection of Brain Tumors in Eloquent Areas. *Journal of Neurosurgery* 126/4, 1323–1333.

Steurs, Frieda/De Wachter, Ken/De Malsche, Evy 2015. Terminology Tools. In Kockaert, Hendrik J./Steurs, Frieda (eds.) *Handbook of Terminology*, vol. 1. Amsterdam/Philadelphia: John Benjamins, 232–249.

Tattersall, Ian 2019. The Minimalist Program and the Origin of Language: A View From Paleoanthropology. *Frontiers in Psychology* 10, Article 677.

Tognini-Bonelli, Elena 2001. *Corpus Linguistics at Work*. Amsterdam/Philadelphia: John Benjamins.

Van Heghe, Hans 2011. *Knowledge Centric Management: Urgent Recommendations and a Practical and Pragmatic Framework to Become a Knowledge Centric Organisation*. London: Panoma Press.

Sven Tarp

Integrated Writing Assistants and Their Possible Consequences for Foreign-Language Writing and Learning

1 Introduction

New disruptive computer and information technologies are invading our daily life. Totally or partially, these technologies are taking over still more tasks and activities that, only a few years ago, were something characteristic and exclusive of human beings. The tendency is irreversible and requires that we adapt to the new reality and make an effort to handle the new distribution of tasks between man and machine. One example of this is the appearance of digital writing assistants designed to support their users when they write and edit texts in both their mother tongue and a foreign language.

A new and highly complex phenomenon like writings assistants can be approached from various angles depending on the objective of the study. In terms of their design, they are the result of interdisciplinary collaboration between specialists from various fields: programmers, designers, corpus linguists and lexicographers, among others. In terms of their usage and the short- and long-term consequences of this usage, specialists in mother-tongue and second-language didactics should be added to the list. Hence, if we had to analyze and describe all relevant aspects of writing assistants, it would, at the least, require an interdisciplinary book with contributions from a range of specialists engaged in the development and use of this new tool. Thus, in the following sections, we will study writing assistants through the optics of only one of the mentioned disciplines, namely lexicography, although other aspects will also be taken into account when relevant.

2 A lexicographical approach

As in other aspects of life, it is of great assistance to know the history of lexicography in order to understand its present challenges. Although history never repeats itself, its development is nonetheless based on regularities that, once they have been discovered, can inspire us when we have to solve current challenges and prepare for future ones. This also holds true for the relationship between lexicography and technology. A considerable body of literature has been published about this relationship, but here it is sufficient to refer to contributions by Hanks (2010, 2013), Rundell/Kilgarriff (2011), Nielsen (2013) and Fuertes-Olivera/Sepstrup/Tarp (2018).

The ideas expressed by these authors show how the introduction of new technologies into lexicography historically implies big changes in the means of presentation of dictionaries; the compilation methods; the design and content of dictionary articles; the distribution and usage made of dictionaries; the topics treated; the number of users; the social role and prestige of lexicographers; as well as the business model that finances new dictionary projects and maintains existing ones. In short, history shows that new disruptive technologies imply a total revolution of the discipline.

The present historical moment is also dramatic. The increasing application of new disruptive technologies has already had a big impact on lexicography as a cultural practice and affects the discipline in its four main dimensions; that is, the presentation, compilation, usage and financing of lexicographical products – see, for instance, de Schryver (2003), Hanks (2012), Tarp (2012), Kilgarriff (2013), Lew/de Schryver (2014), Müller-Spitzer (2014), Kilgarriff et al. (2014), Tarp/Fuertes-Olivera (2016), Rundell (2016, 2018), and Fuertes-Olivera et al. (2018).

Automated or semi-automated compilation methods and the use of Natural Language Processing (NLP) in the selection of phraseology and other data are examples of this development (see Rundell/Kilgarriff 2011; Horák/Rambousek 2018; Gantar/Colman/Parra/Alonso Martínez 2019, among others). The migration to digital platforms and the availability on the Internet are other examples. Completely new products have seen the light. Fuertes-Olivera (2016) has compared the current situation in lexicography with a "Cambrian explosion" where new forms constantly appear and disappear.

We are still in the middle of the digital transformation of lexicography. However, there are already sufficient elements allowing us to conclude that the current changes are much more profound and far-reaching than the ones resulting from the introduction of the printing technology in Europe more than 500 years ago. In a certain way, the discipline is in crisis. In many countries, especially the technologically most advanced ones, the publication of new general dictionaries has decreased dramatically. By way of example, in Spain, if we exclude the 23rd edition of the dictionary of the Real Spanish Academy, no big general dictionary has been published for more than 15 years. This sad reality cannot be explained by a reduced demand of quality dictionaries, as there are more users of dictionaries than ever before. The problem is rather that a majority of users, especially the young generation, are not prepared to pay for the service when they consult dictionaries on the Internet, which has now become the most import means of presentation of new lexicographical works.

Consequently, the traditional business model which until now has financed new lexicographical projects has become obsolete. Still more publishing houses have stopped producing and publishing dictionaries. In some cases, they have even closed down their lexicographical departments due to lack of income. The discipline needs a new business model, which can finance new projects that make full use of the new technologies. It should also guarantee that these projects are carried on until their publication, and even further as continuous updating has become an important lexicographical duty today. Such a model can only be the result of a deep reflection on the relationship between lexicography and technology, a reflection that breaks with the traditional paradigm and looks for new solutions, both to new and to old problems. All this implies that a new lexicographical vision or approach cannot be formulated in a vacuum. On the contrary, it has to be based on a profound knowledge of the drama that takes place before our eyes, even if we are not always aware of it. Let us therefore look at the current tendencies in terms of the presentation of the lexicographical product. A careful observation of these trends unveils four big transformations which are taking place simultaneously:

1) from the *printed dictionary* to the *digital dictionary*, a process that is still ongoing (see Fuertes-Olivera/Tarp 2014);
2) from the *standardized dictionary*, which has characterized lexicography since the introduction of the printing technology, to a more *personalized dictionary* that adapts still more to the user's specific needs in each situation (see Rundell 2010, and Tarp 2011);
3) from the traditional *stand-alone dictionary*, either printed or online, to the *integrated dictionary* – that is, a dictionary integrated into other information tool like e-readers, writing assistants or various types of learning tool (see Tarp/Fisker/Sepstrup 2017);
4) from the *dictionary as such* to *lexicographical data for different uses* – that is, data that is handled without appearing in the form of a dictionary (see Fuertes-Olivera et al. (2018).

These four transformation processes are still developing in a zigzag across a complex lexicographical landscape, but it is becoming still clearer that they are interwoven. As such, and in one way or another, they herald a nearby future of *integrated information tools based on digital platforms and providing personalized service by means of context-adapted lexicographical data*.

In a lexicographical perspective, Fuertes-Olivera/Tarp (2014) have defined personalized service as the provision of the exact amount and types of data required to meet the user's needs in each situation, neither more nor less. This approach requires that the lexicographical data are high quality, that there are enough data, and that data and information overload is avoided. By definition, this goal can only be achieved in the framework of an integrated information tool that is designed to "observe" its users' behavior and *prescribe the exact dose of data that are likely to meet their needs in each concrete case*.

3 The information search process

In essence, dictionaries are consultation tools, or reference works, providing lexicographical data, from which their users can retrieve information that helps them to solve different types of problems occurring in different types of social situation, e.g., the production, reception, translation, and revision of texts in native or non-native languages (see Tarp 2018). In this perspective, the consultation of a dictionary forms part of a much broader information search process. Bergenholtz/Bothma/Gouws (2015) have analyzed the various phases in this process which, schematically, can be illustrated as follows:

A person (who can be characterized as a potential dictionary user):

- experiences an *information need* in a specific situation;
- *becomes aware* of the need;
- decides to *take action* and *consults* an information source – a dictionary, for instance;
- carries out the *consultation*;
- *evaluates* the result – that is, if it is satisfactory;
- *returns* to the situation where the information need originally occurred; and
- *uses* the retrieved information to *solve the problem* that gave rise to the need.

Although information search is something most of us do every day without paying much attention to it, it nonetheless requires a lot of experience and mental efforts from the user to go successfully through the above search phases which are full of challenges. In particular:

- What happens if the person is not aware of the information need?
- What happens if he or she decides not to take action?
- What happens if he or she opts for an inadequate information source?
- What happens if he or she is not satisfied with the information retrieved?
- What happens if he or she is not sufficiently prepared to evaluate the information retrieved?
- What happens if the problem is not solved due to wrong or inadequate information?

In addition to these challenges, it is also necessary to consider the time factor – that is, the time that is required to solve a problem when consulting an information source. Besides, we should not forget that any consultation of an external source, apart from being *time-consuming*, is also *disturbing* because the person performing the consultation may lose his or her concentration, focus, and writing flow. Thus, it would be desirable to develop an information tool that allows the user to *shorten the steps* in the information search process; *reduce the time* spent in external lookups; *maintain* the writing *flow*; and *avoid* that he or she *loses* the concentration and *forgets* what he or she was writing about. In this respect, *time*, *flow,* and *focus* are the key words, to which should be added *quality* of the provided information (see Tarp et al. 2017).

4 Integrated information tools

The solution to the above-mentioned challenges requires the development of integrated information tools in which the user does not have to go a long way in order to get assistance. Various tools of this type are already on the market in connection with the reading, writing, translation, and revision of texts, both in a first (L1) and a second (L2) language. Today, for instance, many e-readers automatically open a pop-up window with a dictionary article when the reader touches a word that he or she does not understand. However, it is problematical that the current generation of e-readers only provide access to traditional, static dictionary articles where the required sense (meaning) is not necessarily the one that is listed first (information overload). During the past few years, research has therefore been conducted in order to develop a method to deduce the meaning of a word from the context by means of neural networks and artificial intelligence, but so far no convincing solution has been presented.

When it comes to tools providing assistance to L1 and L2 writing, there are already several products of this type on the market. Most of them, frequently called *writing assistants*, are combining dictionaries and corpora with different purposes such as academic writing and extraction of collocations and phraseology in order to assist L1 and L2 writing in general, speed up the writing process or support the learning of a foreign language (see Paquot 2012; Wanner/Verlinde/Alonso Ramos 2013; Granger/Paquot 2015; Frankenberg-García 2018; Frankenberg-García et al. 2019). In most cases, the corpora have to be consulted separately, a process that extends the consulting time. Only a few writing assistants are currently integrated into text-processing programs (see Verlinde 2011; Verlinde/Peeters 2012; Tarp et al. 2017). As a result, in most tools the consultation process is still complicated and slow, as writers have to leave the document with which they are working in order to get assistance.

The few tools integrated into such programs have different philosophies, purposes, and functionalities. Some are monolingual and designed either to detect orthographical and grammatical mistakes and suggest corrections or to propose word completions and next words in order to assist text production in L1 or L2. Others like the Belgian *Interactive Language Toolbox*, developed at the Leuven Language Institute, are bilingual and offer equivalents and other assistance primarily aimed at language learning. Only a handful like *WhiteSmoke Writing Assistant*, designed by the US company with the same name, incorporates dictionary consultation as an accessory functionality. To our knowledge, the Danish *Write Assistant* is currently the only one known with such a function integrated into a text-processing program. The use of neural networks in the generation and presentation of lexicographical data in dictionaries integrated into writing assistants is still in an experimental stage, although the first products using this technology may soon see the light.

Writing assistants work on digital devices like laptops, tablets, and smartphones and may, at the least, have the following seven different functionalities, although most of them only have two or three of them:

1) Detective assistance: the tool detects possible problems in the written text and calls the user's attention to these problems;
2) Corrective assistance: the tool corrects mistakes in the written text, either automatically or by providing alternative solutions which the user then can accept or ignore;
3) Predictive assistance: the tool predicts and suggests completions of words when the user has written the first letters, as well as the words that is statistically most likely to follow in the concrete sentence;

4) Applicative assistance: the tool allows the user to automatically introduce a suggested word into the text by a simple click or touch on the screen, thus saving the time-consuming copy and paste actions;
5) Translative assistance: the tool suggests and lists possible L2 equivalents in the statistically most likely order when the user does not know the L2 word to be used and therefore types an L1 word;
6) Consultative assistance: the tool allows the user to consult an integrated dictionary without leaving the text-processing program;
7) Transformative assistance: the tool suggests alternative ways of writing in order to improve the text in terms of syntax, phraseology, style, and formality.

Some of the mentioned functionalities are already known to users of laptops, mobile phones, and tablets where most writing takes place today. Microsoft's well-known *Spelling and Grammar Checker* is, for instance, a tool of this type that offers *detective* and *corrective* assistance to its users. Today, many smartphones and tablets provide *predictive* assistance in several languages allowing their users to improve orthography and accelerate the writing process which is normally carried out with only one or two fingers. Most of these smartphones and tablets also include *applicative* assistance.

5 Write Assistant

In the following, we will discuss *Write Assistant* which has been developed by the Danish high-tech company Ordbogen A/S, a provider of language services and online dictionaries (Fisker 2018). This tool has been designed as an application that can be used together with Microsoft's Office Package as well as other text-processing programs normally used by Danish school children and students. This means that the writer using this application can simultaneously benefit from the advantages of these programs. Write Assistant, therefore, mainly focuses on a combination of *predictive*, *translative*, *consultative*, and *applicative* user assistance as we will see below, but the plan is to also include *transformative* assistance based on neural networks within a period of two or three years, at the most.

Write Assistant connects its users with *big data* in the form of *digital corpora* and *lexicographical databases*. These sources are not directly consulted by the users, but processed by means of a *language model* which makes it possible to provide *instantaneous assistance without the need to consult external information sources*. The language model is the result of cutting-edge programming. It has been *trained* on a big English corpus, a process that takes several weeks. During this *training*, it carries out an automatic analysis of the words contained in the corpus and restructures them in the form of 4-word *tuples* (sequences). As an example, we can take the sequence "I was drawn forward with the prospect of employment" from Samuel Johnson's (1747) *The Plan of an English Dictionary*. This sequence consists of a total of six 4-word tuples:

1) "I was drawn forward"
2) "was drawn forward with"
3) "drawn forward with the"
4) "forward with the prospect"
5) "with the prospect of"
6) "the prospect of employment"

Based on the frequency with which they occur in the corpus, the language model will give each of these six tuples a *score* that indicates the *probability* or *likeliness* of the respective string of four words appearing together in the English language. The current language model based on these principles has three main functions:

1) to complete words when the first letters have been typed;
2) to predict the next words in the sentence; and
3) to prioritize the order of L2 equivalents provided to L1 words.

The assistance provided by the actual version of Write Assistant is furnished in two boxes or windows. The first of these contains the suggestions that are most likely to become the next word in the sentence. This box is always open and moves forward so that the left edge of the word being typed aligns with the left edge of the box (see Fig. 3-1). The second box provides access to an integrated dictionary and only opens when it is activated by a user looking for additional information (see Fig. 3-2).

We will now see how Write Assistant works. In the first example (Fig. 3-1), the user is writing a sentence and types the letters *wo*. In this case, the language model will single out "to a beautiful" and *wo*. By means of a *sorted list* of all the words contained in the language model (and the corpus), Write Assistant now queries all words beginning with *wo*. This could be *work*, *woman*, *world*, *word*, etc. These possible completions of *wo* will then be added to the context *to a beautiful* resulting in the following 4-word tuples:

- "to a beautiful work"
- "to a beautiful woman"
- "to a beautiful world"
- "to a beautiful word", etc.

Each of these 4-word tuples will then be given a score from the model that is proportional to the number of occurrences in the corpus. The completions in the ten tuples with the highest score will be selected and presented to the user in a prioritized order. Although it seems complicated, this process is performed almost instantaneously and the final result will be presented to the user without him or her noting the extremely short time span. In the example discussed here, *woman* is the statistically most likely completion of *wo* in the concrete context:

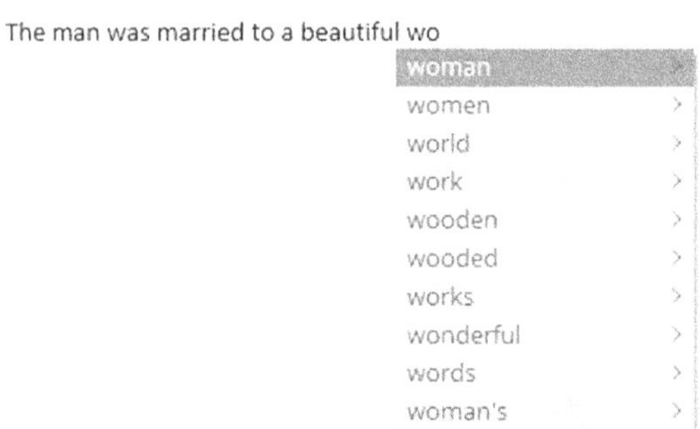

Fig. 3-1: Completion of *wo*.

The second example (Fig. 3-2) shows a situation where a Danish writer (L1) does not know or remember the word, which he or she wants to express in English (L2), and, therefore, types the Danish word *bidrag*. This word will automatically be looked up in the Danish-English dictionary that contains a number of translation candidates such as *donation*, *contribution*, *subscription*, etc. Each of these words are then added to the context *to give a* and the resulting tuples are given a score. Upon this basis, the language model immediately presents the most likely English equivalents in a prioritized order according to the context. Furthermore, if the user has doubts about, or does not know, the meaning of the suggested equivalents, he or she may then activate the integrated dictionary that provides an article with the following definition:

Fig. 3-2: L1 word with L2 equivalents and article from the integrated dictionary.

The two images in Fig. 3-3 furnish another example that illustrates how the language model prioritizes the order of the equivalents depending on the concrete context. In both cases, the writer has typed the Danish word *smuk* which is a polyseme with several equivalents in English. A careful look at the figure will show that the equivalents contained in the two lists are identical, but presented in a slightly different order, because the image to the left refers to a female whereas the one to the right refers to a male. Hence, what has been generated is a tool that is *context-aware* and, as such, marks the first important step towards an *intelligent* and more personalized lexicographical product.

Fig. 3-3: Prioritization of equivalents.

6 Perspectives

In its first published version, Write Assistant is sustained by a language model which is the result of a complex, but nonetheless *traditional* programming, as it has been performed during the past few years. The language model programmed in this way could rightly be called *mechanical* if it is compared to the new versions that are being prepared. As this article is being written, research is being conducted into the application of deep learning based on neural networks – that is, artificial intelligence. The objective is to develop an improved language model which can provide an even better user service. The expectation is that it will be able to handle longer syntactic sequences and more complex grammatical structures. It is also foreseen that it may influence the stylistic level of the text in terms of formality and other parameters.

This new language model will be different from the current grammar checkers which call their user's attention to a possible problem and then refer them to a *general* grammatical-syntactical rule and explanation. The new model is expected to come up with a *concrete suggestion* which the user can then accept and introduce in the text by means of a simple click. In this respect, Write Assistant, as well as other cutting-edge writing assistants under development, will increasingly *compete* with the users' linguistic skills and competences.

Apart from an improved language model, there are also concrete plans to develop the integrated dictionary which should interact in synergy with the language model. By definition, Write Assistant is designed to *assist* writers, but not to *replace* them. Hence, the latter may still need to consult a lexicographical source in order to *verify* some of the suggestions made by the language model.

Write Assistant is originally designed with one main function as defined by Tarp (2008) – that is, to assist its users with *L2 text production*. However, two other usages can be predicted which need to be more explicitly reflected in its design, namely *text revision* (as explained above) and *language learning*. Based on the suggestions from the language model, L2 learners may be inspired to explore meaning, inflectional paradigms, syntactic properties, collocations, phraseology, synonymy, and other aspects relevant to the *learning process*, thus interrupting the writing flow. Such a temporary shift of focus and subsequent immersion in new challenges is expected to characterize many L2 learners and will require a special approach. Users of Write Assistant will therefore still need lexicographically prepared data combined with metalinguistic data on rules and usage.

There is a relatively big body of lexicographical literature on how to assist users in foreign-language writing (see Rundell 1999; Tarp 2004; Bogaards 2005; Chon 2009; Lew 2016, among others). However, the ideas proposed in this literature are in many aspects still influenced by the printed book format. It is therefore necessary to adapt and further develop them in order to serve information tools like Write Assistant. As we saw in Fig. 3-2, in its current design, the integrated dictionary provides a definition, part of speech, inflectional data as well as a link to a number of example sentences. This is clearly not sufficient to meet the challenges mentioned in the previous paragraph. Besides, the problem is not only to include all relevant data in the lexicographical database, but also to find a way of presenting them that adapts to the design and philosophy of Write Assistant. It is above all necessary that the lexicographical data can be accessed and the needed information retrieved as fast and easy as possible.

In Write Assistant, the design and presentation of the integrated dictionary is conditioned by space restrictions, especially on small devices like smartphones and tablets. Even on a laptop, there is only a relatively small window where all relevant lexicographical data can be visualized. In this respect, two criteria, which up to a certain point are conflicting, should be fulfilled. On the one hand, the various types of data overload should be avoided (Gouws/Tarp 2017). This implies above all that as fewer data as possible should be presented simultaneously, and that scrolling down should be reduced to a minimum. On the other hand, the user should not be asked to take too many steps in order to retrieve the required information. This means that a completely new dictionary design has to be developed and that new solutions have to be found to both new and old problems.

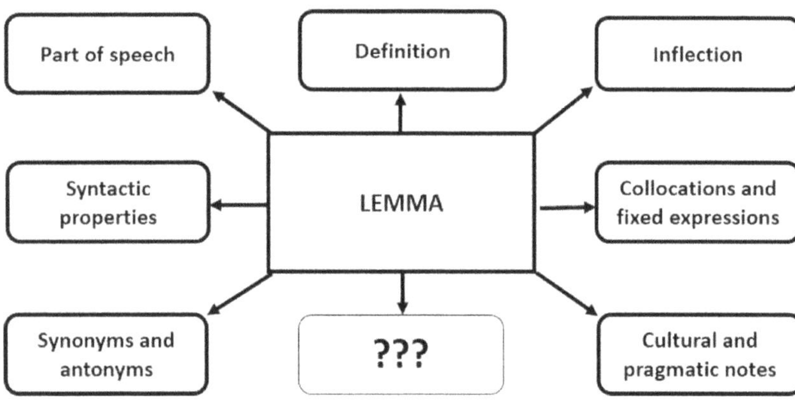

Fig. 3-4: Challenges in terms of a new dictionary design adapted to Write Assistant.

The challenges in terms of such a design are indicated in Fig. 3-4. In the center is the dictionary box that was also shown in Fig. 3-2. It refers to what is traditionally called a *lemma*. In this case, the lemma is a concrete word (in the future also a string of words), which the language model has suggested and the user decided to look up, thereby activating the dictionary function. The question is: Which lexicographical data categories should be put into this box in order to service Write Assistant and meet its users' needs? How should these data be visualized and structured in order to comply with the two criteria mentioned above? The answers to these questions do not only require a lot of research and creativity but should also be tested with real users of Write Assistant.

As mentioned above, in its current version Write Assistant offers two data boxes, one that is automatically shown when the tool is running and another which is activated by the user looking for additional information. These boxes represent two different types of relationship between man and machine, one with a passive and another with an active human role. However, it is already foreseen that an additional third data box will be required. Such a box could automatically pop up providing alerts and notes on special linguistic and cultural challenges which the writer may not be aware of. These challenges could be:

- the different meaning of adjectives in Latin languages which in some cases depends on their position before or after nouns;
- the use of subjunctive or indicative after certain verbs and constructions;
- the use of casus after German prepositions;
- possible cultural misunderstandings related to distant cultures and languages like Chinese and English, etc.

Figure 3-5 shows a prototype of a third box that provides alerts and notes on linguistic or cultural challenges. This functionality can either be activated or deactivated by the user according to individual or didactic preferences.

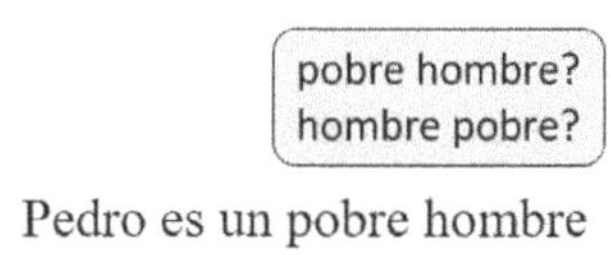

Fig. 3-5: Box with alerts or notes for the Spanish adjective *pobre*.

Let us look at this example where the box is activated and the user writes a simple Spanish sentence: *Pedro es un pobre hombre*. The concrete meaning of the adjective *pobre* depends on its position before or after the noun *hombre* (man). Placed before the noun, it means *sad, unhappy, unfortunate*, whereas it means *without money or means of subsistence* when it is placed behind it. Both positions (*pobre hombre* and *hombre pobre*) are possible and frequent in Spanish. Even the most advanced language model based on artificial intelligence cannot guess the required order of the two words in each concrete case. It is only the writer who knows what he or she wants to express. When *pobre hombre* has been typed, Write Assistant will therefore immediately visualize an alert box which can either be ignored, function as a reminder, or used as a link to lexicographical data that explain the problem.

Another example could be a Chinese writer typing the word *dragon* which is a friendly animal in Chinese culture, whereas it represents the opposite in Western culture. In order to assist the user and avoid unnecessary misunderstandings, it is already envisaged that Write Assistant should be designed to provide alerts and notes on cultural differences of this type.

As can be seen, Write Assistant and similar tools do not only pose new challenges to lexicography. They also open a window to the future with a range of new possibilities which still have to be explored and materialized in the framework of a completely new dictionary design.

7 Challenges

In the autumn of 2018, a Write Assistant designed to help Danish users when writing in English was made available to more than half a million Danish school children – that is, approximately 10 % of the population. They were allowed to use it for free during a three-month period in order to get acquainted with it and promote sales in the framework of a new business model. Similar writing assistants for German, Spanish, Chinese, and other users will soon follow the Danish-English version.

From a technical-practical point of view, the initial experience is positive. It shows that the school children find it very easy to download the application. Because of their general experience with digital tools, they are able to start using Write Assistant within a few minutes without any oral or written instructions. The experience until now also indicates that they generally write faster and more fluently than before and commit fewer mistakes, which was the main objective with the product at this stage. Most of them seem to like the product, and some of them even use it to explore other aspects of the foreign language (English) – that is, they use Write Assistant directly as a *learning tool*. This was not foreseen but should be regarded as a collateral advantage. Moreover, there are indications that Write Assistant may allow some of the *weaker* school children to express other aspects of their personality and improve their self-esteem when writing essays.

It goes without saying that all these results are preliminary. Much more empirical data is needed in order to get a full picture which will probably prove to be very complex. In any case, it is necessary to distinguish between the short-term and long-term consequences of using Write Assistant and similar products. Although the experience until now is generally positive, there are various unknown consequences in the long run. Today, writing, whether in the mother tongue or in a foreign language, is mainly performed on mobile phones, tablets and laptops. Writing skills are above all expressed in connection with the usage of these devices, whereas handwriting is increasingly restricted to the personal sphere. Among the young generation, the consultation of dictionaries in order to solve problems occurring in the writing process is almost exclusively done while they are using these devices. This indicates that future dictionaries should be adapted to this reality and presented with a different and completely new design and functionality.

We can predict that school children, and young people in general, within a very short span of time will use writing assistants, whatever they are told and instructed to do by their teachers. A tool, which is that useful and easy to download and operate, cannot be prohibited, just as it did not make any sense to prohibit the electronic calculator half a century ago. We can also expect that writing assistants, because they shorten the writing process, will allow the school children to dedicate more time and focus more on the content of the texts, with which they are working. This will probably prove to be another didactic advantage in some of their courses.

All this is, undoubtedly, very positive. However, it can be anticipated that the new generations will become more and more dependent on these new digital tools which will serve as crutches for them in the writing process. This dependence will probably increase even more with the introduction of artificial intelligence. It is therefore completely justified to raise the following questions:

- What are the consequences of the continuous externalization of human knowledge and skills?
- Which impact will writing assistants have on school children's writing skills in both L1 and L2?
- Will their writing skills improve if they have to write without these tools? If not, is the growing dependence on these crutches good or bad? And what are the criteria of good and bad?
- With still more sophisticated writing assistants based on artificial intelligence, will it still be relevant that school children are expected to learn orthography, syntax, and grammar in general?
- Which consequences will writing assistants have for the learning of both native and foreign languages?
- Which consequences will all this have for language didactics?
- Will L2 learning be imperative at all, if we can communicate by means of technology in a nearby future?

There is little doubt that externalization of human knowledge and skills to digital devices and robots is an irreversible tendency in a technologically developed society. It is a tendency that we cannot stop but should confront in a creative way in order to get the best out of it. For most of their existence, human beings only had a spoken language, whereas written language is a *relatively recent* innovation. It is a fact that some competences, skills, tools, and topics tend to get outdated and replaced with others with the passing of time. At the end of the day, is it not better to use the brain for other purposes, if we no longer need certain knowledge and competences?

A comparison with the introduction of the calculator more than half a century ago helps us to put the challenges in perspective. In that moment, which seems sun years away, many teachers argued against the use of this tool in the class room, because it would affect the school children's capacity to make calculations in the head. Historically, their arguments have proved to be right in the sense that many young people today are generally not as good to make calculations in the head as they were then. However, it is also a fact that young people today, when they use calculators, can perform far more complex calculations than their parents' and grandparents' generations. The question, which will be left to the readers of this article to answer, is whether this development is positive or negative.

When this is said, there can be little doubt that it is still important to learn languages and master orthography, syntax, and grammar in general. We should not retreat before the machines in these aspects. Language is not only something external used to communicate, but it is also something internal and very intimate that is used to think and reflect about the world. Without language we would not be human beings and capable of navigating in a complex world. However, this does not exclude that new didactic methods are required together with new and better arguments in order to motivate the learners in the current technological environment. If school children and other language learners are not motivated with convincing arguments, many of them will probably be in danger of becoming slaves of the new technologies. That would be an absolute disaster. It is therefore urgent that we start preparing ourselves for the future by means of research and a better understanding of the changes that take place around us as a result of the technological development.

It is above all necessary to *learn to learn by means of technology* – that is, to learn in a different way. It is necessary to have a profound understanding of the new relationship between man and machine as well as the new distribution of tasks. It is necessary to grasp the role of technology in the sense that the machine is there, or should be there, to assist us, but not to take over and replace us. It is necessary to learn to take responsibility, which requires an active role, as passivity will hamper L2 learning. The users of the new writing tools must understand that they are still the only responsible for the final text.

8 Conclusion

Writing assistants are here to stay. As we have seen, they might be highly helpful in various aspects in relation to L2 writing and learning. However, we have also anticipated that there may be undesirable consequences if they are not handled in the right way. All this requires a continuous study combined with a good dose of open-mindedness, flexibility, and creativity.

Future challenges should be met by a combination of improved technology; bigger and better corpora to ensure the quality of the language model; especially adapted lexicographical data; new didactic methods, and convincing arguments in order to motivate language learners. In this respect, everybody should work within their own field of expertise and, simultaneously, engage in interdisciplinary collaboration with colleagues from other fields. Without such collaboration, it would be difficult to set up common goals and successfully confront the new challenges. The gauntlet is down!

References

Bergenholtz, Henning/Bothma, Theo D.J./Gouws, Rufus H. 2015. Phases and Steps in the Access to Data in Information Tools. *Lexikos* 25, 1–30.

Bogaards, Paul 2005. Dictionaries and Productive Tasks in a Foreign Language. *Kernerman Dictionary News* 13, 20–23.

Chon, Yuah V. 2009. The Electronic Dictionary for Writing: A Solution or a Problem? *International Journal of Lexicography* 22/1, 23–54.

De Schryver, Gilles-Maurice 2003. Lexicographer's Dreams in the Electronic-Dictionary Age. *International Journal of Lexicography* 16/2, 143–199.

Fisker, Kasper (ed.) 2018. *Write Assistant. Danish-English*. Odense: Ordbogen A/S.

Frankenberg-García, Ana 2018. Combining User Needs, Lexicographic Data and Digital Writing Environments. Plenary address given at TechLing 2017, University of Bologna, Forlì, Italy, 10–11 November 2017. *Language Teaching*. <DOI: https://doi.org/10.1017/S0261444818000277>.

Frankenberg-García, Ana/Lew, Robert/Roberts, Jonathan C./Rees, Geraint Paul/Sharma, Nirwan 2019. Developing a Writing Assistant to Help EAP Writers with Collocations in Real Time. *ReCALL* 31/1, 23–29.

Fuertes-Olivera, Pedro A. 2016. A Cambrian Explosion in Lexicography: Some Reflections for Designing and Constructing Specialised Online Dictionaries. *International Journal of Lexicography* 29/2, 226–247.

Fuertes-Olivera, Pedro A./Tarp, Sven 2014. *Theory and Practice of Specialised Online Dictionaries: Lexicography Versus Terminography*. Berlin/Boston: Walter De Gruyter.

Fuertes-Olivera, Pedro A./Sepstrup, Peter/Tarp, Sven 2018. New Insights in the Design and Compilation of Digital Bilingual Lexicographical Products: The Case of the Diccionarios Valladolid-UVa. *Lexikos* 28, 152–176.

Gantar, Polona/Colman, Lut/Parra Escartín, Carla/Alonso Martínez, Héctor 2019. Multiword Expressions: Between Lexicography and NLP. *International Journal of Lexicography* 32/2, 138–162.

Gouws, Rufus/Tarp, Sven 2017. Information Overload and Data Overload in Lexicography. *International Journal of Lexicography* 30/4, 389–415.

Granger, Sylviane/Paquot, Magali 2015. Electronic Lexicography Goes Local: Design and Structures of a Needs-Driven Online Academic Writing Aid. *Lexicographica* 31/1, 118–141.

Hanks, Patrick 2010. Lexicography, Printing Technology, and the Spread of Renaissance Culture. In Dykstra, Anne/Schoonheim, Tanneke (eds.) *Proceedings of the XIV Euralex International Congress*. Leeuwarden: Fryske Akademy, 988–1016.

Hanks, Patrick 2012. The Corpus Revolution in Lexicography. *International Journal of Lexicography* 25/4, 398–436.

Hanks, Patrick 2013. Lexicography from Earliest Times to the Present. In Keith, Allan (ed.) *The Oxford Handbook of the History of Linguistics*. Oxford: Oxford University Press, 503–536.

Horák, Aleš/Rambousek, Adam 2018. Lexicography and Natural Language Processing. In Fuertes-Olivera, Pedro A. (ed.) *Routledge Handbook of Lexicography*. London: Routledge, 179–196.

Johnson, Samuel 1747. *The Plan of an English Dictionary*. <https://andromeda.rutgers.edu/~jlynch/Texts/plan.html>.

Kilgarriff, Adam 2013. Using Corpora as Data Sources for Dictionaries. In Jackson, Howard (ed.) *The Bloomsbury Companion to Lexicography*. London: Bloomsbury, 77–96.

Kilgarriff, Adam/Baisa, Vit/Bušt, Jan/Jakubíček, Miloš/Kovář, Vojtěch/ Michelfeit, Jan/Rychlý, Pavel/Suchomel, Vit 2014. The Sketch Engine: Ten Years On. *Lexicography* 1/1, 7–36.

Lew, Robert 2016. Can a Dictionary Help You Write Better? A User Study of an Active Bilingual Dictionary for Polish Learners of English. *International Journal of Lexicography* 29/3, 353–366.

Lew, Robert/de Schryver, Gilles-Maurice 2014. Dictionary Users in the Digital Revolution. *International Journal of Lexicography* 27/4, 341–359.

Müller-Spitzer, Carolin 2014. Empirical Data on Contexts of Dictionary Use. In Müller-Spitze, Carolin (ed.) *Using Online Dictionaries*. Berlin/Boston: Walter de Gruyter, 85–126.

Nielsen, Sandro 2013. The Future of Dictionaries, Dictionaries of the Future. In Jackson, Howard (ed.) *Bloomsbury Companion to Lexicography*. London/New York: Bloomsbury, 355–372.

Paquot, Magali 2012. The LEAD Dictionary-cum-writing Aid: An Integrated Dictionary and Corpus Tool. In Granger, Sylviane/Paquot, Magali (eds.) *Electronic Lexicography*. Oxford: Oxford University Press, 163–185.

Rundell, Michael 1999. Dictionary Use in Production. *International Journal of Lexicography* 12/1, 35–53.

Rundell, Michael 2010. What Future for the Learner's Dictionary? In Kernerman, Ilan/Bogaards, Paul (eds.) *English Learners' Dictionaries at the DSNA 2009*. Jerusalem: Kdictionaries, 169–175.

Rundell, Michael 2016. Dictionaries and crowdsourcing, wikis and user-generated content. In Hanks, Patrick/de Schryver, Gilles-Muarice (eds.) *International Handbook of Modern Lexis and Lexicography*. Berlin: Springer Verlag. <http://michaelrundell.com/wp-content/uploads/2017/05/Crowdsourcing-and-lexicography_MR.pdf>.

Rundell, Michael 2018. Searching for Extended Units of Meaning – and What to Do When You Find Them. *Lexicography* 5/1, 5–21.

Rundell, Michael/Kilgarriff, Adam 2011. Automating the Creation of Dictionaries: Where Will It All End? In Meunier, Fanny/Cock, Sylvie D./Gilquin, Gaëtanelle/Paquot, Magali (eds.) *A Taste for Corpora. In Honour of Sylviane Granger*. Amsterdam/Philadelphia: John Benjamins, 257–282.

Tarp, Sven 2004. Reflections on Dictionaries Designed to Assist Users with Text Production in a Foreign Language. *Lexikos* 14, 299–325.

Tarp, Sven 2008. *Lexicography in the Borderland between Knowledge and Non-knowledge. General Lexicographical Theory with Special Focus on Learner's Lexicography*. Tübingen: Niemeyer.

Tarp, Sven 2011. Lexicographical and Other e-Tools for Consultation Purposes: Towards the Individualization of Needs Satisfaction. In Fuertes-Olivera, Pedro A./Bergenholtz, Henning (eds.) *e-Lexicography: The Internet, Digital Initiatives and Lexicography*. London/New York: Continuum, 54–70.

Tarp, Sven 2012. Theoretical Challenges in the Transition from Lexicographical p-Works to e-Tools. In Granger, Sylviane/Paquot, Magali (eds.) *Electronic Lexicography*. Oxford: Oxford University Press, 107–118.

Tarp, Sven 2018. The Concept of Dictionary. In Fuertes-Olivera, Pedro A. (ed.) *Routledge Handbook of Lexicography*. London: Routledge, 237–249.

Tarp, Sven/Fuertes-Olivera, Pedro A. 2016. Advantages and Disadvantages in the Use of Internet as a Corpus: The Case of the Online Dictionaries of Spanish Valladolid-UVa. *Lexikos* 26, 273–295.

Tarp, Sven/Fisker, Kasper/Sepstrup, Peter 2017. L2 Write Assistants and Context-Aware Dictionaries: New Challenges to Lexicography. *Lexikos* 27, 494–521.

Verlinde, Serge 2011. Modelling Interactive Reading, Translation and Writing Assistants. In Fuertes-Olivera, Pedro A./Bergenholtz, Henning (eds.) *e-Lexicography: The Internet, Digital Initiatives and Lexicography*. London/New York: Continuum, 275–286.

Verlinde, Serge/Peeters, Geert 2012. Data Access Revisited: The Interactive Language Toolbox. In Granger, Sylviane/Paquot, Magali (eds.) *Electronic Lexicography*. Oxford: Oxford University Press, 147–162.

Wanner, Leo/Verlinde, Serge/Alonso Ramos, Margarita 2013. Writing Assistants and Automatic Lexical Error Correction: Word Combinatorics. In Kosem, Iztok/Kallas, Jelena/Gantar, Polona/Krek, Simon/Langemets, Margit/Tuulik, Maria (eds.) *Electronic Lexicography in the 21st Century: Thinking Outside the Paper*. Ljubljana: Institute for Applied Slovene Studies, 472–487.

Jonás Fouz-González

Using the English File Pronunciation App for Pronunciation Training: The Learners' Views

1 Introduction

Throughout history, technological developments have opened up new possibilities regarding the way information and knowledge are accessed and shared. In addition to traditional ways of obtaining information, such as journals, books, newspapers or encyclopaedias, the internet provides people with instant access to virtually unlimited information which is readily available at their fingertips (via search engines like Google; social media like Twitter, Facebook, or Instagram; or video-sharing websites like YouTube). Focusing on language learning, today's learners have access to an extensive range of resources that would have been unimaginable a few decades ago. Today, any foreign language (FL) learner can easily read online newspapers and magazines from any country, watch TV shows and films in the original language, download and listen to podcasts on a wide range of topics (of various lengths and featuring different accents), or look up the meaning of words and expressions using free online dictionaries that they can access from their smartphones.

Nevertheless, just as access to information does not necessarily translate into knowledge, the mere availability of resources does not automatically lead to mastery of an FL. As Healey (1999, cited in Levy/Stockwell 2006: 191) notes, "technology alone does not create language learning any more than dropping a learner into the middle of a large library does". For technology to really facilitate language learning, the tools teachers use or recommend and the tasks they design should always have a sound pedagogical foundation that builds on the findings from previous research on second language acquisition and Computer Assisted Language Learning (CALL). Because the role of technology in language learning is ultimately instrumental, effective implementations of technology should always be based on second language pedagogy (Chinnery 2006). As Nelson and Oliver (1999: 101) write:

> We should not be using a computer just because we can and we should not be using more advanced (i.e., complicated) technologies when something simpler will do. Each technological advancement (since the paper and pen) creates different venues for learning and supports different learning and teaching styles. The computer may or may not be better than teaching on a black-board; it all depends on what the teacher wants students to learn and how they plan to teach.

Hence, technology should not be used just because *it's there* or for the sake of using something new, but because it really contributes to facilitating the development of a given language competence in ways that would not be possible or as effective otherwise. In this respect, of all the competences learners need to master in an FL, pronunciation is probably the one for which technology can be most beneficial. Given the influence of the learners' first language (L1) on their perception and production of the FL sounds and patterns (see Flege 1987, 1995), FL learners often require a great deal of perceptual and productive practice that is difficult to get in a regular classroom due to limitations in classroom time and different learner needs.

There are many ways in which technology can enhance pronunciation training. These range from simply providing learners with access to massive amounts of input or highly variable stimuli, modifying certain elements of the acoustic signal to make them more salient for learners, enhancing features of pronunciation visually (via spectrograms, waveforms, pitch contours or talking faces), or using Automatic Speech Recognition (ASR) software to offer learners automatic feedback on their productions (see Fouz-González 2015 for a review). As Witt and Young (1997) note, because pronunciation is a psycho-motoric action that requires coordination and control over many muscles, the private environment that technology offers seems an ideal solution for students who need a great deal of repetition and are afraid to do so in front of other people. Given that different learners need different types and amounts of exposure and practice, one of the most promising advantages of technology for language learning in general and, for pronunciation training in particular, is the possibility to practise whenever and wherever students need, for as long as they wish. This should allow learners to build up confidence by practising on their own, work individually on those areas they find most problematic, and then put everything into practice in communicative situations in the classroom or in real conversations.

In spite of the above, and because of the need to conduct research under rigorous and controlled conditions, computer assisted pronunciation training (CAPT) studies have traditionally been conducted in rather controlled, laboratory-like settings, using tools and software that learners cannot always access easily outside the classroom/lab. However, in order to really exploit the potential of technology for pronunciation training *anytime, anywhere*, studies should also investigate the possibilities offered by tools that are readily available for learners outside the classroom. In this regard, a promising line of research is the type of training learners can have on their mobile devices, as they can access it whenever they want and wherever they want, with devices they already have and use daily.

Mobile Assisted Language Learning (MALL) "differs from computer-assisted language learning in its use of personal, portable devices that enable new ways of learning, emphasizing continuity or spontaneity of access and interaction across different contexts of use" (Kukulska-Hulme/Shield 2008: 273). Research has explored the possibilities different mobile devices offer for various language learning purposes, and the results have been generally positive. Studies have addressed the potential of portable consoles to work on listening and reading skills (Kondo et al. 2012), FaceTime conversations through iPads to foster oral skills practice (Lys 2013), or sending SMSs (Kennedy/Levy 2008) or e-mails (Thornton/Houser 2005) to teach vocabulary. As far as pronunciation is concerned, studies have shown the potential of mobile-based High Variability Phonetic Training (HVPT) paradigms (Uther et al. 2007), iPods for shadowing practice (Foote/McDonough 2017), or mobile speech recognisers to offer learners feedback on their pronunciation (Liakin/Cardoso/Liakina 2015). However, despite the wide range of apps aimed at pronunciation training available (see, for instance, Fouz-González 2012; Kaiser 2018), there are no studies addressing the learners willingness to use apps for autonomous pronunciation training or evaluating their potential to help learners improve aspects of their pronunciation empirically.

In light of the above, this study was set to explore the potential of and the learners' views towards a commercial smartphone app (English File Pronunciation app – EFP app henceforth) designed to help learners work on English pronunciation autonomously (Oxford University Press, 2012). The empirical data evaluating the app's potential to foster improvements in FL learners' pronunciation has been presented in Fouz-González (2020). This chapter aims at furthering such research and therefore explores the learners' willingness to use apps for language learning outside the classroom, their perceptions towards the EFP app and the approach adopted, as well as the students' recommendations to improve the training offered by the app.

2 Using a smartphone app for perceptual training outside the classroom

The results obtained in Fouz-González (2020) show that the perceptual training offered by the app yielded significant differences in the improvement made between participants who used the app and those who did not, both in perception and in production. The gains fostered by the app-based training were considered to be very positive, as the target aspects addressed were a range of segmental features that tend to be fossilised in the interlanguage of advanced English as a Foreign Language (EFL) learners (/æ/ /ɑː/ /ʌ/ /ə/ /z/) and were considered to be very difficult to modify without training. Nevertheless, before supporting the use of a particular tool or approach for language learning, it is also vital to explore the learners' willingness to adopt such approaches and their perceptions towards this type of training. As Cenoz and García Lecumberri (1999) note, investigating the learners' perspectives is very relevant for language acquisition because their attitudes and beliefs are very likely to affect the learning process. If learners do not perceive activities to be useful or are not willing to spend time or money on them, it is not worth exploring their potential because they will simply not use them. In fact, in some of the studies in which participants have been given the choice to use either a mobile device or a computer, participants have expressed their misgivings about the mobile version due to reasons such as screen or keypad size, or cost (see Stockwell 2007, 2008). With the increase in smartphones screen size and the widespread use of internet data on mobile devices, this seems to have become less of a problem for learners, as the results of recent studies addressing the potential of language learning apps and the learners' perceptions towards them have been generally positive (see Amer 2014; Castañeda/Cho 2016; Rosell-Aguilar 2016, 2018; among others).

Studies addressing the learners' views on pronunciation teaching and the acquisition of pronunciation in FL contexts show that students are aware of the difficulty FL pronunciation entails (Cenoz/García Lecumberri 1999; Calvo Benzies 2013) and that learners do not think pronunciation receives the attention it should in FL classes (Calvo Benzies 2013). In fact, in a study conducted with 157 students from Italy, Spain, and Poland, 76 % of the informants claimed that they usually worked on pronunciation on their own (Nowacka 2012).

Research has shown that perceptual training techniques such as ear training are often amongst teachers' preferred choices (Henderson et al. 2015). Furthermore, numerous studies have explored the potential of different perceptual training paradigms and the results have been generally very positive (see Gómez-Lacabex/García-Lecumberri/Cooke 2008; Aliaga-García/Mora 2009; Rato 2013; Wong 2015; Carlet 2017; among others). However, when learners practise at home, they do not make use of such techniques and opt for *listen and repeat* activities, reading aloud, or listening to authentic speech and imitating it (Nowacka 2012; Calvo Benzies 2013). This may be due to learners not being aware of the existence of other alternatives, to their reluctance to spend money on some of the resources available (such as apps), or to their unwillingness to use other resources because they do not consider them to be adequate or reliable.

3 Research questions

In light of the above, this chapter seeks to answer the following research questions:

RQ1: Are learners willing to use apps for language learning outside the classroom?
RQ2: What are the learners' perceptions towards the English File Pronunciation (EFP) app?
RQ3: What are the learners' perceptions towards the approach adopted?
RQ4: What are the learners' recommendations to improve the training offered by the app?

4 Methodology

4.1 Participants

There were 63 participants in this study, 48 females and 15 males (mean age 19.2; SD = 0.88). They were 52 EFL learners recruited from a phonetics course in the second year of an English studies degree and 11 first-year students enrolled in various English courses from other degrees (Translation, Hispanic Studies, and Medicine). Students from the degree in English studies had a B2 level according to the Common European Framework of Reference for Languages (CEFR). Students from the other degrees ranged between B1 and B2. Of the 63 participants who volunteered to participate in the study and used the app, 59 completed the initial questionnaire and 48 completed the final one.

4.2 Data collection instruments

Two questionnaires were administered to participants, one before and another one after the EFP app training (see Appendices 1 and 2). These questionnaires contained a combination of close and open-ended questions, and a series of 5-point Likert-type statements (1 = totally disagree; 5 = totally agree). The surveys were created with Google Forms and distributed via email.

4.3 Training procedure

The EFP app includes an interactive sound chart to help users to become familiarised with the sound system of English and two activities for practice. The sound chart features English sounds in isolation, in sample words, and in sentences. The first activity is a sound identification activity in which users are presented with words in isolation, and they have to identify the sound they hear out of two possibilities (see Fig. 4-1, left section). In the second activity, users are presented with words in orthography (without any audio illustration) and they have to identify which of the two sounds that are shown on the screen is featured in the target words (see Fig. 4-1, middle section). Users receive immediate feedback on the choices they make (a green tick if their choice is correct, a red cross if it is wrong), and a progress screen is shown every 10 items with a summary of their scores for those ten words (see Fig. 4-1, right section).

Participants were asked to use the EFP app over a period of two weeks. They could use the app wherever they wanted and at the time of day that was most convenient for them. However, in order to make training as homogeneous as possible for all participants, they were asked to complete the same number of activities a day. They were told to (i) explore the target sounds in the phonemic chart; (ii) compare sounds they considered to be problematic; and (iii) complete ten progress screens on each of the two activities offered in the app. This three-stage process was estimated to take around 20 minutes per day. In order to monitor task completion, students were required to take screenshots of every progress screen and to share them with the researcher via Dropbox.

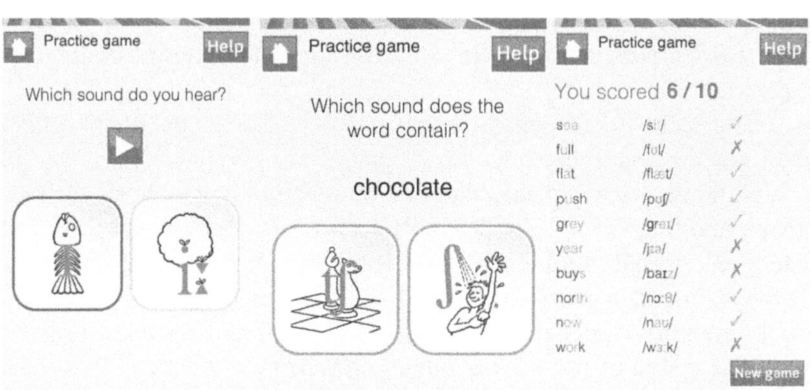

Fig. 4-1: Screenshots from the EFP app. Activity 1 (left), activity 2 (middle), and progress screen (right).

5 Results and discussion

This section presents the participants' responses to the initial and final questionnaires. The results and the discussion are divided into four subsections that coincide with the research questions in section 3.

5.1 Willingness to use apps for language learning

The number of smartphone owners among the respondents and the time they spend using mobile devices daily suggests that incorporating approaches like this into their routine should not be problematic. Of the 59 informants who completed the initial questionnaire, 58 (98.3 %) owned a smartphone. The only student who did not have one used her mother's phone to complete the activities. As regards the time learners spend using their smartphones daily, 37 students (62.7 %) said that they use them for more than two hours a day, 15 (25.4 %) use them between one and two hours, four (6.8 %) between 30 minutes and an hour, two (3.4 %) between 15 and 30 minutes, and only one (1.7 %) uses them less than 15 minutes a day. The smartphone ownership figures are very positive and in line with studies in other countries (Rosell-Aguilar 2016; Stockwell/Liu 2015). The fact that most students today have these devices and spend so much time using them suggests that encouraging practice with devices like this is a way of making training very accessible for learners, as opposed to having to go to a computer lab, for example.

The learners' responses to the 5-point Likert-type items reflect their willingness to use apps for language learning ($M = 4.3$, $SD = 1$) and show that they consider apps to be potentially beneficial for language learning ($M = 4.2$, $SD = 0.9$). In fact, 24 participants (40.7 %) had already used mobile applications for language learning purposes. In the open-ended items, they mentioned that they often used dictionary apps, automatic translators, apps aimed at helping users learn English irregular verbs, or apps for phonetic transcription practice. This indicates that, despite initial scepticism towards using this type of device for educational purposes (see, for instance, Stockwell 2008), students are starting to accept them as potential educational tools, which is in line with the results obtained by Amer (2014), Tan and Teo (2015), or Rosell-Aguilar (2018). Previous research has shown that among the aspects students value most about apps are the fact that they are easy to use and access, or the possibility to receive specific training on language areas students may find difficult (see Rosell-Aguilar 2016). While smartphone screens may not be as suitable for activities that require reading long texts, for example, they seem particularly well suited to work on areas such as vocabulary, grammar, or pronunciation.

Finally, when asked about the daily amount of time they would be willing to spend using language learning apps, one participant (1.7 %) said "more than one hour a day", 16 (27.1 %) said "between 30 minutes and an hour", 40 (67.8 %) said "between 15 and 30 minutes", and two (3.4 %) said "less than 15 minutes a day". The amount of time learners devote to practising different language competences autonomously will undoubtedly vary depending on their needs. The majority of participants in this study said they would be willing to practise for around 15–30 minutes a day. Perceptual training studies using HVPT have found very positive effects of training with similar time spans in five (Carlet/Cebrian 2015) and eight sessions (Thomson 2011). Thus, although the training offered by the EFP app does not include the variability of an HVPT paradigm (and therefore longer training periods would probably be necessary for substantial improvements to take place), the fact that learners are willing to practise with activities like this on a daily basis suggests that this type of app-based training can be very suitable for pronunciation.

5.2 Learners' perceptions towards the EFP app

The learners' responses to items addressing their perceptions towards the EFP app revealed that they considered the app to be useful ($M = 4.4$; $SD = 0.8$) and that the contents were perceived as relevant to the students' daily use of English ($M = 4.2$; $SD = 0.8$). Participants believed that the app had helped them to improve their perception ($M = 4.6$; $SD = 0.6$)

and production ($M = 4.3$; $SD = 0.8$) of the target sounds, which is in line with the empirical data reported in Fouz-González (2020).

The mean scores in the items exploring the participants' views regarding the number of sample words in the phonemic chart ($M = 3.6$; $SD = 1.2$) or the activities ($M = 3.4$; $SD = 1.1$) are slightly lower, which indicates that learners would appreciate a wider range of lexical items to illustrate the target sounds, both in the sound chart and in the activities. Nevertheless, the feedback offered by the app was considered to be adequate ($M = 4.1$; $SD = 1.2$) and suitable to inform learners why their answers were wrong when they made mistakes ($M = 4.2$; $SD = 1$).

As regards usability, the learners' responses suggest that they thought the app was easy to use ($M = 4.8$; $SD = 0.6$) and that they did not find the activities to be difficult ($M = 1.7$; $SD = 0.8$ –in a statement claiming that the activities were difficult), which implies that this type of perceptual practice could be very suitable for autonomous practice. Nevertheless, the mean scores in items stating that students enjoyed using the app ($M = 3.8$; $SD = 0.9$) or that the app was entertaining and that they did not get bored while using it ($M = 3.7$; $SD = 1.1$) are slightly lower. This may be due to the fact that the type of training offered in the activities is always the same (i.e., a two-alternative forced-choice), using a limited range of sample words, and without really exploiting gamification elements that could help maintain motivation. Even though the mean score in the statement suggesting that the training offered by the app is monotonous is not very high ($M = 3.3$; $SD = 1.3$), the participants' responses to the open-ended questions revealed that some of them did find the app to be somewhat monotonous. The mean score in the item addressing the learners' intention to continue using the app after the study was over was not very high either ($M = 3.8$; $SD = 1$). Nevertheless, their answers were much more positive when asked about their willingness to continue using the app if new levels and activities were released ($M = 4.4$; $SD = 0.9$).

One participant mentioned that it would be interesting to be able to see how many games had been played as well as the scores received. As explained above, the app shows a progress screen every 10 stimuli, but it does not keep a record of the users' scores over time, nor does it offer the possibility to keep track of the learners' progress or time spent using the app. Moreover, the type of training offered by the app does not imply increasing difficulty or progression through a series of levels like the ones usually found in games, which may be perceived by users as something "too open" and without clearly defined stages. Creating a progress-screen where learners could see their performance over time, previous answers, and scores (if possible using trophies or a similar gamification system to motivate users) would improve the app substantially, as it would make it more appealing for longer instructional periods, and it would help learners to monitor their progress and devote further work to those aspects they need to reinforce.

Finally, when asked whether they would pay 5.5€ for this app, 13 students (26.5 %) said that they would, although one pointed out that it was "a bit expensive" for what it offered. The remaining 35 replied that they would not buy this app: 14 (28.6 %) because it is too expensive and 21 (42.9 %) because they never spend money on apps. When asked about the ideal price for this app, seven students (14.3 %) recommended between 1 and 2€, 13 (26.5 %) recommended between 2 and 3€, 11 (22.4 %) between 3 and 4€ and 9 (18.4 %) between 4 and 5€. Although the learners' opinions differ, their responses offer an idea of the amount of money they are willing to spend on this type of software. A somewhat surprising finding is the fact that, while they are generally willing to use apps for language learning, the majority claimed to never spend money on apps.

5.3 Learners' perceptions towards the approach adopted

When asked about the amount of time they were required to use the app daily, 45 (91.8 %) said it was appropriate and four (8.2 %) mentioned that it was excessive. One of the open-ended questions addressed the amount of time they considered necessary in order to master the target sounds with the app. Their responses ranged from ten minutes to an hour, but they have been grouped into four broad categories for the sake of simplicity: three students (6.1 %) suggested time-slots between 45 minutes and an hour, three (6.1 %) between 30 and 45 minutes, 32 students (65.3 %) between 15 and 30 minutes, and 11 students (22.4 %) suggested 15 or less than 15 minutes. Thus, the vast majority considered the time recommended to be appropriate.

As for the duration of the study, 38 participants (79.16 %) considered it to be 'just right'. However, five (10.41 %) claimed that some more days would have been desirable in order to consolidate the target sounds addressed and five (10.41 %) said it was a bit long. The results in Fouz-González (2020) show that while training fostered improvements in the participants' perception and production of the target features, the differences between groups did not reach statistical significance for every sound in every task and, in general, there was still room for improvement. Thus, while learners considered the length of training to be enough, it seems that for more substantial improvements, longer training periods are needed.

One student recommended addressing one sound each day. However, research has shown that training with a wider range of sounds is more beneficial than training with a small set (Nishi/Kewley-Port 2007), as learners are exposed to greater stimulus variability – one of the key elements for perceptual training to be most effective (see Logan/Lively/Pisoni 1991). Thus, training with groups of sounds that exemplify different phonetic categories seems to be more beneficial than focusing on just one. In this regard, the EFP app does not allow users to choose the sounds with which they want to practise, but rather, it presents them with a randomised set of words featuring the whole range of English sounds featured in the app. This means that learners are presented with a randomised set of words featuring different English sounds and that the target sounds only appear occasionally. While this can be very useful to help them become familiarised with the phonemic inventory of English, it limits the amount of exposure to the target sounds considerably. Other apps, like *Sounds* (Macmillan Publishers Ltd., 2011), offer users the opportunity to choose the sounds they want to practise with, the number of trials they want to have, as well as the possibility to buy word lists dealing with a range of topics. If future updates of the app incorporated the possibility to let users choose the sounds that they want to focus on, it would certainly facilitate the integration of this type of training over a whole course or semester, as learners would be able to receive a much more focused type of training every day, with many more instantiations of the target features in the same training session.

5.4 Participants' recommendations on how to improve the training offered in the EFP app

In the open-ended items, 16 participants (32.7 %) suggested the inclusion of more sample words to exemplify the target sounds. Several participants mentioned that because the words exemplifying the target sounds were limited to a small set, training felt somewhat monotonous. As a case in point, in the trial run carried out to examine the app's stimuli for the target sounds reported in Fouz-González (2020), there were only twelve words for /æ/, ten for /ɑː/ and /ʌ/, nine for /z/, and 22 for /ə/. If the app is to be used for long training periods, this can be rather repetitive. Moreover, adding more sample words for each sound would facilitate the generalisation of improvements to words that do not appear in training and it should facilitate the creation or reinforcement of adequate phonetic categories for the FL sounds, as learners would be exposed to a wider range of instantiations of the target features and to more stimuli variability.

Regarding feedback, although the learners' responses to the Likert-type items reported above show that they considered it to be adequate in order to inform them of their mistakes, participants offered some suggestions for improvement. They mentioned the fact that it would be beneficial to be able to hear the words again when their answers were wrong, which is in fact the way feedback is commonly offered in perceptual training paradigms to help learners notice why their answers are wrong and help them associate stimuli to the right answer (Logan/Pruit 1995). Another student said that it would be very helpful if sounds that were identified incorrectly during the activities could be played back at the end of each level, which could serve as some kind of revision. Furthermore, one participant would have appreciated to see the transcription of the words immediately after making a mistake, as waiting until the end of the 10-word block to see the right transcription was not perceived as effective as receiving feedback immediately.

Finally, one participant also suggested adding more options as distractors, as (s)he considered the two-alternative forced-choice to be too easy. Perhaps it would be interesting to divide the training offered by the app into levels of increasing difficulty, giving two options in the first levels of the app and adding more possibilities as learners progress. Additionally, two participants mentioned that the training routine was always the same and recommended adding more activities, such as transcription practice, identification practice with the sounds in sentences, or activities that addressed other pronunciation aspects, such as intonation.

6 Conclusions

With the arrival of smartphones and the possibility to install applications that make use of the different functionalities of the device, pronunciation training is more accessible than ever. The fact that apps can make use of the phone's audio, video, recorder, or even speech recogniser offers promising prospects for pronunciation training. Today's smartphones are like mini-computers which can run all sorts of programmes, from simple quizzes to state-of-the-art games. While software for pronunciation practice has been around for a long time in computers, the emergence of pronunciation apps brings pronunciation practice literally to the students' fingertips. The fact that learners can practise in devices they already have and use, and which are always *on*, makes this type of training very accessible to learners. Students no longer need to go to a language laboratory to practise pronunciation; they do not even have to sit at their desk, but they can simply take their phone and practise wherever they are.

It is important to note that apps are not free from limitations. As Kaiser (2018) points out, they are not always developed by pronunciation experts – which may be partly due to the fact that they do not undergo the same quality controls that other materials do before being published. Furthermore, apps are not always updated as regularly as operating systems. Users may spend months without being able to use them until the new version is released, something that would never be a problem with other platforms, such as books or web-based applications like Thomson's (2018) English Accent Coach, or the one used by Qian, Chukharev-Hudilainen and Levis (2018).

However, the possibilities apps offer are many, as they can provide learners with various types of training and immediate feedback on their performance, both in terms of perception (Uther et al. 2007; Fouz-González 2020) and production (Liakin/Cardoso/Liakina 2015). Even if ASR technology cannot yet provide reliable feedback on FL learners' spontaneous productions, apps can easily incorporate perceptual training paradigms that offer learners instant, reliable feedback on their performance. Because of the positive effects perceptual training has on the learners' perception and production (Rato 2013; Wong 2015; Carlet 2017; Thomson 2011), it seems that apps are the perfect way of incorporating perceptual training into the learners' routines. This would allow them to work on their perception of the FL and create adequate perceptual targets for the FL sounds and patterns, which should eventually lead to improvements in their ability to monitor their own pronunciation and, consequently, to improvements in their production.

The results reported by Calvo-Benzies (2013) show EFL learners' dissatisfaction with the way pronunciation is addressed in EFL textbooks and call for other types of pronunciation activities, with a third of the informants claiming that the activities often available in textbooks hardly ever helped them to improve their pronunciation. As pointed out above, if learners feel that something is not useful, they will simply not invest time in it. The results of this study show that learners considered training to be effective and that they are willing to incorporate this type of training into their routine. Some of the commonly mentioned reasons why students have been sceptical about adopting mobile devices for language learning in the past were screen and keypad sizes, as well as the high cost of internet data and applications (Stockwell 2008). Nevertheless, the fact that screens in smartphones are increasing in size and that data plans are much more affordable these days is making these reasons less of a limitation, with a great number of students placing a higher value on aspects such as portability or ubiquitous learning (Ko 2017).

This study has focused on the perceptions of a specific group of FL learners towards one particular app for pronunciation training. However, users' perceptions towards an app may differ depending on their interests, their mastery of the language, their background, or even their age. Future research should continue to explore how different types of learners perceive different apps as well as the language learning potential different apps have to facilitate the improvement of various pronunciation features.

The vast majority of participants in this study owned a smartphone and claimed to use it for more than two hours a day. As opposed to approaches in which teachers decide when to deliver information, which may not always be convenient for learners, apps offer learners the possibility to practise whenever and wherever they decide. Most participants in this study claimed that they would be willing to use apps like this for 15–30 minutes a day, which suggests that incorporating training paradigms like this as a complement to classroom instruction should not be difficult. Thus, given the challenging nature of pronunciation and the fact that learners often feel shy when they have to speak in front of their classmates, apps can be the perfect support for pronunciation homework. Learners could adopt approaches like this to work autonomously on those aspects that they find most challenging, build up self-confidence, and eventually put what they learn at home into practice in communicative interactions in the classroom or in real conversations with other speakers.

Appendix 1. Initial questionnaire (abridged)

Encuesta inicial
*Obligatorio

1. Sexo *
   - Hombre
   - Mujer
2. Edad *
3. ¿Qué carrera/estudios oficiales estas cursando actualmente? *
   - Grado en Estudios Ingleses
   - Grado en Traducción e Interpretación
   - Grado en Lengua y Literatura Españolas
   - Grado en Medicina
   - Otro:
4. ¿Cuánto tiempo pasas al día en internet? *
   - Menos de 15 minutos
   - Entre 15 minutos y 30
   - Entre 30 minutos y 1 hora
   - Entre 1 y 2 horas
   - Más de 2 horas
5. ¿Desde qué dispositivo sueles conectarte a internet? *
   - Desde el móvil (por la calle)
   - Desde el móvil (en casa)
   - Tablet
   - Ordenador
   - Otro:
6. ¿Qué modelo de teléfono tienes? *
   Por favor, especifica marca y modelo (ejemplo: Samsung Galaxy Ace 2)
7. ¿Es un smartphone? *
   Un smartphone es un teléfono con pantalla táctil que permite descargar aplicaciones
   - Sí
   - No

8. ¿Qué sistema operativo tiene? *
   - Android
   - iOS (iPhone)
   - Windows
   - Otro:
9. ¿Cuánto tiempo utilizas tu teléfono al día? *
   (para hablar, chatear, navegar por internet, estar en redes sociales, etc.)
   - Menos de 15 minutos
   - Entre 15 y 30 minutos
   - Entre 30 minutos y 1 hora
   - Entre 1 y 2 horas
   - Más de 2 horas
10. ¿Has utilizado alguna vez aplicaciones móviles con fines educativos? *
    - Sí
    - No
11. Si la respuesta anterior es afirmativa, por favor, indica para qué asignatura/tema
12. ¿Cuál es tu postura sobre las siguientes afirmaciones? *
    Totalmente EN DESACUERDO 1 2 3 4 5 Totalmente DE ACUERDO
    - Me gustaría utilizar aplicaciones móviles para aprender idiomas.
    - Considero que una aplicación móvil puede resultar útil para aprender idiomas.
    - Considero que una aplicación móvil puede ser útil para ayudarme a mejorar la pronunciación
13. ¿Cuánto tiempo estarías dispuesto a utilizar una aplicación móvil para aprender idiomas? *
    - Menos de 15 minutos al día
    - Entre 15 y 30 minutos al día
    - Entre 30 minutos y 1 hora al día
    - Más de 1 hora al día
    - Otro:
14. ¿Cuál es tu postura sobre las siguientes afirmaciones? *
    Totalmente EN DESACUERDO 1 2 3 4 5 Totalmente DE ACUERDO

- Presto atención a cómo la gente pronuncia en inglés y me comparo con ellos (La forma en que acentúan las palabras, cómo pronuncian los sonidos, la entonación que usan, etc.)
- Cuando cometo fallos de pronunciación, me doy cuenta.
- Cuando cometo fallos de pronunciación, soy consciente de cuál es el problema.
- Cuando cometo fallos de pronunciación, soy capaz de corregir el problema yo mismo.

15. ¿Cómo describirías tu nivel de inglés? *
    (Siendo realista, nivel obtenido, no cursando actualmente) Los niveles entre paréntesis son los descriptores del Marco Europeo de Referencia
    - Completamente bilingüe o casi bilingüe (nivel C2)
    - Muy alto (nivel C1)
    - Avanzado (nivel B2)
    - Intermedio (nivel B1)
    - Elemental (nivel A2)
    - Principiante (nivel A1)
    - Otro:
16. ¿Tienes algún título oficial que certifique el nivel de inglés que mencionas arriba? *
    - Sí
    - No

Appendix 2. Final questionnaire (abridged)

Encuesta final
*Obligatorio

1. Antes de este estudio, ¿has utilizado otras aplicaciones móviles con fines educativos? *
   - Sí
   - No

2. Si la respuesta anterior es afirmativa, por favor, indica para qué asignatura/s o temas y el tipo de actividad realizada.
   Ejemplo: para matemáticas, para aprender a hacer divisiones.

3. Por favor, indica tu postura sobre la siguientes afirmaciones *
   Totalmente EN DESACUERDO 1 2 3 4 5 Totalmente DE ACUERDO
   - Después de esta experiencia me gustaría utilizar aplicaciones móviles para aprender inglés
   - En general, la aplicación me ha parecido útil
   - Considero que el contenido visto en la aplicación me va a resultar útil en mi uso cotidiano del inglés
   - Creo que la aplicación me ha ayudado a DISTINGUIR mejor los sonidos estudiados
   - Creo que la aplicación me ha ayudado a PRONUNCIAR mejor los sonidos estudiados
   - He disfrutado utilizando la aplicación
   - Los aspectos tratados me parecen interesantes
   - La aplicación me ha parecido entretenida, no me aburría
   - La aplicación me ha parecido monótona
   - La aplicación me ha parecido fácil de manejar
   - El número de palabras ejemplo para cada sonido en el cuadro de fonemas me parece suficiente
   - El número de palabras ejemplo en las actividades me parece suficiente
   - El diseño de la aplicación me ha parecido atractivo
   - Pienso seguir utilizando la aplicación una vez que acabe el estudio
   - Si sacan niveles y actividades nuevas, estoy dispuesto a usarlos
   - Las actividades me han parecido difíciles
   - El feedback que me indicaba si mis elecciones eran correctas o no me ha parecido adecuado
   - Cuando daba una respuesta incorrecta, el feedback me ha ayudado a saber por qué mi respuesta era incorrecta

4. ¿Te ha parecido apropiada la duración del estudio (10 días)? *
   - Sí, el tiempo justo.
   - Sí, pero me hubieran venido bien unos días más.

- Un poco largo, con unos días menos habría estado bien.
- Otro:

5. Por favor, indica el grado de utilidad que le ves al cuadro de fonemas de la app
   NADA ÚTIL 1 2 3 4 5 MUY ÚTIL
6. Por favor, indica el grado de utilidad que le ves a la actividad 1 (con sonido) de la app
   NADA ÚTIL 1 2 3 4 5 MUY ÚTIL
7. Por favor, indica el grado de utilidad que le ves a la actividad 2 (sin sonido) de la app
   NADA ÚTIL 1 2 3 4 5 MUY ÚTIL
8. ¿Has utilizado la función de grabación para repetir después del modelo? *
   - Sí
   - No
9. ¿Has repetido en voz alta las palabras después del modelo para intentar imitar su pronunciación?
   - Siempre
   - Con frecuencia
   - A veces
   - Casi nunca
   - Nunca
10. Si yo no te hubiera dicho cómo utilizar la app, ¿cómo la habrías utilizado tú? *
    (¿habrías utilizado las mismas actividades, el mismo orden, etc.?)
11. ¿Conocías ya el vocabulario que sale en la App? *
    - Sí
    - No
    - No lo sé, no me he fijado
12. Por favor, indica tu postura sobre la siguiente afirmación (contesta ÚNICAMENTE si te has fijado en el vocabulario que salía)
    El vocabulario que sale en la app me ha parecido útil
    Totalmente EN DESACUERDO 1 2 3 4 5 Totalmente DE ACUERDO
13. ¿Crees que se repiten las palabras que salen en la App? *
    - No, nunca.
    - A veces.

- Bastante.
- Mucho.
- No lo sé, no me he fijado

14. ¿Te ha parecido apropiado el tiempo que tenías que usar la App cada día? *
(La práctica con el cuadro de fonemas más los 10 niveles de cada actividad)
    - Sí
    - No, ha sido demasiado.
    - No, ha sido poco.
    - Otro:
15. Por favor, indica cuánto tiempo diario con la App consideras necesario para aprender los sonidos que hemos visto *
16. En los resúmenes de nivel (donde te indica los fallos y aciertos que has tenido), ¿te fijabas en los fallos que tenías con intención de mejorar? *
    - Sí, siempre.
    - Sí, a menudo.
    - Sí, a veces.
    - Rara vez.
    - Nunca.
17. ¿Qué recomendaciones me darías para mejorar futuras ediciones de este curso? *
(sobre la duración, cómo utilizar las actividades, u otras cosas que se te ocurran)
18. Pensando en cómo está diseñada la aplicación, ¿cambiarías algo? *
(Algo que notes que le falta, algún fallo que hayas visto y quieras comentar).
19. ¿Pagarías 5,50€ por esta aplicación? *
    - Sí, merece la pena.
    - No, es demasiado caro.
    - No, porque nunca compro aplicaciones, pero si comprase me parece un precio razonable.
    - Otro:
20. ¿Qué precio le pondrías tú a esta aplicación? *
(Teniendo en cuenta el precio de otras aplicaciones del mercado)

21. Por favor, indica qué momento del día preferías para utilizar la app y por qué *
22. Por favor, si hay algo que quieras comentar o sugerir, hazlo aquí:

References

Aliaga-García, Cristina/Mora, Joan Carles 2009. Assessing the Effects of Phonetic Training on L2 Sound Perception and Production. In Watkins, Michael/Rauber, Andreia/Baptista, Barbara (eds.) *Recent Research in Second Language Phonetics/Phonology: Perception and Production*. Newcastle: Cambridge Scholars Publishing, 2–31.

Amer, Mahmoud 2014. Language Learners' Usage of a Mobile Application for Learning Idioms and Collocations. *CALICO Journal* 31/3, 285–302.

Calvo-Benzies, Yolanda 2013. Spanish EFL University Students' Views on the Teaching of Pronunciation: a Survey-Based Study. In Ciarlo, Chiara/Giannoni, David (eds.) *Language Studies Working Papers* (vol. 5). Reading: University of Reading, 41–49.

Carlet, Angelica 2017. *L2 Perception and Production of English Consonants and Vowels by Catalan Speakers: The Effects of Attention and Training Task in a Cross-Training Study*. Unpublished doctoral dissertation. Barcelona: Universitat Autònoma de Barcelona. <https://ddd.uab.cat/record/180084>.

Carlet, Angelica/Cebrian, Juli 2015. Identification vs. Discrimination Training: Learning Effects for Trained and Untrained Sounds. In The Scottish Consortium for ICPhS 2015 (ed.) *Proceedings of the 18th International Congress of Phonetic Sciences*. Glasgow: University of Glasgow, paper number 752, 1–4. <https://www.internationalphoneticassociation.org/icphs-proceedings/ICPhS2015/Papers/ICPHS0752.pdf>

Castañeda, Daniel/Cho, Moon-Heum 2016. Use of a Game-Like Application on a Mobile Device to Improve Accuracy in Conjugating

Spanish Verbs. *Computer Assisted Language Learning* 29/7, 1195–1204.

Cenoz, Jasone/García Lecumberri, María Luisa 1999. The Acquisition of English Pronunciation: Learners' Views. *International Journal of Applied Linguistics* 9/1, 3–17.

Chinnery, George 2006. Emerging Technologies: Going to the MALL: Mobile Assisted Language Learning. *Language Learning & Technology* 10/1, 9–16.

Flege, James 1987. Effects of Equivalence Classification on the Production of Foreign Language Speech Sounds. In James, Allan/Leather, Jonathan (eds.) *Sound Patterns in Second Language Acquisition*. Dordrecht: Foris, 9–39.

Flege, James 1995. Second-Language Speech Learning: Theory, Findings and Problems. In Strange, Winifred (ed.) *Speech Perception and Linguistic Experience: Theoretical and Methodological Issues in Cross-Language Speech Research*. Timonium: York Press, 233–277.

Foote, Jennifer/McDonough, Kim 2017. Using Shadowing with Mobile Technology to Improve L2 Pronunciation. *Journal of Second Language Pronunciation* 3/1, 34–56.

Fouz-González, Jonás 2012. Can Apple's iPhone Help to Improve English Pronunciation Autonomously? State of the App. In Bradley, Linda/Thouësny, Sylvie (eds.) *CALL: Using, Learning, Knowing, EUROCALL Conference, Gothenburg, Sweden, 22–25 August 2012, Proceedings*. Dublin: Research-publishing.net, 81–87.

Fouz-González, Jonás 2015. Trends and Directions in Computer-Assisted Pronunciation Training. In Mompean, José Antonio/Fouz-González, Jonás (eds.) *Investigating English Pronunciation: Trends and Directions*. Basingstoke/New York: Palgrave Macmillan, 314–342.

Fouz-González, Jonás 2020. Using Apps for Pronunciation Training: An Empirical Evaluation of the English File Pronunciation App. *Language Learning & Technology* 24/1, 62–85.

Gómez-Lacabex, Esther/García-Lecumberri, María Luisa/Cooke, Martin 2008. Identification of the Contrast Full Vowel-Schwa: Training Effects and Generalization to a New Perceptual Context. *Ilha do Desterro* 55, 173–196.

Henderson, Alice/Curnick, Lesley/Frost, Dan/Kautzsch, Alexander/Kirkova-Naskova, Anastazija/Levey, David/Tergujeff, Elina/Waniek-Klimczak, Ewa 2015. The English Pronunciation Teaching in Europe Survey: Factors Inside and Outside the Classroom. In Mompean, José Antonio/Fouz-González, Jonás (eds.) *Investigating English Pronunciation: Trends and Directions*. Basingstoke/New York: Palgrave Macmillan, 260–292.

Kaiser, DJ 2018. Mobile-Assisted Pronunciation Training: The iPhone Pronunciation App Project. *IATEFL Pronunciation Special Interest Group Journal* 58, 38–52.

Kennedy, Claire/Levy, Mike 2008. L'italiano al Telefonino: Using SMS to Support Beginners' Language Learning. *ReCALL* 20/3, 315–330.

Ko, Myong-Hee 2017. Learner Perspectives Regarding Device Type in Technology-Assisted Language Learning. *Computer Assisted Language Learning* 30/8, 844–863.

Kondo, Mutsumi/Ishikawa, Yasushige/Smith, Craig/Sakamoto, Kishio/Shimomura, Hidenori/Wada, Norihisa 2012. Mobile Assisted Language Learning in University EFL Courses in Japan: Developing Attitudes and Skills for Self-Regulated Learning. *ReCALL* 24/2, 169–187.

Kukulska-Hulme, Agnes/Shield, Lesley 2008. Overview of Mobile Assisted Language Learning: Can Mobile Devices Support Collaborative Practice in Speaking and Listening? *ReCALL* 20/3, 271–289.

Levy, Mike/Stockwell, Glenn 2006. *CALL Dimensions. Options and Issues in Computer-Assisted Language Learning*. Mahwah: Lawrence Erlbaum.

Liakin, Denis/Cardoso, Walcir/Liakina, Natallia 2015. Learning L2 Pronunciation with A Mobile Speech Recognizer: French /y/. *CALICO Journal* 32/1, 1–25.

Logan, John/Lively, Scott/Pisoni, David 1991. Training Japanese Listeners to Identify English /r/ and /l/: A First Report. *Journal of the Acoustical Society of America* 89/2, 874–886.

Logan, John/Pruitt, John 1995. Methodological Issues in Training Listeners to Perceive Non-Native Phonemes. In Strange, Winifred (ed.) *Speech Perception and Linguistic Experience: Theoretical and Methodological Issues*. Baltimore: York Press, 351–378.

Lys, Franziska 2013. The Development of Advanced Learner Oral Proficiency Using iPads. *Language Learning & Technology* 17/3, 94–116.

Macmillan Publishers Ltd 2011. *Sounds*: *The Pronunciation App* (Version 3.0). [Mobile application software]. <https://itunes.apple.com/gb/app/sounds-the-pronunciation-app/id442713833?mt=8>

Nelson, Terri/Oliver, Walter 1999. Murder on the Internet. *CALICO Journal* 17/1, 101–114.

Nishi, Kanae/Kewley-Port, Diane 2007. Training Japanese Listeners to Perceive American English Vowels: Influence of Training Sets. *Journal of Speech, Language, and Hearing Research 50*, 1496–1509.

Nowacka, Marta 2012. Questionnaire-Based Pronunciation Studies: Italian, Spanish and Polish Students' Views on their English Pronunciation. *Research in Language* 10, 43–61.

Oxford University Press 2012. *English File Pronunciation* (Version 1.1). [Mobile application software]. <https://itunes.apple.com/es/app/english-file-pronunciation/id520767531?mt=8>

Qian, Manman/Chukharev-Hudilainen, Evgeny/Levis, John 2018. A System for Adaptive High-Variability Segmental Perceptual Training: Implementation, Effectiveness, Transfer. *Language Learning & Technology* 22/1, 69–96.

Rato, Anabela 2013. *Cross-Language Perception and Production of English Vowels by Portuguese Learners: The Effects of Perceptual Training*. Unpublished doctoral dissertation. Braga: Universidade do Minho. <http://repositorium.sdum.uminho.pt/handle/1822/28100>.

Rosell-Aguilar, Fernando 2016. User Evaluation of Language Learning Mobile Applications: A Case Study with Learners of Spanish. In Palalas, Agnieszka/Ally, Mohamed (eds.) The International Handbook of Mobile-Assisted Language Learning. Beijing: China Central Radio & TV University Press, 545–581.

Rosell-Aguilar, Fernando 2018. Autonomous Language Learning through a Mobile Application: A User Evaluation of the *Busuu* App. *Computer Assisted Language Learning* 31/8, 854–881.

Stockwell, Glenn 2007. Vocabulary on the Move: Investigating an Intelligent Mobile Phone-Based Vocabulary Tutor. *Computer Assisted Language Learning* 20/4, 365–383.

Stockwell, Glenn 2008. Investigating Learner Preparedness for and Usage Patterns of Mobile Learning. *ReCALL* 20/3, 253–270.

Stockwell, Glenn/Liu, Yi-Chun 2015. Engaging in Mobile Phone-Based Activities for Learning Vocabulary: An Investigation in Japan and Taiwan. *CALICO Journal* 32/2, 299–322.

Tan, Emelyn/Teo, Debbie 2015. Appsolutely Smartphones: Usage and Perception of Apps for Educational Purposes. *Asian Journal of the Scholarship of Teaching and Learning* 5/1, 55–75.

Thomson, Ron 2011. Computer Assisted Pronunciation Training: Targeting Second Language Vowel Perception Improves Pronunciation. *CALICO Journal* 28, 744–765.

Thomson, Ron 2018. *English Accent Coach* [Computer program] (Version 2.3). <www.englishaccentcoach.com>.

Thornton, Patricia/Houser, Chris 2005. Using Mobile Phones in English Education in Japan. *Journal of Computer Assisted Learning* 21/3, 217–228.

Uther, Maria/Uther, James/Athanasopoulos, Panos/Singh, Pushpendra/Akahane-Yamada, Reiko 2007. Mobile Adaptive CALL (MAC). A Lightweight Speech-Based Intervention for Mobile Language Learners. *Proceedings of INTERSPEECH 2007*, 2329–2332.

Witt, Silke/Young, Steve 1997. Language Learning Based on Non-Native Speech Recognition. In *Eurospeech '97. Proceedings of the 5th European Conference on Speech Communication and Technology*, 633–636. <ftp://mi.eng.cam.ac.uk/pub/reports/auto-pdf/witt_euro97.pdf>.

Wong, Janice Wing Sze 2015. Does Proficiency Matter? The Effects of L2 Vowel Training on Cantonese ESL Learners with High and Low Proficiency Levels. In Mompean, José Antonio/Fouz-González, Jonás (eds.) *Investigating English Pronunciation: Trends and Directions*. Basingstoke/New York: Palgrave Macmillan, 219–240.

Carmen Sancho Guinda

The Discourse of Engineering Students' Entrepreneurial Proposals at the *Universidad Politécnica de Madrid*

1 Entrepreneurship and innovation in higher education: Why do they matter?

Entrepreneurship is one of the key lifelong learning competencies furthered by the Bologna Process in many European countries. The European Reference Framework proposed by the European Parliament and the Council (2006: Annex) speaks of "a sense of initiative and entrepreneurship", which tends to go hand in hand with "innovation", another buzzword in higher technical education and, increasingly, in secondary schools. The definition and relationship of the two constructs, nonetheless, remain ambiguous, since they overlap at some points. What is not difficult to perceive is that, in actual fact, both subsume other life-long competencies, such as a basic knowledge of science and technology, the exercise of problem-solving, a critical use of information, communication in the mother tongue and in foreign languages, and certain digital prowess. They involve, in sum, the four transversal skills (Sancho Guinda/Breeze 2017) that we university teachers aim to foster among our students: creativity, critical thinking, motivation, and autonomy.

Attempts to pinpoint the differences between entrepreneurship and innovation have been recent. According to a thematic criterion, the "Innovation Pedagogy" of Putkonen, Kairisto-Mertanen and Penntilä (2010) defines innovation as academic scientific knowledge, and entrepreneurship as the capacity to solve practical and application problems. Likewise, Zhao (2005), Crossan and Apaydin (2010), Shane (2012), and Maritz and Donovan (2015) associate innovation with technology, the renewal and enlargement of products and services, methods, and markets, as well as with knowledge and intellectual property management, whereas entrepreneurship has to do with the detection, evaluation, and exploitation of profitable opportunities, in which technology plays a secondary role. A second criterion is the placement of each area along a stasis-dynamism continuum: innovation is seen as a "process" rather than a product. It starts with the proposal of new ideas and finishes with the commercial exploitation of their outcomes (Marín-García/Pérez-Peñalver/Watts 2013), be they products, services, methods of any kind, the opening of new markets, business models, or novel management procedures. Entrepreneurship, albeit susceptible to being improved and nowadays included in educational syllabi, seems rather to be popularly conceived of as an innate quality of some individuals. A third criterion is social impact: entrepreneurship lays emphasis on the individual actor in start-ups, while innovation seeks a balance between individual and organisational action (Kontio 2010; Maritz/Donovan 2015). Fortunately, beyond these traditional dichotomies, personal and communal variables have been incorporated into a scoring rubric called "INCODE barometer" (Watts/García-Carbonell/Andreu-Andrés 2013), which evaluates students' entrepreneurial capacities and skills at individual, interpersonal, and networking levels, the latter referring to multi-disciplinary and multicultural environments. A fourth and last criterion is functional subservience: some regard innovation as an entrepreneurial tool (Zhao 2005) and others view entrepreneurship as an outcome of the innovation process – as a final commercialisation of the innovation (Crossan/Apaydin 2010).

Yet, whatever the perspective, and despite the substantial importance of entrepreneurship and innovation in higher education, particularly in those degrees revolving around technical contents, it is surprising to find a notable dearth of subject matters and supplementary training conducive to the development of entrepreneurial and innovative mentalities and abilities. In my work environment, the *Universidad Politécnica de Madrid* (henceforth UPM), the ACTÚA-UPM contest (see Fig. 5-1), a competition of business ideas among the different schools, intends to mitigate this teaching gap.

The contest intends to encourage team work diversity, as (under) graduates may co-work with masters and doctoral students, teachers, researchers, administrative and maintenance personnel, and professionals outside the institution, and consists of four major stages: 1) the screening

Fig. 5-1: ACTÚA-UPM advertising posters for 2018 and 2019.

phase of succinct communication of business ideas, 2) a competition for the best business model, 3) a *pre-hatching* stage or competition for the best start-up of the year, and 4) a *hatching* and *acceleration* stage devoted to financing, sponsor networking, and promotional dissemination. Seminars, courses, meetings, and specialised training are facilitated at every stage of the process, but awards are given only to the best business ideas (€1,000 for each of the best ten) and the three best start-ups (with prizes of €5,000; €10,000 and €15,000). Strikingly, however, participants do not receive specific instruction regarding the succinct communication and the promotional dissemination steps involved. As a generic competence, communication is indeed acknowledged to be crucial in the construction and dissemination of ideas (Marín-García et al. 2013) and equated with other competences of that sort, such as "action" and "negotiation" (Kontio 2010: 1, 5), but the descriptors of "good communication" are still too vague when it comes down to building fine-grained rubrics. The INCODE barometer, for one, speaks of "creative and enthusiastic" presentations at the individual level, and of an "effective transmission of ideas" on the interpersonal plane, without detailing them further. In addition, classic works of the literature on innovation and entrepreneurship, such as Dundon's (2002) *Seeds of Innovation,* just recommend "giving the major highlights" (p. 164), defining the vision statement "in words that have meaning" (p. 102), "adding credibility" (pp. 122–123), "repacking your idea" (p. 172), or "igniting passion" (pp. 144–145). The "passion supporters" listed to provide readers with a repertoire of expressions are, by the way, too colloquial and consequently inappropriate for the formal register of a written proposal.

Motivated by this panoramic picture, the present study analyses student output at the very first stage of the ACTÚA-UPM contest, that of the succinct communication of ideas, to detect communicative needs and establish the bases for a permanent collaboration between language and content teachers.

1.1 What type of communication is required?

The form to be filled out for the communication of business ideas (see Fig. 5-3) consists of two parts, respectively entitled *Tu proyecto en una línea* ("Your project in one line") and *Breve descripción de la idea* ("Brief description of the idea"). For the first, a total of around 20 words is recommended. For the second, no more than 250. This requisite is quite an exercise of concision and resembles the format of a similar contest at a national level: *Think Big-Telefónica,* but whereas the latter provides contestants with specific rhetorical guidance for the description of their business model (see Fig. 5-2), ACTÚA-UPM does not.

Fig. 5-2: *Think Big-Telefónica's* exemplar of rhetorical and content guidelines for contestants (my translation from the original in Spanish).

ACTÚA-UPM participants must, therefore, discover by themselves what information to include (i.e. what *rhetorical moves*) and select the register and tone they deem most appropriate, which is not always easy and even less when promotional discourse intervenes. If the standard conventions of engineering proposals were taught, for example, participants could at least regard the contest form as a condensed variant, since both texts are opportunities for "giving face" (Sales 2006: 152) to their

Campus de Excelencia Internacional	**Documento de trabajo** **Formulario en pruebas XIV *actúaupm*** **Competición de Creación de Empresas**	actúaUPM

TU PROYECTO EN UNA LÍNEA *(Se recomiendan unas 20 palabras)*

BREVE DESCRIPCIÓN DE LA IDEA

Esta información puede ser utilizada con fines promocionales. Describe bien tu idea, evitando incluir información de carácter confidencial en este apartado. Sé claro y conciso, lo importante es que cualquier persona no involucrada en el proyecto, ni experta en la materia, pueda entender de una forma fácil cuál es la necesidad o el problema a resolver que habéis detectado. También brevemente, en qué se basa vuestra solución. Se recomiendan unas 250 palabras.

Fig. 5-3: Registration form for the first stage of ACTÚA-UPM.

authors, who try to convince readers of their problem-solving capacities and, in the case of full-fledged engineers, their high standards of professional practice. In principle, these readers are alike in the two genres: on the one hand, what is known as "chief readers" (Sales 2006: 126); that is, committee members who make decisions in the process of selection and may not be engineers but have commercial or procurement expertise. On the other hand, "team readers" (Sales 2006: 126); that is, specialists (usually engineers) with the same knowledge background as the writers and who scrutinise and veto parts of the proposal.

Although the contest form (Fig. 5-3) is not, as Robert Ellis (1997: 166) remarks, a "selling document" like the engineering proposal, it should also be highly persuasive, which entails inspiring credibility by means of a solid background together with accuracy and rigour, being expressed in a comprehensible, simple, and concise way and carrying a *hook* or appeal that makes it attractive and memorable. It is intriguing how UPM students may try to convey such appeal, whether grammatically, by direct adjectival and adverbial qualification, noun and verb choices and emphasis devices, or discursively, by instilling emotion or employing proximisation strategies (Cap 2013). Do they choose an overtly sales-pitched overall tone, or resort to more subtle persuasion ploys? This unknown constitutes the overarching research question of the study.

1.2 What register and tone should we expect?

In a semi-structured interview with Pepa Casado Pérez, Technical Entrepreneurship Advisor at *Compluemprende – Oficina Complutense del Emprendedor*[1] (the Entrepeneur's Office of the Universidad Complutense de Madrid, hereafter UCM), some concrete communicative difficulties

1 URL <http://www.ucm.es/compluemprende>; E-Mail: emprende@ucm.es. This office serves the UPM in their joined masters' programmes at their common Campus of Excellence *(Campus de Excelencia),* whose facilities they share in downtown Madrid. The interview with Ms. Casado was held on March 7, 2019, and pivoted around the following issues: 1) Major communicative difficulties encountered by student entrepreneurs; 2) Type of communicative training offered by the institution; and 3) Impact of communicative performance on the evaluators' verdicts.

experienced by student entrepreneurs emerged. These comprised discriminating key from peripheral information and not getting lost in technical details (i.e. mostly when writing "one-line summaries"); presenting the message in a cohesive and coherent way; shifting registers to adapt to different audiences, genres, and media; and presenting the information creatively and enthusiastically. She noted an abuse of "story-telling" and the importance of punctuation to delimit ideas and dissolve ambiguity. The training provided by the Office underlined the selection of content and attention-getting and interest-raising strategies. The weight of proposal communication in board decisions was reported to be "very high", with special attention paid to clarity, coherence, and "staging" (both in oral presentations and written introductions stating the centrality of the project).

From all this it follows that, without any guidance, students are left to their own intuition to set a suitable promotional tone. As Bliss (2001: 16) notes, undergraduates are asked by faculty to produce two types of writing: descriptive and persuasive, which most often are interpreted as mutually exclusive. Nothing farther from the truth, though: according to Houp et al. (1980: 41), technical writing unfolds along a "persuasive continuum" in whose poles locate the factual non-argumentative text (Kirkman 1992), termed "restrained persuasion" by Sales (2006: 137), and an emotionally biased, one-sided sales-pitched style very much shunned by engineers (Sales 2006). In between these objectivity and subjectivity poles there is an "area of reasonable argument" through narrative, description, exposition, and argumentation proper. This middle zone is precisely the most difficult one for students, who are at a loss when it comes to expressing opinion or signalling the pros and cons of a certain solution or situation. This fact might be a consequence of their continued exposure to academic writing and its associated dogma of formality and impersonality (Swales/Feak 1994; Hyland 2006; Biber/Conrad 2009), which implies an avoidance of explicit appraisal and attitudes and low emotivity (Dzung Pho 2013).

Another component of the UPM students' background is engineering writing, characterised by a "complex simplicity" and "restrained persuasion" (both terms coined by Sales 2006). Syntax is, in effect, simple but burdened with dense nominalization strings, and subjective evaluative language is discouraged – for example, the use of tropes, tabloid-like titles, and sales-pitched style – in favour of empirical data, explanations, equations, and formulae. The third influence on UPM students' writing is computer-mediated communication, basically informal (Puschmann 2015) and oriented to emotional marketing and branding (Gómez Cabranes 2013) and author foregrounding (Maier/Engberg 2013). Because these three writing traditions (i.e. academic, engineering and computer-mediated) are acting upon students' writing, it is reasonable to expect a hybrid style with features of all of them. To describe these predictable expectations more accurately, the stylistic hybridity mentioned above is presumed to concern two fronts: linguistic and discursive. The former, leaving cross-linguistic influences aside, would involve, in Rod Ellis' (1997: 45–46) terms, a "grammatical foreign talk" whose characteristic traits might be, on the one hand, short sentences and an avoidance of syntactic subordination and complex constructions in general, and, on the other, an unnecessarily elaborated language use with phrasal and sentence lengthening to make meaning clear. Differently put, the lack of concision that is typical of novice writers, native and non-native users of English alike.

From a discursive standpoint, the main difficulties may concern manoeuvres of register shift, partly due to a lack of training and to a factor of "psychological distance". This means that, in spite of the authenticity of the Actúa-UPM writing task, student writers do not engage with a particular range of discourses along the stylistic continuum as a self-identified social group, since the communication being managed takes place within an institutional academic frame and motivation seems therefore strictly academic, not social. This prevents addressers from envisaging their intended readers. For all these reasons, and drawing on Selinker's (1972) notion of *interlanguage* (i.e. the learner's mental system of foreign language knowledge), we could expect a *discursive interlanguage* in engineering students' proposals.

2 Method

This small-scale study is essentially qualitative and corpus-based, and tries to answer the research question posed at the end of section 1.1; that is, whether UPM students promote their innovations with an overt sales-pitched tone or deploy more subtle persuasion strategies. It reports on the analysis of ten contest-registration forms (five initial texts and their revised final versions) written and voluntarily submitted by students enrolled in the subject "Advanced Design and Solid Surfaces" as part of the Masters' course in Industrial Design Engineering. As proposal forms divide into a one-line summary of the idea and a more extended description, the two parts were examined separately. One-line summaries were manually scrutinised and extended descriptions (a corpus totalling 2,292 word tokens and 664 word types),[2] both manually and electronically, with the aid of the freeware AntConc. 3.2.1w (Anthony 2007). All samples were instances of candid writing, with no previous training in proposal writing.

The theoretical framework adopted is eclectic and combines Classical Rhetoric, Narratology, Hyland's (2005) Metadiscourse Model, Pragmatics through Proximisation Theory (Cap 2013), and Positioning Theory (van Langenhove/Bertolink 1999). The reason for this choice has been their inter-connectivity: there are convergent points between them above their diverse foci. For example, through metadiscourse and pragmatic devices writers may comply or not with the Gricean and politeness maxims; also, proximisation (the creation of deictic centres) contributes to the adoption of points of view and narrative focalisation (i.e. the perceptual and/or conceptual vantage point or perspective of the telling, according to Bal 1985; Genette 1988; or Herman 2009). Such connectivity gives a larger and more consistent picture than restricting analysis to a single theory and a particular discursive feature.

The three persuasive strategies from Classical Rhetoric (i.e. *logos*, *ethos*, *pathos*) have been taken as broad categories of analysis subsuming more concrete rhetorical and lexico-grammatical features detected in the corpus, although the aspects researched under each of them are by no means exhaustive:

2 Initial versions comprised 1,048 word tokens and 463 word types, whereas final ones consisted of 1,244 word tokens and 554 word types.

Logos
- Metadiscourse
- Restrained persuasion (data and predictions)

Ethos
- Type of beginning and rhetorical organisation
- Narrative focalisation
- Contrast

Pathos
- Subjective evaluation
- Emotional load
- Proximisation strategies (deictics, reader pronouns and particularisation)

Moreover, in my adoption of the three Aristotelian principles or appeals, I will attend to Toye's (2013: 43) observation that they are not clear-cut categories, as their boundaries "can be blurred" and their functions polyvalent.

3 Findings and discussion

On the whole, and as expected, the samples examined showed a blend of features from academic and engineering writing and computer-mediated communication. Final versions gained specificity and incorporated restrained persuasion (i.e. data, formulae, technical facts), but tended to use nominalisation to achieve a formal register. Curiously, metadiscursive changes were few from the initial to the revised final versions.

3.1 Discursive features of the one-line summaries

All of the initial one-line summaries are noun phrases, which stylistically remind of the noun-phrase abstracts of some U.S. patents.[3] It is

3 "A double clutch transmission with an electric unit, as well as a method for operating the transmission", Pels et al (Oct. 21, 2003), USPTO patent

not likely, however, that authors have had previous contact with those phrasal abstracts. It rather seems that the decision to use noun-phrase structures is an utterly spontaneous summarising device, derived from their continued exposure to engineering writing during their degree years. Table 5-1 displays variation between the initial a) and final b) versions of each proposal, which are identical in the first instance (Proposal 1). As can be seen, only one sample was turned into a clause in its final version (3b). The rest of lexico-grammatical transformations comprise *substitutions* of different kinds, *simplifications* and *particularisations*.

Substitution is found in proposals 2–5, but for different reasons: out of the need to establish a "credibility credential" through a more nominal or "serious" register (in Proposal 3, "to create" becomes "for the creation of" in the final version), "politeness" (euphemisms such as the substitution of "Third World" in the initial version with "developing countries" in the final version of Proposal 2), or "semantic accuracy", as shown in the final version of Proposal 3, which shifts the agency focus away from the product's properties, metaphorically assuming human action in the initial version ("clothes able to reuse the material of used garments") to place it on a human collectivity in the final one, by means of the company's brandname, thus foregrounding human agency/intention ("con el fin de reutilizar"), which translates as "with the aim/purpose of reutilising".

Simplification (either through deletion or expansion) pursues facilitating comprehension for mixed and lay audiences. Deletion frequently concerns the elimination of technical jargon (e.g. "polymeric recyclable fibres" in the initial version of Proposal 3 turns into merely "recyclable fibres" in its final version), while expansion carries a somewhat emphatic nuance that spells out or glosses content to stress a given quality or aspect, normally relative to broad applicability or versatility. The specification of the type of containers in the final version of Proposal 5 ("in home and community containers alike") aptly illustrates this strategy: it leads us to envisage a wider range of dimensions and uses than "Dustbin […] in the homes" (initial version of Proposal 5).

No. 6,634,247. Retrieved from the United States Patent and Trademark Office website https://www.uspto.gov/patents-application-process/search-patents.

Tab. 5-1: One-line summaries of five ACTÚA-UPM proposals submitted to the 2018 contest edition.

Proposal	One-line versions
1 Ecological furniture	*a) Mobiliario ecológico que se realice con partes de automóviles que ya no tienen ningún uso en la industria automotriz.* *b) Mobiliario ecológico que se realice con partes de automóviles que ya no tienen ningún uso en la industria automotriz.*
2 Recipient for food storage	*a) Recipiente para el almacenamiento y la conservación de alimentos en el Tercer Mundo.* *b) Recipiente para el almacenamiento y la conservación de alimentos en países en vías de desarrollo.*
3 Recyclable clothing	*a) Firma de ropa a partir de fibras poliméricas reciclables capaz de reutilizar el material de las prendas usadas para crear nuevos productos.* *b) Syncy es una empresa fabricante de ropa a partir de fibras reciclables con el fin de reutilizar las prendas usadas para crear nuevos productos.*
4 Recycling drinks vending machine	*a) Máquina expendedora de bebidas que da a sus usuarios la posibilidad de utilizar su propio recipiente, beneficiándose así de descuentos.* *b) Máquina expendedora de batidos que da a sus usuarios la posibilidad de utilizar su propio recipiente, beneficiándose así de descuentos.*
5 Residue-compressing dustbin	*a) Cubo de basura con sistema para comprimir los residuos plásticos en los hogares minimizando así su volumen.* *b) Sistema de comprimido de residuos en contenedores, tanto caseros como comunitarios.*

Particularisations may consist in the hyponymic specification of objects, materials, etc. to gain accuracy (e.g. "milk shakes" instead of "drinks") or the mention of the business' commercial brand for promotional reasons (*"Syncy"* in the final version of Proposal 2), instead of a general description of the type "this company/business is/has/does…".

It is somehow surprising that even the final versions are redundant and/or verbose, with clausal modifiers ("which do not have any use in the automotive industry", see 1a in Tab. 5-1) instead of lexical (e.g. "useless/unutilised/no longer used"), which would make a much more economic alternative. Analogously, roundabouts (e.g. "that gives its users the chance of using", both initial and final versions in Proposal 4) are preferred over the more concise "that enables users to use" or "that permits using/allows for using"), or embedded meanings (e.g. "recyclable" is logically included in "reuse", see the two versions of Proposal 3).

One would not expect the use of data or much metadiscourse in one-line descriptions, as the *logos* component of discourse should be sufficiently materialised in concise lexical choices and clear syntax. In this corpus of one-line summaries, however, a couple of appositive gerund clauses work as conventional metadiscourse items, performing the function of explanatory glosses to ensure a promotional effect: "this one benefitting from discounts" (4a) and "thus benefitting from discounts" (4b). All five samples are expanded noun phrases, but, in contrast with engineering writing, noun-based modifiers qualify the nominal core in right-branching collocations, not as left-branching premodifiers. Other interesting *logos*-related findings affecting comprehension are that the average number of words does not vary from the initial to the final versions (18.2), so there are no concision gains via text reduction, and the difference between mean lexical densities is very scarce (0.53 and 0.52), which suggests little explicitness because the use of grammatical words is similarly low in both versions. The average number of finite verbs slightly increases (three in the initial versions and four in the final ones) and that of subordinate clauses decreases (seven in the initial versions and four in the final ones). These facts indicate a small evolution towards syntactic simplicity and immediacy. The number of passive sentences stays equal (just one) in both versions.

So far we have seen that *ethos* is stylistically attained with a formal register based on nominalisation, but also through interpersonal distance in the form of *dictionary entry* defining the proposal, with a direct rhetorical structure consisting of category + usefulness. There is no contrast with former situations or proposals.

Finally, *pathos* is minimum. The few adjectives used are intended to be classifying (e.g. "ecological", "recyclable", "new"), although they convey a considerable positive load, as do verbs such as "benefit", "minimise", "reuse", and the noun "preservation".

3.2 Discursive features of the extended descriptions

In the longer accounts of the proposals, *logos* relies fundamentally on restrained persuasion, present in 40 % of all samples (initial and final) and in 60 % of the final versions. Probably because of this trend (i.e. the increase of data in the final versions), added to the imposed textual brevity, metadiscourse displays fluctuating reader-deference patterns in the corpus, as empirical data speak for themselves and "do the job". A case in point is excerpt (1), which corresponds to the extended final version of Proposal 3. That is, there seems to be no real need to spell out content through code glosses, to announce goals, cite sources, or interact with the reader if data can justify the importance of the proposed idea and bridge inferential leaps.

(1) *Se puede reciclar hasta un 80 % de tejido con estos procesos, y solo en la fabricación de una camiseta se ahorrarán hasta 27.000 L de agua y se emitirán 3,2 Kg menos de* CO_2.
Up to 80 % of fabric can be recycled with these processes, and only in the production of a t-shirt up to 27,000 l of water will be saved and 3.2 kg less of CO_2 will be emitted. (Extended final version of Proposal 3)

If the low use of code glosses (see Fig. 5-4) when addressing a mixed audience, as is that of ACTÚA-UPM, can be attributed to the explanatory power of restrained persuasion, the scantiness of goal announcers appears to be caused by the brevity of the text and its inherent rhetoric of problematisation. Certainly, even though this rhetoric is not explicit, every start-up proposal tries to overcome a technical obstacle and/or fulfil an unattended social need. Sequencers are also scarce because just two proposals (the first and the third ones) expose a procedural description, enumerate arguments (only the initial version of Proposal 5, with the Spanish equivalents of "firstly", "in parallel", and "finally"), or stage discourse to offer an overview of forthcoming contents, as in the final version of Proposal 1 ("next we explain to you how our simplest table model is made", in Spanish *os explicamos a continuación cómo se fabrica nuestro modelo de mesa más simple*).

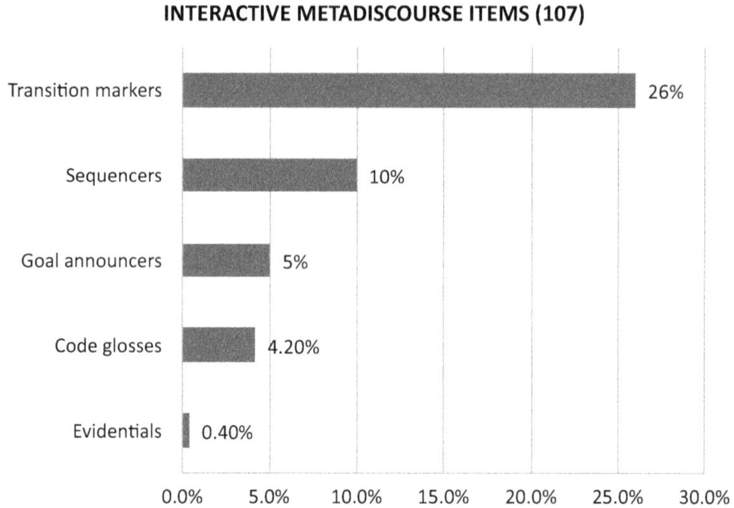

Fig. 5-4: Percentages of interactive metadiscourse items in all samples.

Another thought-provoking finding involving interactive metadiscourse concerns the use of evidentials, which serve to shake off responsibility for expressions conveying a strong emotional load (see excerpt 2, small caps added).

> (2) *Cada día mueren aproximadamente 24.000 personas a causa de la falta de alimentos o por las malas condiciones en las que estos alimentos son consumidos. Teniendo en cuenta que el total de muertes diarias (en todo el Mundo) son aproximadamente de 150.000 personas, las muertes por hambruna alcanzan el 16 % del total* SEGÚN EL 'PROYECTO HAMBRE DE LAS NACIONES UNIDAS'. *Esta causa de muerte suele ser propia en países del Tercer Mundo.*
> Every day approximately 24,000 people die of starvation or because of the bad conditions under which food is consumed. ACCORDING TO THE 'FAMINE PROJECT' OF THE UNITED NATIONS, deaths out of famine reach 16 % of the total, this being approximately 150,000 daily (round the world). This death cause is typical of/often occurs/tends to happen in Third World countries. (Extended final version of Proposal 2)

This example shows that the drama tinge imprinted by the vocabulary of death, which states the start-up's relevance via extreme problematisaton of the type "death(s) (of starvation)"/"die", in Spanish *muerte(s) (por hambruna)/mueren,* is toned down by the evidential reference "according to the Project Hunger of the UN".

Last, transition markers predominate because the limited length of the document appears to favour the construction of brief sentences/clauses, interrelated by means of connectives pre-empting conceptual gaps, such as *pues* and *ya que,* both translatable into English as "since", "as", or "given that", in the original *pues* and *ya que* (excerpt 3, my small caps). Other frequent items are "thus" *(así, de esta manera),* "which", "where/thereby" (*lo cual*) and "due/owing to" and "because of" (*por ello/esto* and *debido a* in Spanish). Transition markers, in this context, reflect concern for the audience's comprehension and border on interactional metadiscourse.

(3) *[...], PUES parte de los consumidores optarán por rellenar sus propios recipientes, YA QUE les saldrá más barato. [...] Con estas máquinas se disminuirá el volumen de residuos generados con el envasado, LO CUAL aminorará el impacto ecológico.* [...], SINCE part of the consumers will opt for filling up their own recipients, AS this will be cheaper for them, [...] With these machines the volume of residues generated by the bottling/packaging will be reduced, WHICH will mitigate ecological impact. (Extended final version of Proposal 4)

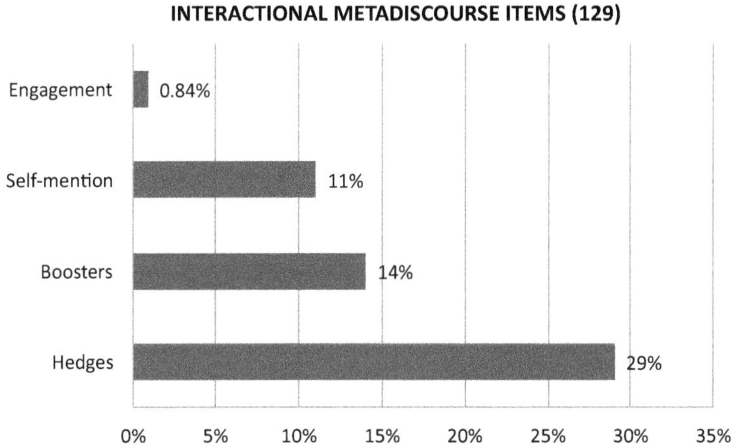

Fig. 5-5: Percentages of interactional metadiscourse items in all samples.

Let us now turn to interactional metadiscourse proper (typified in Hyland's 2005 taxonomy). As can be observed in Fig. 5-5, the most prominent items are hedges (due to the incipient status of the business idea or model, whose relevance and future efficacy must not be enunciated arrogantly or in a dogmatic way). Hedges (see excerpt 4, my small caps) may mitigate certainty, frequency, and quantification, either in the service of problematisation or to praise the proposal's strongpoints. Between parentheses I attach the translation of hedging items into English to the sample provenance.

(4) *[…] YA QUE en "Furni-car" CREEMOS QUE fabricar productos obsolescentes no es ético ni sostenible.*
[…] SINCE in "Furni-car" WE BELIEVE/THINK THAT manufacturing obsolescent products is neither ethical nor sustainable. (Extended Proposal 1, final version: "we believe/think that")
Cada día mueren APROXIMADAMENTE 24.000 personas […] Esta causa de muerte SUELE SER propia en países del Tercer Mundo.
Every day APPROXIMATELY 24,000 people die […] This death cause OFTEN OCCURS/IS TYPICAL OF/TENDS TO HAPPEN IN Third World countries. (Proposal 2, initial + final: "approximately", "is often/tends to be")
[…] PUEDE causar un grave impacto medioambiental. Los envases de plástico y bebidas generan GRAN CANTIDAD DE residuos.
[…] MAY cause a grave environmental impact. Plastic containers and beverages generate A LARGE AMOUNT/GREAT DEAL OF waste. (Proposal 4, initial + final: "may", "a large amount/great deal of")

The instances of booster use reveal variety and bifunctionality: there appear subjective lexical intensifiers of evaluative adjectives and value-laden nouns (e.g. *gran, totalmente, considerablemente, completamente, bastante, muy,* whose English translations are "great/large/big", "totally", "considerably", "completely/utterly/totally", "quite", and "very"), but there is also grammatical intensification through tense choice, specifically through the future simple, which imbues the writing with a promotional quality of certainty and success (see excerpt 5), exploited by Proposals 3 and 4 (small caps mine). Verbs conjugated in the future simple denote predictable beneficial actions (e.g. "reduce", "diminish", "alleviate") and introduce negative direct-object referents such as "costs" or "pollution":

(5) *SUPONDRÁ un gran ahorro para […] Las empresas REDUCIRÁN su gasto […], ya que les SALDRÁ más barato. Con esta máquinas se DISMINUIRÁ el volumen de residuos generados con el envasado, lo cual AMINORARÁ el impacto ecológico de las empresas.*
IT/THIS WILL RESULT IN large savings for […]. Companies WILL REDUCE their expenses […], as it will be cheaper for them. With these machines the volume of residues generated by the bottling/packaging WILL BE REDUCED, which WILL MITIGATE the ecological impact of companies. (Proposal 4, initial + final)

There is, nevertheless, a sort of *reversibility* in the use of boosters and hedges: a dual function whereby the frequency, quantification, or certainty hedges form part of a problematisation statement that boosts the start-up's value. Or the obverse – a boosting expression whose intensifying effect resides in imprecision, as is the case of verbs in the simple future, which express "*sine die* certainty" when not accompanied by empirical data and time frames backing up the prediction.

The proportion of engagement items is negligible. No questions or directives were found, and a single expression of shared knowledge (see excerpt 6, my small caps) was detected. The reason is that, as already mentioned, data are attention-getters *per se,* and when additionally impressive, they even implicitly raise questions about their causes and effects and function as a "shared perception" that triggers "shared reflection". Here too, restrained persuasion "does the job".

(6) *[…] con toda la repercusión* QUE YA SABEMOS *que estas producen en el medio ambiente.*
[…] with all the repercussion THAT WE ALREADY KNOW these produce on the environment. (Proposal 5, final version; translation: "that we already know")

Ethos is conveyed, first and foremost, through problematisation, this being the generalised beginning or "description opener" (see Fig. 5-6).

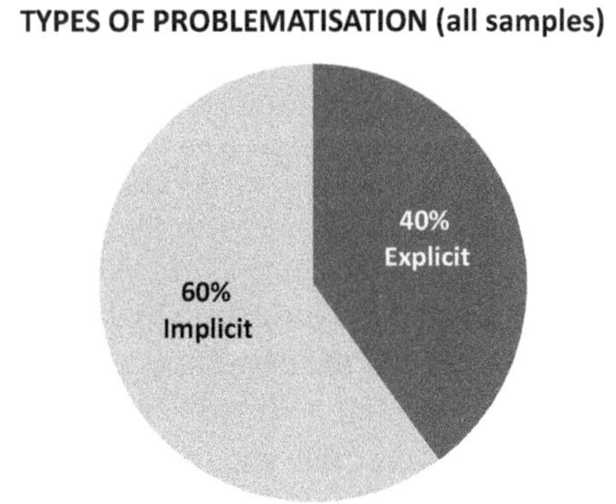

Fig. 5-6: Percentages of samples using problematisation types in all versions (initial and final).

Problem-posing is not only a distinctive rhetorical feature of engineering writing (of the disciplinary mentality it mirrors) but also a strategy to earn credibility: problematising proposals aim to solve a technical issue of importance or meet a specific social need, and thus contribute to the common welfare. Therefore, those start-ups deserve attention because their authors deal with serious – sometimes urgent and grave – matters, which portrays them as committed individuals.

Interestingly, it is not extremely frequent to find problematisation explicitly marked by signalling nouns such as "problem", "repercussion", "impact" or "solution". Problems are instead raised with more or less subtle negatively loaded verbs, nouns or phrases, such as *residuos, muerte, zonas más pobres, dañar el medio ambiente, hambruna, mala gestión, espacio innecesario en los hogares* (in English "residues", "death", "poorer areas", "harm the environment", "poor management", "unnecessary space in the homes"), as well as with lexis denoting amendment or improvement of a taken-for-granted situation that constitutes tacit knowledge and therefore is not mentioned (e.g. *reciclar, reciclaje, reutilizar, conservar, sostenibilidad, ecodiseño,* in English "recycle", "recycling", "reuse", "preserve", "sustainability" and "eco-design"). Little wonder, then, that in the word-list ranking yielded by AntConc, the first negatively loaded word, *residuos* ("residues") does not appear until position 31, and the first positively loaded term *ahorro* ("cost savings") ranks 67.

Indirect problematisation may be in turn associated with contrasts and/or predictions (see excerpt 7):

(7) *A diferencia de otros negocios de esta categoría, se recuperarán y reutilizarán los materiales de las prendas vendidas para crear nuevos productos.*
Unlike other businesses of this category, the sold garments' materials will be recovered and reused to create new products. (Proposal 3, initial version)

This kind of implicit criticism draws attention to the distinctiveness of the proposal and shows expertise of the entrepreneurial field by describing the level or behaviour of potential competitors. In this fashion, authors tacitly position themselves as credible and trustworthy "experts" who are technically knowledgeable and simultaneously exhibit moral authority. They "tell", as they are the narrators of a situation needing improvement or redress, but also filter or "focalise" the narrative in various ways through evaluation: they tell us what they think or perceive, not what is thought or perceived by others. The problem-solution progression, for instance, resorted to more or less overtly by all proposals, is a sort of macro-evaluation act that appraises an undesirable societal situation or need, and hence carves out a niche for the start-up. In such encompassing act embed two other evaluations that also profile the authors' *ethos*: that of the proposal (along an objectivity-subjectivity continuum with varying degrees of subjectivity and emotion) and of the communication act itself, which positions the writer(s) and the readers. In all these evaluations, the borderline between *ethos* and *pathos* becomes fuzzy. Logical reasoning (*logos*) and emotion (*pathos*) shape *ethos* as well, as indicators of reasoning and communicative competence and engagement with readers and society.

Tab. 5-2: Evaluative expressions promoting ACTÚA-UPM proposals.

Proposal	Idea evaluators
1 Ecological furniture	1a) *[…] para no dañar más al medio ambiente.* 1b) *Este diseño es estético, funcional, robusto y duradero.*
2 Recipient for food storage	2a) *[…] fácil de transportar* 2b) *[…] fácil de transportar […] con un cierre seguro y compacto.*
3 Recyclable clothing	3a) *[…] empresa autosuficiente* 3b) *[…] modelo de negocio totalmente novedoso, basando su producción en la sostenibilidad y ecodiseño.*
4 Recycling drinks vending machine	4a) *[…] supondrá un gran ahorro[…] más barato.* 4b) *[…] supondrá un gran ahorro[…] más barato.*
5 Residue-compressing dustbin	5a) *[…] la tarea del reciclaje se hace más amena […] mecanismo sencillo, útil y eficiente […]capaz de comprimir los envases de forma mecánica y rápida. Será un producto universal y económico […]* 5b) […] *mecanismo universal, sencillo, útil y ecoeficiente […] capaz de comprimir los envases de forma mecánica y rápida.*

So far we have seen that the words chosen to depict problematic societal scenarios may be emotion-laden and express *pathos* (e.g. "death", "starvation", "harmful", "residues", "emissions", etc.), but a growing sense of authorial presence, in the form of subjectivity or focalisation (see Tab. 5-2), is also present in the evaluations of the idea (excepting Proposal 4, whose evaluators stay unchanged in the final version). Definitive versions contain evaluators as subjective as "aesthetic" (1b), "universal" and "ecoefficient" (3b), or "totally novel" (5b), the latter, curiously, being the only use of innovation for promotional purposes in the corpus. Finally, the shortening of interpersonal distance through proximisation strategies (e.g. proximal deictics, personal pronouns, and particularisation; that is to say, the reiterated mention of the newly created commercial brand in the final versions – *Furni-car* in 1b, *Syncy* in 3b, and *Ecoenvas* in 4b) creates an impression of nearness and mutual engagement between writer and reader. Figure 5-7 itemises the proximisation devices employed in all samples.

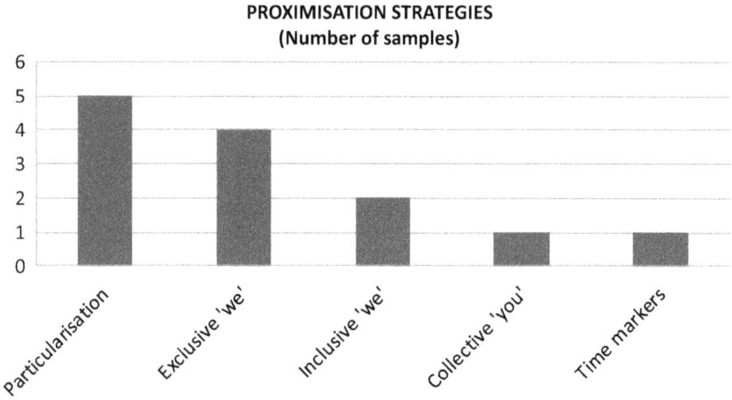

Fig. 5-7: Concrete proximisation strategies in ACTÚA-UPM proposals.

The bar chart reflects that the proximisation strategy most preferred by UPM students is the specification of their brand names (particularisation), followed by the use of collective pronouns. But the pronoun "we" is much more employed excluding the readers (e.g., when referring to difficulties, achievements or actions undergone or performed by the group of student innovators) than including them (e.g., as beneficiaries of the innovation or to show solidarity towards their needs and plights, which the innovation will supposedly solve). A collective use of "you", primarily for sympathising with the potential consumers' needs and offering them the benefits of the innovation, is less resorted to, and the use of proximal deictics of space and time ranks last among all other strategies to bring the invention near the potential consumer or the technology gatekeepers, in this case the members of the contest examining board.

There is only one proposal (number 3) impersonally written (in other words, having zero focalisation), although the increased interpersonal distance seems to be made up for with more subjective adjectives. The rest of texts speak of "our idea/proposal/device" with an exclusive first-person plural pronoun, present also in their mission statements "we will try/intend to develop", "we seek to solve", "we believe/think", and "we propose". Only one document (1b) mentions the reader, but incidentally as a disadvantaged interlocutor who needs to be instructed about the production process ("next we explain to you how our most simple table model is made"). With this double-edged didactic deference towards the addressee, authors markedly take up the role of experts and create a fictitious inequality, a knowledge breach between both participants. This approach to the intended reader stands in stark contrast with an ambiguous use of "we" which may be inclusive and embrace the reader as actor/sponsor/consumer and part of the team behind the idea in Proposal 2a: "In this way, we make possible that the people in these poorer areas can keep food under better conditions [...]".

4 Concluding reflection

To recapitulate, the candid entrepreneurial discourse of the UPM proposals under study corroborates the expectation of stylistic hybridity or *promotional interlanguage*, because it gathers features of engineering writing (restrained persuasion and nominalisation), academic writing (little explicit evaluation, low emotivity, and formality) and computer-mediated communication (author foregrounding and emotional marketing). Restrained persuasion and authorial presence appear mostly in the final versions, more reflected upon after being read, as if authors had only then realised about the promotional nature of the message and the competitiveness fostered by the context. In answer to the study's research question, formulated at the end of section 1.1, both sales-pitched items going beyond mere functionality and usefulness (e.g. "aesthetic", "universal", "totally novel", "great cost savings", "ecoefficient") and subtle persuasive tactics (i.e. indirect problematisation, reader mention) are few.

With this small-scale study, I would like to make the case for a narrow collaboration between content and language instructors, who should co-teach the discourse of the discipline and support content learning by exploiting "language-related episodes" (Basturkmen/Shackleford 2015), here prolonged throughout the ACTÚA-UPM competition and in pursuit of an appropriate promotional style. To this end, applied linguists and sci-tech professionals could synergise their respective expertise to help students curb redundancy and gain concision, especially by detecting implicit meanings, honing their idea descriptions with precise definitory nouns in order to economise expression, and finding engaging developments of the problem-solution progression, to avoid knowledge rifts as much as a patronising tone, and to advertise the start-up without incurring over-promotion.

References

Anthony, Laurence 2007. *AntConc 3.2.1w*. <http://www.antlab.sci.waseda.ac.jp/software.html>.

Bal, Mieke 1985. *Narratology: Introduction to the Theory of Narrative*, 3rd edition. Toronto: University of Toronto Press.

Basturkmen, Helen/Shackleford, Nick 2015. How Content Lecturers Help Students with Language: An Observational Study of Language-Related Episodes in Interaction in First-Year Accounting Classrooms. *English for Specific Purposes* 37/1, 87–97.

Biber, Douglas/Conrad, Susan 2009. *Register, Genre, and Style*. Cambridge: Cambridge University Press.

Bliss, Anne 2001. Rhetorical Structures for Multilingual and Multicultural Students. In Panetta, Clayann Gilliam (ed.) *Contrastive Rhetoric Revisited and Redefined.* Mahwah, NJ: Lawrence Erlbaum, 15–30.

Cap, Piotr 2013. *Proximization: The Pragmatics of Symbolic Distance Crossing.* Amsterdam: John Benjamins.

Crossan, Mary M./Apaydin, Marina 2010. A Multidimensional Framework of Organizational Innovation: A Systematic Review of the Literature. *Journal of Management Studies* 47/6, 1154–1191.

Dundon, Elaine. 2002. *Seeds of Innovation: Cultivating the Synergy that Fosters New Ideas.* New York: American Management Association.

Dzung Pho, Phuong. 2013. *Authorial Stance in Research Articles.* Houndmills, Basingstoke: Palgrave Macmillan.

Ellis, Robert A. 1997. *Communication for Engineers.* London: Arnold.

Ellis, Rod 1997. *Second Language Acquisition.* Oxford: Oxford University Press.

European Parliament and the Council. 2006. *Recommendation of the European Parliament and of the Council of 18 December 2006 on Key Competences for Lifelong Learning (2006/962/EC).* <http://eur-lex.europa.eu/legal-content/EN/TXTn/?uri=celex:32006H0962>.

Genette, Gérard 1988. *Narrative Discourse Revisited.* Ithaca, NY: Cornell University Press.

Gómez Cabranes, Leonor 2013. Las Emociones del Internauta. In Flamarique, Lourdes/D'Oliveira Martins, Madalena (eds.) *Emociones y Estilos de Vida: Radiografía de Nuestro Tiempo* Madrid: Biblioteca Nueva, 211–243.

Herman, David 2009. *Basic Elements of Narrative.* Oxford: Wiley-Blackwell.

Houp, Kenneth W./Pearsall, Thomas E./Tebeaux, Elizabeth/Dragga, Sam 1980. *Reporting Technical Information*, 4th edition. Encino, CA: Glencoe Publishing.

Hyland, Ken 2005. *Metadiscourse. Exploring Interaction in Writing.* London: Continuum.

Hyland, Ken. 2006. *English for Academic Purposes. An Advanced Resource Book.* London: Routledge.

Kirkman, John 1992. *Good Style: Writing for Science and Technology*. London: E. & F.N. Spon.

Kontio, Juha 2010. Inspiring the Inner Entrepreneur in Students – A Case Study of Entrepreneurship Studies in TUAS. In *Proceedings of the 6th International CDIO Conference*. École Polytechnique, Montréal, June 15–18, 2010. <http://cdio.org/knowledge-library/documents/inspiring-inner-entrepreneur-students-case-study-entrepreneurship-studie>.

Maier, Carmen Daniela/Engberg, Jan. 2013. Tendencies in the Multimodal Evolution of Narrator's Types and Roles in Research Genres. In Gotti, Maurizio/Sancho Guinda, Carmen (eds.) *Narratives in Academic and Professional Genres*. Bern: Peter Lang, 149–173.

Marín-García, Juan A./Pérez-Peñalver, M. José/Watts, Frances 2013. How to Assess Innovation Competence in Services: The Case of University Students. *Dirección y Organización* 50, 48–62.

Maritz, Alex/Donovan, Jerome 2015. Entrepreneurship and Innovation. Setting and Agenda for Greater Discipline Contextualisation. *Education + Training* 57/1, 74–87.

Puschmann, Cornelius 2015. A Digital Mob in the Ivory Tower? Context Collapse in Scholarly Communication Online. In Bondi, Marina/Cacchiani, Silvia/Mazzi, Davide (eds.) *Discourse in and through the Media*. Newcastle upon Tyne: Cambridge Scholars, 22–45.

Putkonen, Ari/Kairisto-Mertanen, Liisa/Penntilä, Taru 2010. Enhancing Engineering Students' Innovation Skills through Innovation Pedagogy Experiences in Turku University of Applied Sciences. *International Conference on Engineering Education ICEE*, July 18–22, Gliwice, Poland. <http://www.ineer.org/Events/ICEE2010/papers/T11E/Paper_987_1232.pdf>.

Sales, Hazel E. 2006. *Professional Communication in Engineering*. Houndmills, Basingstoke: Palgrave Macmillan.

Sancho Guinda, Carmen/Breeze, Ruth 2017. Introduction: Making Essential Competencies Visible in Higher Education. In Breeze, Ruth/Sancho Guinda, Carmen (eds.) *Essential Competencies for English-Medium University Teaching*. Cham: Springer, 1–16.

Selinker, Larry 1972. Interlanguage. *International Review of Applied Linguistics* 10, 209–231.

Shane, Scott 2012. Reflections on the 2010 AMR Decade Award: Delivering the Promise of Entrepreneurship as a Field of Research. *Academy of Management Review* 25/4, 217–226.

Swales, John M./Feak, Christine B. 1994. *Academic Writing for Graduate Students. Essential Tasks and Skills*. Ann Arbor, MI: The University of Michigan Press.

Toye, Richard 2013. *Rhetoric: A Very Short Introduction*. Oxford: Oxford University Press.

Van Langenhove, Luk/Bertolink, R. 1999. Positioning and Assessment of Technology. In Harré, Rom/van Langenhove, Luk (eds.) *Positioning Theory*. Oxford: Blackwell, 116–126.

Watts, Frances/García-Carbonell, Amparo/Andreu-Andrés, M. Ángeles (eds.) 2013. *Innovation Competences Development. INCODE Barometer and User Guide*. Turku: Turku University of Applied Sciences.

Zhao, Fang 2005. Exploring the Synergy between Entrepreneurship and Innovation. *International Journal of Entrepreneurial Behaviour & Research* 11/1, 23–41.

Part 2: Internationalisation

Elspeth Jones

The Role of Languages in Transformational Internationalisation

1 Introduction

Today's interconnected, globalised world demands that our students graduate with skills for living and working in multicultural societies. Universities increasingly view this as one driver for a focus on internationalisation, alongside other more economic, quality and reputational concerns. Internationalisation appears annually to grow in importance in institutional, regional and national strategies, and has now "moved from the fringe of institutional interest to the very core" (Brandenburg/ De Wit 2015: 15).

But what are the real and potential outcomes of a transformational form of internationalisation for our students, one which aims to develop their global and intercultural perspectives within the curriculum? What are the factors involved in delivering this, and what role do languages have to play? How can language study be helpful in perspective change? Can programmes delivered using English as a medium of instruction in non-Anglophone countries make a contribution to the internationalisation agenda?

These are the questions at the heart of this chapter, which begins by examining various dimensions of internationalisation, including the outcomes and benefits of student mobility. It then considers how a more inclusive approach can deliver an internationalised curriculum *at home*. Using appropriate learning outcomes and offering opportunities for *interculturalisation* through "constructive engagement with otherness" (Daloz, 2000: 110), we can create a context in which all students are able to benefit from internationalisation, not merely the mobile minority.

2 Internationalisation

Building on a previous definition by Jane Knight (2004), De Wit, Hunter, Howard and Egron-Polak (2015: 29) describe internationalisation as:

> The intentional process of integrating an international, intercultural or global dimension into the purpose, functions and delivery of postsecondary education, in order to enhance the quality of education and research for all students and staff, and to make a meaningful contribution to society.

Since mobility has long been the major focus of internationalisation efforts for universities around the world, this includes a welcome and unambiguous statement that we must consider all stakeholders, not simply the mobile elite (Wiers-Jenssen 2011). The definition makes clear the purpose of internationalisation, and specifies its importance for all students and staff, in addition to society at large (Brandenburg/De Wit/Jones/Leask 2019). It encourages us to reflect on previous practice and to broaden internationalisation efforts from what may have been a rather narrow focus on mobility.

But why do governments, policy makers and institutions too often settle on the idea that internationalisation, as far as students are concerned, is synonymous with study abroad or other forms of credit mobility? In the European context this may, to some extent, be a result of the success of the Eramus+ scheme, which has boosted the numbers taking part to unprecedented levels. Mobility also offers a relatively easy measure of success if we are merely interested in quantitative input-output results. However, simply counting the number of students (and staff) participating tells us nothing about what they have gained from the experience; in other words, the qualitative outcomes of international mobility also need to be measured. Yet it seems that stating and achieving target numbers is often thought to be enough to indicate a university's commitment to internationalisation.

As for students who study their whole programme in another country, again it is assumed that outcomes will include intercultural learning along with the qualification. Institutions are keen to receive international students, partly for economic reasons. But this results in yet another numerical indicator, with the assumption that the presence of international students on campus will support internationalisation at home – the higher the number, the more internationalised the campus. Yet there is negligible evidence of this being effective as one study after another shows little integration between international and domestic students (e.g. Volet/Ang 1998; Leask 2010; Montgomery 2010). Furthermore, the inability to make local friends is one element limiting the positive experience of international students (Ammigan/Jones 2018).

There are, however, good reasons to value international mobility, and these will be considered next.

3 Transformational internationalisation

When the outcomes of international experiences are evaluated rather than a simple count of the numbers taking part, there are clear benefits for those who do so. Putting aside any language skills or intercultural competence that may develop, there are two other important sets of outcomes which are widely reported as resulting from mobility.

Firstly, in terms of academic achievement, a recent UK study demonstrated a clear influence of study abroad on the grades achieved at graduation (Cardwell 2019). This echoed an earlier finding on improved grades in a study which also showed that graduates received higher salaries and were less likely to be unemployed following a mobility experience than those who did not take part (UUKi 2016).

Secondly, numerous international studies show international experience to offer significant gains, especially with regard to transferable employability skills (Jones 2013b). International study, work placement or volunteering can develop not only personal and intercultural skills, but also those which are highly sought by employers (see Tab. 6-1). It has been shown that such skills can be developed even through relatively short international experiences, from two weeks to one semester (Jones 2010; Mellors-Bourne/Jones/Lawton/Woodfield 2015).

Tab. 6-1: Skills developed through international experience (adapted from Jones 2010, 2012a, 2013a, 2015).

Personal & self-efficacy skills	Interpersonal & employability skills
Adaptability to complex social & cultural contexts	Communication skills
Being globally & interculturally informed	Cross-cultural empathy & communication
Challenging personal stereotypes	Decision-making & communicating decisions which may be unpopular
Commitment & motivation	Fluency, accuracy & appropriateness of language use (L1 or L2)
Coping strategies	Initiative & enterprise
Creativity	Mediation skills & conflict resolution
Flexibility	Networking & forging relationships
Humanity	Planning & organising
Humility & respect	Problem solving
Independence	Project management
Integrity	Taking responsibility
Non-judgmental observation	Team work
Open-mindedness	Team leadership
Patience	
Risk-taking	
Self-awareness	
Self-confidence	
Self-management	
Sense of identity	
Sensitivity	
Willingness to learn	

The Erasmus Impact Study (European Commission 2014) found that 92 % of employers are looking for these kinds of transversal skills in their employees. It noted, perhaps unsurprisingly, that these skills are developed through international study and exchange, for example the Eramus+ scheme. All of this confirms the finding that employers are seeking graduates with first-hand experience of living and working among other cultures (Fielden/Middlehurst/Woodfield 2007), although perhaps without clearly understanding the skills developed as a result. This requirement will surely continue to grow as migration and other social change results in ever more diverse societies and workplaces.

If they are to capitalise on the skills identified in Tab. 6-1 and achieve employment, students may need to go beyond simply describing their experiences by recognising the precise nature of the skills they have developed. They must also understand how to express those skills in a meaningful way using the kind of language potential employers will value. As argued by De Wit and Jones (2014: 1):

> Maybe we should use the word 'internationalisation' less and connect it more to the international and intercultural dimensions of personal transferable skills and learning outcomes.

Directly applying the language used and understood in an employment context would allow universities and students to better articulate the transformational impact of international experiences both to employers and the wider society. It would facilitate a clearer and more direct linkage between the outcomes of mobility and graduate employability which, as we have seen, can be substantial.

4 Inclusive internationalisation for all students

While these benefits clearly accrue to students who have international experiences, what can be done to achieve more inclusive outcomes from internationalisation for all our students, not just a mobile elite? The European target for 2020 of 20 % of graduates having had a mobility experience (European Commission Education and Training, n.d.) will still mean, even if achieved, that 80 % of students will not have an international experience during their programme of study, placing them at a potential disadvantage compared to their mobile peers.

So the question is this: how can an internationalised curriculum "at home" present similar benefits for the static majority of students, both in terms of skills development and the wider outcomes of internationalisation? As yet, there is limited evidence to suggest whether the international element or experiential learning (Kolb 1984) is more important in the transformational outcomes noted above.

With his concept of *transformative learning* Mezirow (1978) suggests that "disorienting dilemmas" offer a catalyst for "perspective transformation". Such dilemmas occur when experiences do not fit or align with our expectations and we need to adjust our worldview in order to understand them. International travel and encounters with cultural others provide many such experiences and are thus ideal sources of these dilemmas.

Internationalisation at Home is built on the premise that disorienting dilemmas can be replicated in domestic contexts, resulting in transformative learning through "constructive engagement with otherness" (Daloz 2000: 110). In this respect, the term *interculturalisation* might be more appropriate, since the "international" is not a requirement of such an approach.

Internationalisation at Home (IaH) therefore seeks to involve students in purposeful engagement with cultural others in our own localities. It aims to support the transformation of mindsets, which can result from international experience, without travelling to other countries. The concept is essentially the same as Internationalisation of the Curriculum (Leask 2015), although that term has not gained as much ground throughout Europe as it has in other parts of the world. Both focus on international and intercultural learning outcomes as a way to enhance transformative learning. They are used interchangeably in this chapter. The definitions are similar, with Internationalisation at Home defined as:

> The purposeful integration of international and intercultural dimensions into the formal and informal curriculum for all students within domestic learning environments. (Beelen/Jones 2015: 76)

Tab. 6-2: Ten key elements of Internationalisation at Home (adapted from Jones/ Reiffenrath 2018).

	Element	Explanation
1	Offers all students global perspectives within their programme of study, whether or not they spend time abroad.	IaH is not to be considered a substitute or a "second-best option" for students who may not be internationally mobile during their studies. By targeting all students within their respective programmes of study, IaH integrates global perspectives, thereby enriching the quality of a study programme. Moreover, IaH can be an effective means of *actively including diverse student cohorts* – both internationally mobile incoming students and local students from a variety of backgrounds – into teaching and learning processes.
2	Moves beyond electives or specialised programmes.	IaH does not merely target students who may already be interested, but the entire student cohort. Elements of internationalisation are integrated systematically into the compulsory curriculum.
3	Involves developing international and intercultural perspectives through internationalised learning outcomes in the formal curriculum.	International and/or intercultural dimensions are integrated into learning outcomes within the discipline, e.g. "Students demonstrate understanding of the basic principles of production ecology and agrosystems modelling and their implications for diverse cultural and location-specific contexts"; or "In diverse teams, students are capable of debating the local as well as global impact of relevant risk management strategies".
4	Is supported by informal (co-) curriculum activities across the institution.	As learning not only takes place within formal classroom settings, more informal activities, such as intercultural communication workshops, buddy programmes, language tandems, service learning activities or cultural programmes lend substantial strength to IaH and can help deliver comprehensive internationalisation.
5	Makes purposeful use of cultural diversity in the classroom for inclusive learning, teaching and assessment practice.	In this respect, IaH is strongly learner-oriented. Using cultural diversity as a classroom resource includes finding ways of integrating experiences and knowledge of both internationally mobile students and local students from diverse backgrounds.

(*continued on next page*)

Tab. 6-2: Continued

	Element	Explanation
6	Creates opportunities for student engagement with 'cultural others' in local society.	IaH motivates students to seek "the intercultural" as well as "the international", and to acknowledge effects of globalisation, migration, and cultural diversity on their doorstep. Formal learning scenarios, such as community research projects, might go hand in hand with service learning, excursions or class visits by community members.
7	Involves all staff, not only academics and international officers.	Since teaching and the curriculum are at the heart of IaH, teaching staff and academics play a crucial role and need to take ownership over IaH measures. However, they also need support from colleagues across the university – including *international officers*, educational developers, quality assurance officers and faculty administrators.
8	May or may not include teaching in English or another lingua franca.	IaH entails a shift in orientation, not merely translation of an existing curriculum. The adoption of new viewpoints and consideration of global contexts is not language-dependent and may be delivered either through local language or English-medium programmes.
9	Can include virtual mobility through online working with partner universities.	Virtual collaborations, shared teaching materials or even low-threshold activities such as virtual guest lectures expand perspectives in classroom discussions and sensitise students to other forms of knowledge production as well as modes of conducting scientific research. Students gain access to knowledge and material not available on their home campus or, in more collaborative formats, enhance their communicative and social skills.
10	Fosters purposeful engagement with international students.	In both formal and informal learning settings, teaching activities and assignments are designed to stimulate exchange and collaboration among students from diverse backgrounds, whether they are "domestic" or international. Successful IaH does not depend on the presence of international students.

While Internationalisation of the Curriculum is seen as:

> [...] the incorporation of international, intercultural and/or global dimensions into the content of the curriculum as well as the learning outcomes, assessment tasks, teaching methods, and support services of a program of study. (Leask 2015: 9)

Both definitions assume that global, international and intercultural perspectives can be introduced and developed through creative learning, teaching and assessment approaches in the local context. Students' comfort zones can be extended in a controlled manner, by working with their peers as cultural others, in the relatively safe yet challenging space offered by higher education (Jones/Caruana 2010). Internationalisation of the curriculum at home thus has the potential to challenge cultural assumptions, extend knowledge and adjust mindsets by valuing the role of cultural diversity within a broader internationalisation framework.

Table 6-2 outlines ten key elements of internationalisation at home, as identified by Jones and Reiffenrath (2018), and is intended to illustrate this approach in practice.

Recent work by the Council of Europe, based on its notion of *intercultural dialogue* (Council of Europe, 2008), has resulted in an interesting model of twenty competencies required for democratic culture and intercultural dialogue (see Fig. 6-1). The knowledge, skills, values and attitudes identified by this project appear to be in line with values-based rationales for internationalisation (Jones/Killick 2007) which are often at the heart of curriculum internationalisation.

To summarise, if we continue to concentrate on international mobility for the minority who take part, it will distract us from the need to internationalise the curriculum for all students. Mobility should not be seen as the main focus of our internationalisation efforts but, instead, as adding value (for a few students) to a curriculum which already incorporates global, international and intercultural perspectives. An article in *China Daily* sums up the reasons why this is important.

> Students that [sic] are globally competent should be able to formulate and explore globally significant questions and create a coherent response that considers multiple perspectives and draws useful and defensible conclusions. They should also recognize that they have a particular perspective and that others may or may not share it. They should be able to articulate and explain the perspectives of others and compare them with their own perspective to construct a new point of view....

> They should see themselves as being capable of making a difference and be able to recognize opportunities in which they may do so. They should be able to weigh options based on evidence and insight, assess the potential effects and be able to act and reflect on the consequences of their actions. (Jackson 2012: 5)

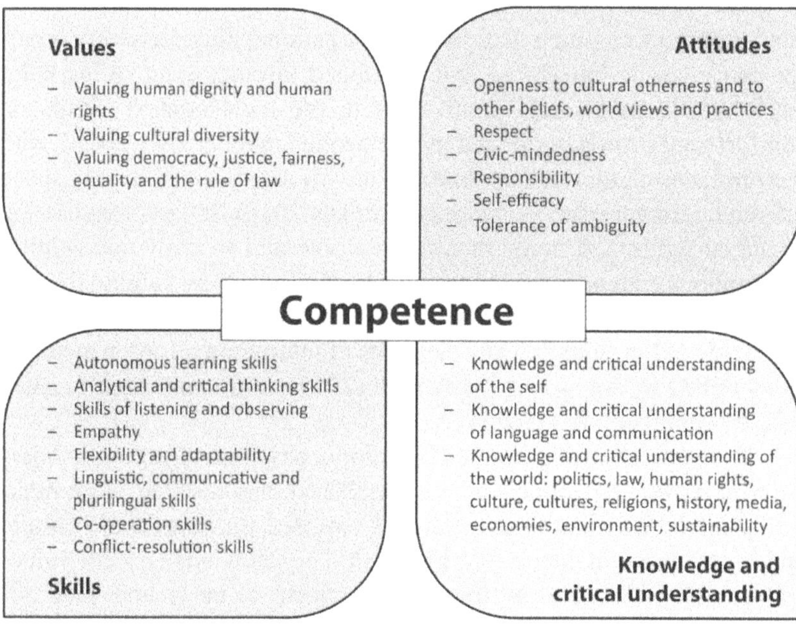

Fig. 6-1: A model of the competences required for democratic culture and intercultural dialogue (Council of Europe 2018: 38).

5 Internationalisation and the role of languages

The chapter now turns to consideration of the extent to which transformational internationalisation and languages are intertwined.

5.1 English as a lingua franca

It is important to bear in mind that much of what we think of as internationalisation would not be possible without a lingua franca and, for the moment, that is English. The internationalisation of higher education, by definition, requires communication across a range of countries through international conferences, the development of institutional partnerships, mobility programmes, collaborative research and publication (across all subjects) and in the development of internationalisation as a field of scholarship and research. These have all been facilitated by the use of a lingua franca when interlocutors do not speak one another's language.

In terms of student mobility English has been the great facilitator, enabling the movement of students to study in countries where English is the majority language, or used as a medium of instruction (EMI) in others where they do not speak the local language. Yet the questions arising have rarely been problematised in the literature beyond those who are involved in EMI programmes, who are researchers, speakers or teachers of languages other than English, or studying the many issues associated with the use of English as a lingua franca. Scholars beyond those fields "tend to be unaware of the manifold complexities relating to language use" (Jenkins 2019: 15):

> These include issues such as the role of language in identity, the causes and effects of language ideologies, and the influence of language attitudes, as well as English-specific phenomena such as the gatekeeping function that English performs and the entire question of whether it is reasonable for an 'international' university to teach only in the medium of English rather than in multiple languages. (Jenkins 2019: 15)

So, while the use of English as a lingua franca has been beneficial to the internationalisation agenda, it should not simply be normalised and assumed as standard practice. Jenkins (2017) argues for using English within a context of multilingualism, while Pratt (2010) calls for the emergence of "new heterolingual practices", and asserts that:

> [w]hile many people who think about language are thinking about globalization, the people who think about globalization never think about language. Language has not been a category of analysis in the literature on globalization. (Pratt 2010, cited in Jenkins 2019: 15)

5.2 Second language study

If we focus solely on internationalisation, it is clear that competence in another language can assist international travel and interpersonal communication with speakers of that second language. But more importantly, for the purposes of this chapter, the wider consequences of language study are allied to values-based rationales for internationalisation, in addition to those which are more pragmatically based (Jones/Killick 2007).

Specifically, the kind of paradigm shift needed to speak and think in a different language can transform mindsets in important ways. It can support the development of intercultural perspectives by challenging our assumptions, as outlined in section 3, and clarified in this quotation.

> Language study encourages us to deconstruct the linguistic world as we know it, to tolerate ambiguity, and to embrace cultural "otherness". .... Linguists understand that apparently direct translations are fraught with potential misunderstanding and we learn that cultural "others" may not see the world in the same way.... Fluency in another language takes us beyond mere tolerance of "otherness" and requires us to engage with alternative world views as a matter of course. (Jones 2012b: n.p.)

Almost by definition, study of another language causes us to think internationally more than locally:

> Of all areas of the curriculum, in Higher Education but also in other contexts, foreign language teaching is particularly well-placed to respond to this [intercultural dialogue] drive in internationalisation because it entails contact with a language different from the mother tongue and also contact with people who speak or use this language, involving not only a linguistic dimension but also different values, beliefs and worldviews. (Porto 2020: 151)

One respondent to a survey in Jones (2015: 18) put it this way:

> I think that learning a language is a humbling experience. It makes you put things into perspective. As we discover that there is no right or wrong way of saying things, [and] concepts [we don't know], we realise how arbitrary our views and assumptions are within our native culture, how narrow-minded and ignorant we can be at times, and ultimately how small we are as individuals. It forces you to open your mind and be more critical and, as much as possible, objective.

These examples of transformative learning are a natural consequence of different ways of thinking brought about by language study. Byram's (1997) model of intercultural communicative competence, as expressed in five *savoirs*, has been influential in summarising some of the broad capabilities involved in intercultural communication and can be linked both to *intercultural dialogue* (Council of Europe 2008) and the competencies for democratic culture (Council of Europe 2018) seen in Fig. 6-1. Although speaking another language may not be a requirement for the development of these skills, Byram (1997) argues that language competence represents an important element in his five *savoirs*:

- *Savoirs* denotes knowledge of self and other, and the processes of interaction between individuals and within society.
- *Savoir être* suggests curiosity, reflection and openness in intercultural learning while relativising the self. Sometimes described as "attitudes".
- *Savoir apprendre* indicates the skills of discovery and learning through social interaction.
- *Savoir comprendre* relates to skills of interpreting and relating, interpreting cultural practices or documents in relation to those which are more familiar.
- *Savoir s'engager* refers to critical cultural awareness, the ability to make informed evaluations of other cultures in comparison to one's own, or others.

Byram (2012, 2018) also argues for the importance of languages as a foundation for more internationalist perspectives in higher education.

> Internationalisation might provide the opportunity for demonstrating the importance of language teaching and learning, but it is crucial that an internationalist perspective is added to the language teaching agenda if it is to make a convincing argument for a role not merely in an internationalised university but in a university which is internationalist. (Byram 2012: 6)

Knowledge of another language is valuable in its own right but, as we have seen, it can also help develop intercultural communicative competence and the transformation of mindsets. Yet it is neither necessary nor sufficient to speak another language in order to develop these competences. Plenty of monolinguals are clearly proficient and comfortable communicating across cultures, operating effectively and appropriately in international contexts. Equally, specialist linguists sometimes rely on their ability to speak the other's language, finding it more difficult to communicate with cultural others from different linguistic backgrounds. The challenge may be to move forward from culture-specific knowledge, language and skills to become less specialised *interculturalists* (Jones 2011).

5.3 English as a medium of instruction

The practice of using English as a medium of instruction (EMI) in universities has grown exponentially in recent years. Initially intended as a means of making curriculum attractive and accessible to those who do not speak the local language, it has grown to become synonymous, just as with mobility, with internationalisation itself. EMI programmes have certainly supported efforts to recruit international students in countries where lesser taught and less widely used languages are spoken.

Some practitioners see delivering programmes in another language as internationalising the curriculum. But teaching disciplinary content programmes through English is a vehicle for internationalisation, not a goal in itself. Simply translating the curriculum from one language to another will not internationalise it (Leask 2015; Jones 2017). As suggested earlier, a minimum requirement for curriculum internationalisation is for students to be able to reflect on internationalised or interculturalised content, and to consider alternative perspectives through the teaching and learning process. Relevant internationalised learning outcomes and appropriate assessment practices can then demonstrate achievement of those planned outcomes (Jones/Killick 2013; Leask 2015):

> Simply providing a program in English is insufficient for it to be considered an internationalised curriculum. If the program content and learning outcomes are not internationalised, and remain the same as in the original language, merely changing the language of instruction will not make them so. (Beelen/Jones 2015: 64)

Although EMI programmes are now widespread, there are many issues associated with the decision to deliver programmes in English which have only recently begun to be explored in detail (see, for example, Barnard/Hasim 2018; Bradford/Brown 2018; Henriksen/Holmen/Kling 2019; Murata 2019). The question of English used as a lingua franca and the use of *world Englishes* compared to native speaker norms has, of course, been debated for much longer (see, for example, Brumfit 2001; Kirkpatrick 2010; Jenkins 2014; Jenkins/Baker/Dewey 2017). Indeed the function and role of English in the globalised world continues to mutate, with more second than first-language speakers. Jenkins (2014: 10) cites Brumfit (2001: 120) who refers to a shift in English education:

> [...] away from English as part of an education that inducts you into a humanistic tradition, to an education that facilitates your communication for whatever you want with whoever you want: a shift towards a notion of communicative competence where the communication is defined by the capacity of individuals of different cultures to interact.

The consequences and outcomes of large scale use of English for the delivery of university programmes are still underexplored, and may take some time to be fully understood. But some of the issues for students, teachers and the institution are illustrated in Tab. 6-3.

Socio-political implications may also arise in cases where EMI dominates in higher education, and there may be consequences for local (possibly indigenous) languages. For instance, there was an outcry when the Politecnico di Milano announced its intention to deliver from 2014 all Masters programmes in English, with the result that the decision was eventually rescinded. There was societal concern at the undermining of national identity as embodied by the Italian language, and the resulting devaluation of Italian as an academic language and a vehicle for research and publication.

There may also be wider implications for the secondary education system. Pre-university levels of language competence for local entrants will need to be at a suitable level. Students will require sufficient capability on entry to work alongside those who may be native speakers of English. Indeed, widespread university-level instruction through English may limit access to higher education programmes from lower socio-economic groups, leading to potential societal divisions.

This section has considered various aspects of the role of languages in transformational internationalisation. These include the benefits of language study for developing alternative international and intercultural perspectives. Languages can also be beneficial in supporting

Tab. 6-3: Some issues in the implementation of EMI programmes.

For the student	For the teacher	For the university
• Assumed superiority of native speakers – issues for mixed classes of native and non-native speakers	• Assumed superiority of native speaker teachers – implications for those who are not	• Expectations of allowable threshold standards for language competence
• Willingness of those with higher level language skills to undertake assessed group work and other activities with those who are less proficient	• Chosen language/ culture can shape learning and teaching approach (Luxon/ Peelo, 2009), and there may be different ways of conveying information in different languages	• Quality and standards relating to teaching and assessment may be an issue where neither teachers nor students are native speakers
• Preparedness to speak out in class if lacking confidence in language skills	• Lack of confidence may result in a return to more traditional teaching styles	• Selection and recruitment of academics who can rise to the demand of teaching in another language
• May need language development as well as understanding of disciplinary content to ensure progression and achievement	• Language development and support needs – academic delivery is very different from more general language use	• Support, resources and staff development
	• For those teachers with weaker language skills it may be difficult to deliver all disciplinary aspects of the curriculum within the time allotted	• Policy on the place of translation, writing and proofreading services, or support by native speakers
	• EMI may have been introduced "top-down" by policy makers rather than through consultation with key stakeholders and implementation issues may not have been thought through, resulting in high workloads	• Signage, websites and other implications if a bilingual campus is the aim
		• Ensuring continued use of the local language as a vehicle for academic thought and publication

internalisation processes and activities, despite some of the pitfalls and issues associated with using English as a medium of instruction.

One final aspect to consider relates to our sorry failure as English-speaking scholars of internationalisation to seriously examine the literature produced in languages other than English. This may offer quite different perspectives. If we are lucky enough to understand articles written in another language, that is already a first step. In due course, machine translation is likely to make it easier to search across languages. We could also make more effective use of international students or research assistants in this regard.

6 Summary

This chapter has reflected upon internationalisation, in particular the role of mobility, in the development of students' transversal and employability skills. It has argued that in order for all students to benefit from the potential offered by international experiences, a more inclusive internationalisation of the curriculum at home must be implemented. It has suggested a number of ways in which this can be achieved in local contexts, with transformative learning, as well as developing intercultural competence, as its objectives. Crucially, it noted that intercultural engagement does not require an international dimension and that local, multicultural contexts may offer the disorienting dilemmas which can lead to perspective transformation. Thus diversity in the domestic classroom and local population can offer opportunities to work across cultures through *interculturalisation* at home.

The role of languages in internationalisation was then examined, and its value was noted along with some drawbacks. It was suggested that one challenge for linguists is to be open to the notion that language study is not the only route to intercultural communicative competence, nor is a period of study abroad a prerequisite. Some of the issues associated with delivering programmes through English were identified, and it was emphasised that simply translating a curriculum does not result in its internationalisation.

Helping students to develop the kind of knowledge, skills and attitudes they will need for living and working in our increasingly interconnected, globalised world is one of the most important purposes of higher education. Similarly, if we are to solve major global problems, crossing boundaries using international and intercultural knowledge, communication skills and critical thinking will be essential. Furthermore, this will require a commitment to ethical practice, global responsibility and an understanding of and respect for cultural others, regardless of origin and background. The relatively safe space for debate represented by higher education presents an ideal opportunity to achieve these important goals, and language study may provide one route to this kind of transformational internationalisation.

References

Ammigan, Ravichandran/Jones, Elspeth 2018. Improving the Student Experience: Learning From a Comparative Study of International Student Satisfaction. *Journal of Studies in International Education* 22/4, 283–301.

Barnard, Roger/Hasim, Zuwati (eds.) 2018. *English Medium Instruction Programmes: Perspectives from South East Asian Universities*. London: Routledge.

Beelen, Jos/Jones, Elspeth 2015. Redefining Internationalization at Home. In Curaj, Adrian/Matei, Livia/Pricopie, Remus/Salmi, Jamil/Scott, Peter (eds.) *The European Higher Education Area: Between Critical Reflections and Future Policies*. Dordrecht: Springer, 67–80.

Bradford, Annette/Brown, Howard (eds.) 2018. *English-Medium Instruction in Japanese Higher Education: Policy, Challenges and Outcomes*. Bristol: Multilingual Matters.

Brandenburg, Uwe/De Wit, Hans 2015. The End of Internationalization. *International Higher Education* 62, 15–17.

Brandenburg, Uwe/De Wit, Hans/Jones, Elspeth/Leask, Betty. 2019. Internationalisation in Higher Education for Society. *University*

World News, 20 April. https://www.universityworldnews.com/post.php?story=20190414195843914.

Brumfit, Christopher 2001. *Individual Freedom in Language Teaching: Helping Learners to Develop a Dialect of Their Own*. Oxford: Oxford University Press.

Byram, Michael 1997. *Teaching and Assessing Intercultural Communicative Competence*. Bristol: Multilingual Matters.

Byram, Michael 2012. A Note on Internationalisation, Internationalism and Language Teaching and Learning. *The Language Learning Journal* 40/3, 375–381.

Byram, Michael 2018. An Essay on Internationalism in Foreign Language Education. *Intercultural Communication Education* 1/2, 64–82.

Cardwell, Paul J. 2019. Does Studying Abroad Help Academic Achievement? *European Journal of Higher Education*, 1–17. <https://doi.org/10.1080/21568235.2019.1573695>

Council of Europe 2008. *White Paper on Intercultural Dialogue "Living Together As Equals in Dignity"*. Strasbourg. <https://www.coe.int/t/dg4/intercultural/source/white%20paper_final_revised_en.pdf>.

Council of Europe 2018. *Reference Framework of Competences for Democratic Culture. Volume 1 Context, Concepts and Model*. Strasbourg. <https://rm.coe.int/prems-008318-gbr-2508-reference-framework-of-competences-vol-1-8573-co/16807bc66c>.

Daloz, Laurent A. Parks 2000. Transformative Learning for the Common Good. In Mezirow, Jack (ed.) *Learning as Transformation: Critical Perspectives on a Theory in Progress*. San Francisco: Jossey-Bass, 103–123.

De Wit, Hans/Hunter, Fiona/Howard, Laura/Egron-Polak, Eva 2015. *Internationalisation of Higher Education*. Brussels. <http://www.europarl.europa.eu/RegData/etudes/STUD/2015/540370/IPOL_STU(2015)540370_EN.pdf >.

De Wit, Hans/Jones, Elspeth 2014. We Need to Change the Language of Internationalisation. *University World News*, 14 November. <https://www.universityworldnews.com/post.php?story=20141112125546605>.

European Commission 2014. *The Erasmus Impact Study. Effects of Mobility on the Skills and Employability of Students and the*

Internationalisation of Higher Education Institutions. Luxembourg. <https://publications.europa.eu/en/publication-detail/-/publication/13031399-9fd4-11e5-8781-01aa75ed71a1>.

European Commission Education and Training n.d. *Mobility and Cooperation*. <https://ec.europa.eu/education/policies/higher-education/mobility-and-cooperation_en>.

Fielden, John/Middlehurst, Robin/Woodfield, Steve 2007. *Global Horizons for UK Students (Project Report)*. London: Industry and Higher Education. <https://eprints.kingston.ac.uk/6900/>.

Henriksen, Birgit/Holmen, Anne/Kling, Joyce 2019. *English Medium Instruction in Multilingual and Multicultural Universities: Academics' Voices from the Northern European Context*. London: Routledge.

Jackson, Anthony 2012. Today's Students Need Global Outlook, *China Daily*, 3 March. <http://europe.chinadaily.com.cn/opinion/2012-03/03/content_14746069.htm>.

Jenkins, Jennifer 2014. *English as a Lingua Franca in the International University: The Politics of Academic English Language Policy*. London: Routledge.

Jenkins, Jennifer 2017. Not English but English-within-Multilingualism. In Coffey, Simon/Wingate, Ursula (eds.) *New Directions for Research in Foreign Language Education*. London: Routledge, 65–78.

Jenkins, Jennifer 2019. The Internationalization of Higher Education. But What About Its Lingua Franca? In Murata, Kumiko (ed.) *English-Medium Instruction from an English as a Lingua Franca Perspective. Exploring the Higher Education Context*. London: Routledge, 15–31.

Jenkins, Jennifer/Baker, Will/Dewey, Martin (eds.) 2017. *The Routledge Handbook of English as a Lingua Franca*. London: Routledge.

Jones, Elspeth 2010. "Don't Worry about the Worries": Transforming Lives through International Volunteering. In Jones, Elspeth (ed.) *Internationalisation and the Student Voice: Higher Education Perspectives*. New York: Routledge, 83–97.

Jones, Elspeth 2011. *Global Perspectives and the Role of Languages. Shaping the Future: Online Resources for Internationalisation*. London: University Council of Modern Languages.

Jones, Elspeth 2012a. Challenging Received Wisdom. In Beelen, Jos/De Wit, Hans (eds.) *Internationalisation Revisited: New Dimensions in the Internationalisation of Higher Education*. Amsterdam: Centre for Applied Research on Economics and Management (CAREM), 35–45.

Jones, Elspeth 2012b. In Praise of Languages for Internationalization. *The Chronicle of Higher Education*, 9 February. <https://www.chronicle.com/blogs/worldwise/in-praise-of-languages-for-internationalization/29132>.

Jones, Elspeth 2013a. Internationalisation and Student Learning Outcomes. In De Wit, Hans (ed.) *An Introduction to Higher Education Internationalization*. Milan: Vita e Pensiero, 107–115.

Jones, Elspeth 2013b. Internationalization and Employability: The Role of Intercultural Experiences in the Development of Transferable Skills. *Public Money & Management* 33/, 95–104.

Jones, Elspeth 2015. Culture Change and Exchanging Culture: The Role of Languages in Internationalisation. In Orme, Mark (ed.) *Supporting Internationalisation through Languages and Culture in the Twenty-First Century University*. Bern: Peter Lang, 11–22.

Jones, Elspeth 2017. Internationalisation of the Curriculum: Challenges, Misconceptions and the Role of Disciplines. In Casper-Hehne, Hiltraud/Reiffenrath, Tanja (eds.) *Internationalisierung der Curricula an Hochschulen: Konzepte, Initiativen, Maßnahmen*. Bielefeld: Bertelsmann Verlag, 21–38.

Jones, Elspeth/Caruana, Viv 2010. Nurturing the Global Graduate for the 21st Century: Learning from the Student Voice on Internationalisation. In Jones, Elspeth (ed.) *Internationalisation and the Student Voice: Higher Education Perspectives*. London: Routledge, xv–xxiii.

Jones, Elspeth/Killick, David 2007. Internationalisation of the Curriculum. In Jones, Elspeth/Brown, Sally (eds.) *Internationalising Higher Education*. London: Routledge, 109–119.

Jones, Elspeth/Killick, David 2013. Graduate Attributes and the Internationalized Curriculum. *Journal of Studies in International Education* 17/2, 165–182.

Jones, Elspeth/Reiffenrath, Tanja 2018. *Internationalisation at Home in Practice. Curriculum & Teaching*. <https://www.eaie.org/blog/internationalisation-at-home-practice.html>.
Kirkpatrick, Andy (ed.) 2010. *The Routledge Handbook of World Englishes*. London: Routledge.
Knight, Jane 2004. Internationalization Remodeled: Definition, Approaches, and Rationales. *Journal of Studies in International Education* 8/1, 5–31.
Kolb, David A. 1984. *Experiential Learning: Experience as the Source of Learning and Development*. Englewood Cliffs, NJ: Prentice Hall.
Leask, Betty 2010. "Beside me is an Empty Chair": The Student Experience of Internationalisation. In Jones, Elspeth (ed.) *Internationalisation and the Student Voice: Higher Education Perspectives*. London: Routledge, 3–17.
Leask, Betty 2015. *Internationalizing the Curriculum*. London: Routledge.
Luxon, Tony/Peelo, Moira 2009. Academic Sojourners, Teaching and Internationalisation: The Experience of Non-UK Staff in a British University. *Teaching in Higher Education* 14/6, 649–659.
Mellors-Bourne, Robin/Jones, Elspeth/Lawton, William/Woodfield, Steve 2015. *Student Perspectives on Going International*. London: British Council. <https://www.britishcouncil.org/sites/default/files/iu_bc_outwd_mblty_student_perception_sept_15.pdf>.
Mezirow, Jack 1978. Perspective Transformation. *Adult Education* 28/2, 100–110.
Montgomery, Catherine 2010. *Understanding the International Student Experience*. London: Palgrave Macmillan.
Murata, Kumiko (ed.) 2019. *English-Medium Instruction from an English as a Lingua Franca Perspective. Exploring the Higher Education Context*. London: Routledge.
Porto, Melina 2020. Intercultural Citizenship as an Opportunity for Bottom-Up Intercultural Dialogue Internationalisation in South America. In Lundgren, Ulla/Castro, Paloma/Woodin, Jane (eds.) *Educational Approaches to Internationalization through Intercultural Dialogue: Reflections on Theory and Practice*. London: Routledge, 150–168.

UUKi 2016. *Gone International 2016: The Value of Mobility*. <http://www.universitiesuk.ac.uk/policy-and-analysis/reports/Pages/gone-international-2016-value-mobility.aspx>.

Volet, Simone E./Ang, Grace 1998. Culturally Mixed Groups on International Campuses: An Opportunity for Inter-cultural Learning. *Higher Education Research & Development* 17/1, 5–23.

Wiers-Jenssen, Jannecke 2011. Background and Employability of Mobile vs. Non-Mobile Students. *Tertiary Education and Management* 17/2, 79–100.

Carmen Carracelas-Juncal

Service-Learning and Social Networks in Study Abroad Contexts: Engaging International Students in the Host Communities

1 Introduction

This chapter discusses the current challenges facing study abroad programs. Home institutions can do much to prepare students to be ready for their study abroad experience through required pre-departure as well as abroad follow-up components (Jackson 2018; Jones 2018; Marijuan/Sanz 2018; Moreno Bruna 2018). However, they cannot ensure students' meaningful interactions with native speakers nor membership in host country social networks. Jackson (2018: 5) suggests that "much more attention needs to be paid to what is actually happening on stays abroad". I could not agree more. It is paramount to extend that attention to encompass host country course offerings. This chapter argues that there is a need to critically examine and revise host country curricula in order to better meet the current needs of study abroad students. It further argues that service-learning should be added to the study abroad curriculum, since it allows students to have meaningful interaction with native speakers and become valued members of already established native speaker social networks.

2 Study abroad research findings

Current research shows that study abroad students may not attain a high level of achievement from their sojourn abroad. Jackson (2018: 4) notes that:

> While some individuals experience gains in L2 proficiency, intercultural competence, and global-mindedness, many others do not appear to have benefited from their stay in the host country, at least not in the immediate aftermath.

Contrary to expectations, a study abroad setting does not guarantee student interaction with people of the host country (Kinginger 2009). Some studies show that the language gains of study abroad students most often do not surpass those of students enrolled in regular language programs at home (Freed/Segalowitz/Dewey 2004; Segalowitz/Freed/Collentine/Lafford/Lazar/Díaz-Campos 2004). The average study abroad student does not seem to spend more time speaking the target language than students enrolled in other types of language programs at home. It also appears that interaction with native speakers in the study abroad contexts does not lead to greater language gains or better intercultural learning and/or communication than peer-to-peer non-native interaction (Martisen/Baker/Dewey/Brown/Johnson 2010). Furthermore, research shows that for a variety of reasons some study abroad students might close themselves off from their host culture (Kinginger 2011: 66). The study abroad experience may result in "reinforced stereotypes and little interest in using their second language (L2) to engage in intercultural dialogue" (Jackson 2018: 4), an enhanced "sense of national superiority" (Marijuan/Sanz 2018: 191), or more xenophobic attitudes than prior to their experience abroad (Jones 2018). It is clear that student gains in L2 proficiency and cultural competence during study abroad are not automatically guaranteed (Kinginger 2011; Jackson 2018).

In light of these results, researchers highlight the need for more home institution involvement before, during, and after the study abroad experience. Jackson (2018: 3) points out that:

> Largely due to the expectation of immersion and a strong belief in the transformative dimension of international experience, most university students are still sent abroad with very limited intercultural guidance or preparation for the use of the host language in informal, social situations.

Students need guidance in setting realistic pre-departure goals and identifying learning strategies and activities while abroad that will help them achieve those goals. They also need to know how to manage the experience of living in a different culture, to be aware that things might not be easy, and obtain some strategies to manage their feelings and reactions. Pointing specifically to the importance of more home institution involvement during student stay in the host country, Jackson (2018: 5) has created courses "designed to enhance the language and intercultural learning of student sojourners and returnees". She calls for an intervention in study abroad programs "to bring about more positive sojourn outcomes, such as higher levels of sociopragmatic awareness, intercultural competence, and constructive intercultural relationships" (Jackson 2018: 4). More institutions are adding pre-departure preparation in intercultural strategies to their program (Coleman 2015; Marijuan/Sanz 2018), as well as in-country follow-up courses during the study abroad period (Jackson 2018; Moreno Bruna 2018), and post-study abroad debriefing sessions (Jones 2018) with seemingly positive results. Nevertheless, it is important to examine the challenges study abroad students currently face during their host-country stay before discussing further steps study abroad programs can take to bring positive results for all students while abroad.

3 Current study abroad reality: "Abroad is less abroad than it once was"

The ease, low cost, and speed of connecting to support networks at home, added to the extensive use of social media, have certainly changed the study abroad experience. It is true that "thanks to telecommunications technologies, abroad is less abroad than it once was" (Coleman/Chafer 2010: 165) and that evolving "social and technological changes" continually impact study abroad so that " 'abroad' today is not the 'abroad' of even five or ten years ago" (Coleman 2015: 35). Home language use with family and friends at home and peer social networks abroad, as well as the presence of English as a lingua franca among international students, have exacerbated the ever present challenge to the hoped-for study abroad immersion experience.

It is well documented that students use their native language while abroad, whether communicating with family and friends back home or with fellow students abroad. Study abroad students tend to make friends with peers from their home institution or home country (Martinsen et al. 2010; Magnan/Lafford 2012; Coleman 2013, 2015). Study abroad peer networks seem to play an important role in helping students manage the culture shock involved in moving to their host country. Both home and study abroad peer networks fill a necessary support role since most host institutions do not involve themselves in the student acculturation process. As Jackson (2018: 3) points out "the host institution may offer a welcoming session for international students, but then the newcomers are generally expected to adapt to the new environment on their own". Also, "Wilkinson (1998) notes that spending time with other students allows an individual to process the overwhelming newness of their surroundings" (Martinsen et al., 2010: 57). Contrary to what may seem otherwise, students' need to speak their native language and socialize with their peers does not show a lack of motivation or disregard for their learning experience abroad. It may not detract from their learning; in fact it might help them benefit more from their study abroad experience (Martinsen et al. 2010; Magnan/Lafford 2012; Coleman 2013). However, it can also be "a potential obstacle to achieving the immersion which is necessary for the learning objectives to be attained" (Coleman 2013: 30).

The need to be connected with home, speak the home language, and make friends with peers from the home country is nothing new. What has changed is the speed of communication due to the Internet and virtual social networks. A more recent challenge is the generalized use of English among international students and its steady growth as the language of instruction in a greater number of university course offerings abroad (Coleman 2013). This is especially significant for study abroad students whose native language is English. As Kinginger (2009: 74–75) points out, these students "will find it increasingly difficult to find both informal and formal situations where they may practice their foreign language" and, when they do, "their interlocutors may insist upon using English as a way of furthering their own learning". Kinginger (2009: 75) fears that due to the generalized used of English, students "may decide that there is little reason to pursue advanced competence in other languages". It might be counterproductive and unrealistic to expect or demand study abroad students not to use their native language and/or English to communicate with others. However, both the use of the home language and English while abroad do present a great challenge that can minimize the target language use and host culture immersion of all study abroad students. As Coleman (2013: 29) points out:

> [...] the social networks a student establishes, maintains and develops while abroad are crucial to learning outcomes, since they can determine access to linguistic and cultural input, and the quantity, nature and functional coverage of target language interactions.

Study abroad programs need to "address the issue of social networks" (Coleman 2015: 34). They should focus their efforts not on reducing first language (L1) or English language use, but on making it necessary for all students to interact in the target language and participate in the local culture. When this happens, the use of the L1 and/or English by study abroad students may naturally diminish in favor of the target language (Coleman 2013).

The challenge then resides in getting study abroad students to frequently engage in meaningful target language interactions with native speakers. What can study abroad programs do to ensure that students maximize their use of the target language and get more involved in their host communities?

4 Study abroad native speaker interaction and host country social networks

Previous research findings point to the need for students to maximize their language use and cultural immersion while abroad, and the effects that involvement in host country social networks may have on language development and intercultural competence (Magnan/Lafford 2012). Kinginger (2011) found that the most successful study abroad students take advantage of every opportunity to interact in the language and get involved in host country social networks. However, as discussed earlier, student interaction with native speakers abroad is much less frequent than expected, and it can be mostly of a transactional type that does "not result in extensive or meaningful conversations with native speakers" (Martinsen et al. 2010: 58). These findings highlight the need of promoting more meaningful contact with native speakers while abroad. Isabelli-García (2006) and Kinginger (2009, 2011) observed that the students who create social networks with native speakers have a higher level of language and culture attainment. In their study abroad research review Marijuan/Sanz (2018: 196) found that "social networks seem to be a critical factor in language and cultural development". In his review, Pinar (2016: 90) noted that students who have the ability to create social networks:

> [...] have greater advances in communicative competence and a stronger cultural knowledge than those who prefer to spend free time interacting with speakers of their own language or maintaining constant contact with the country of origin through the internet and virtual social networks.

I would like to argue that a great majority of study abroad students would rather make friends with native speakers and join host country social networks if they could, as evidenced by their pre-departure goals and initial enthusiasm (Isabelli-García 2006; Jackson 2018). And yet for a variety of reasons, creating or joining host country social networks is not an easy task for the average study abroad student (Isabelli-García 2006; Kinginger 2009, 2011).

Individual variables like personality, motivation, attitude, self-image and initiative, among others can affect the establishment of native speaker social networks. This may lead to feelings of frustration and disillusionment with the study abroad experience, causing the student to retreat from seeking out new opportunities to interact in the language (Isabelli-García 2006; Kinginger 2009; Magnan/Lafford 2012; Marijuan/Sanz 2018). It is important also to consider the receiving communities' values, attitudes, degree of acceptance, and beliefs towards study abroad students. They can influence whether students feel welcome in the community, affecting their degree of confidence to engage in interactions, and find opportunities to join host country social networks (Kinginger 2009). Coleman (2013: 30) reminds us that "students have more to gain from interactions than do locals (unless the latter are linguistically motivated), and that the expected outcomes are frequently not realized". The transient state of the study abroad student can condition and limit the outcomes of the study abroad experience. Study abroad program length adds a time constraint to the naturally lengthy and involved process of establishing social networks with native speakers.

Current literature shows that one semester abroad does not seem to allow sufficient time for most students to develop social networks with native speakers (Dwyer 2004; Isabelli-García 2006; Magnan/Lafford 2012). Referring to language gains, Lafford (2006: 17) observed that those students who benefit most from their study abroad experience are those who spend an academic year abroad, "students say that they are just "getting the system down" after a semester, when they have to leave to go home". This assertion may be extended as well to their ability to establish social networks with native speakers. In Isabelli-García's (2006: 237) study, only one study abroad student out of four was able to participate in a multiplex social network with native speakers through his contact with a friend of a friend, which "considerably increased" his opportunities "of observing and participating in prolonged interaction" in the target language. Isabelli-García (2006: 258) suggested in her conclusions that "programs could benefit from ways to successfully create social networks". Coleman (2015: 42) concurs and identifies social networks as "a major influence on the variability of study abroad experience: Greater contact with the local community leads to greater gains".

Study abroad host institution curricula should take into account current students' needs and challenges. Host institution course offerings should be revised to provide different built in opportunities for all study abroad students to have access to established native speaker social networks. How can study abroad programs facilitate this process? One way may be by integrating service-learning in the host institution curriculum. This issue is further explored in the next section.

5 Service-learning and the study abroad curriculum

Service-learning is an approach to teaching that connects academic learning with life experience outside of the classroom. It encompasses the "various pedagogies that link community service and academic study so that each strengthens the other" (Campus Compact 2003: 8). The three main components of service-learning are:

- reciprocity of benefits for both the students and the community they serve;
- the careful alignment of academic objectives with the service-learning experience; and,
- student reflection.

Many universities have a community engagement office with already established long-term relationships with community organizations, facilitating the process of adding service-learning courses to the curriculum. Service-learning is an ideal addition to the study abroad curriculum that brings about positive results (Marijuan/Sanz 2018) and provides a curricular built-in social context for meaningful target language interaction with native speakers. Service-learning positions students inside host country social networks, allowing them to be "socialized into using language" as they are also "socialized through language into local ways of 'acting, feeling, and knowing, in socially recognized and organized practices associated with membership in a social group' " (Kinginger 2009: 32).

Service-learning can help to minimize the possible negative effects of individual and community variables on student gains. It places study abroad students at the same starting point, neutralizing individual variables. Service-learning gives all participants equal access to a native speaker social network and opportunities for meaningful interaction in the target language. Kinginger (2011: 60) observed that study abroad student success depends not only on "the attributes and intentions of the student but also [on] the ways in which the student is received within his or her host community". She further pointed out that a student "who is welcomed as a person of consequence, worthy of the hosts' time and nurture, is likely to succeed" (Kinginger 2011: 60). At the service-learning site each study abroad student is welcomed, accepted, and valued in their new native speaker social network. Regardless of individual variables, they can feel appreciated for their personal contribution, possibly influencing study abroad outcomes.

Service-learning bypasses the time constraints inherent to study abroad programs that hinder the process of creating native speaker social networks. It expands students' initial social circles abroad, usually made of co-nationals and other international students (Coleman 2013, 2015), to include a native speaker social network within the first weeks of their arrival in the host country. Service-learning seems to be a successful "attempt to short-circuit the natural process, to jump directly from the inner to the outer circle" of study abroad student social networks (Coleman 2013: 32). Through service-learning, students have the opportunity to join a multiplex network that, as Isabelli-García (2006: 236) points out, requires them "to speak to each member in various capacities" allowing them to engage in meaningful interactions. These "interactions with native-speaker members help the learners' interlanguage reach a close approximation of the L2 faster" (Isabelli-García 2006: 236).

In their service-learning site students may safely learn to overcome their fears of linguistic inadequacy and acquire confidence in their communicative and social skills. The service-learning network might also allow students to develop friendships within the network that may give them access to additional native speaker networks, although one semester may still not be enough time. Regardless of whether or not they are able to develop friendships, the service-learning experience might help study abroad students feel more confident to interact with other people from the host community and create their own social networks with native speakers. As shall be seen in the next sections, the results of this study confirm previous research findings: service-learning gives students the opportunity to be immersed in meaningful language and culture exchanges with positive results, positioning them as welcomed members of native speaker social networks abroad.

6 Host country service-learning course case study

At The University of Southern Mississippi (USM), my home institution, I regularly teach service-learning courses and I am actively involved with study abroad programs. I have advised students to participate in our exchange programs, directed our summer programs in Spain several times, and developed, coordinated and supervised our new semester program in Spain. However, I had never taught a service-learning course in a study abroad context. Curriculum wise, I had always been on the home institution side of the study abroad experience, since our partner host institutions provided all classroom instruction. This changed when I received an invitation from the *Instituto de Lengua y Cultura Españolas* (ILCE) at Universidad de Navarra (UNav) to help with their new service-learning curricular initiative. With the consent of my home institution I became a visiting professor and researcher hosted by ILCE. For almost a year and a half, from September 2017 to December 2018, I had the opportunity to teach a service-learning course every semester of my stay. This was an eye opening experience for me. I thought I knew what my students went through while abroad. However I realized I really did not truly know until I began teaching international students myself at UNav in Pamplona, Spain. At ILCE I was now on the host institution side of the study abroad experience. Planning and designing my study abroad courses made me realize how crucial the host institution curriculum is to be able to provide study abroad students with the opportunities for a successful experience. The invitation from ILCE has been a unique opportunity to research the effects of integrating service-learning into the host institution study abroad program.

6.1 Purpose and methodology of the study

From advising exchange students and supervising the semester abroad program at my home institution, I was aware that interacting with native speakers and making friends in the host country were not automatic and that the study abroad experience was highly variable and particular to each student. The first semester at UNav, I gave my service-learning students a questionnaire. The purpose was to know them a little better and find out about their language level, some personality traits, and their goals and hopes for the semester. I was also curious about the extent of their target language use outside the classroom and what their involvement with local people might be. Their answers made me realize how rare their target language interactions in the community were, mostly limited to shopping, and ordering drinks and *pintxos* when going out. This led me to reflect on the importance of host institution course offerings and to explore the impact service-learning could have upon the student experience abroad. This research became, and still is, a work in progress since each semester I had to refine the questions I needed to ask as I reflected on student and course outcomes.

6.2 Study abroad service-learning course description

The service-learning course was titled *Inmersión Sociocultural en Pamplona: Aprendizaje Servicio y Comunicación en Español*. It had already been incorporated into the ILCE curriculum the previous academic year. It was offered as an elective course and did not have a language level requirement. In the Fall 2017, the classroom content was initially organized as a conversation and culture course. This allowed the inclusion of different topics of interest to the students as well as those relevant to the students' service-learning experience. The course title did not change, but throughout the three semesters the course content evolved. It shifted to reflect the interests of each new group of students, but it also incorporated the previous semester's important topics and experiences. This was done to match the academic content with the reality of the service-learning sites and to better prepare students for their service-learning experience. In the second semester I gave priority to the topic of immigration, which stood out during the service-learning experience in the first semester, and the characteristics of the Spanish school system, a topic that the second-semester students wanted to explore. During the second semester, I saw the need to discuss at-risk families and children in Spain as well, which I added to the discussion topics in the third semester. The third semester students also requested to go over vocabulary on different subjects and discuss other cultural topics (like types of families, relationships, and traditional celebrations) that they wanted to include in their interactions during their service-learning visits.

6.3 Service-learning sites and time distribution

The site selection was facilitated by the help of the staff from Tantaka, the community engagement office at UNav. The main criteria in selecting the sites were to make sure that the course participants would be involved in the same type of service-learning experience. This would ensure that class discussions of service-learning individual experiences would be engaging to all and that the participants could give relevant feedback in return. Two different organizations were selected to allow the participants some choice. Students could choose between two similar service sites in Pamplona that offered after-school support. Site 1 only served elementary school age children while site 2 served elementary, middle-school, and high school students, as well as adult immigrants learning Spanish. In the second or third week of class, one class day was dedicated to visiting both sites as a group and meeting the coordinator of each site. The third semester only site 2 was included, due to the late starting time of site 1.

The number of visits to the service-learning sites were limited by the late starting date of the Spanish school system, which determined the after-school programs dates, and the early start and end of UNav semesters. In Fall 2017 (Fall 1) there were a total of eight service-learning visits in a period of six weeks, in Spring 2018, eight visits in seven weeks, and in Fall 2018 (Fall 2), nine visits in eight weeks. In Fall 1 students visited the service-learning sites twice during two weeks, and Spring and Fall 2 students, during one week. In the first weeks of each semester students met in the classroom twice a week to discuss different topics and prepare themselves for the service-learning experience. After the preparation weeks, students met once a week in the classroom and spent two hours at their service-learning site. In the last two weeks of the semester, students met again twice a week in the classroom to complete their final projects. During the third semester, the time spent in the classroom changed from one hour to two hours due to a course credit increase.

6.4 Course participants

There were a total of thirty students enrolled in the course (nine in Fall 1, twelve in the Spring semester, and nine in Fall 2) from different countries in Europe, Africa, Asia, and North America. All were enrolled in the ILCE Spanish language program. Most students were taking concurrent language courses at the B level, with significant variation in their communicative skills. There was one A2 student each during the Fall 1 and Spring semesters and one A1 student in the Spring semester. In Fall 2, there were three C1 students enrolled as well. There were four females and five males in Fall 1 semester, ten females and two males in the Spring, and nine females in Fall 2. Most participants in Fall 1 and Spring chose site 2 for their service-learning experience, except five students, two in Fall 1 and three in the Spring semester that chose site 1. Regarding age preference, in Fall 1, three course participants mentored elementary school children, and six mentored adolescents. In the Spring, seven mentored elementary age children; four mentored adolescents; and one chose to work with the adult class. In Fall 2, four participants chose to mentor elementary age children, and five, adolescents.

6.5 Data collection

The data for this study come from class assignments, observations, one questionnaire distributed at the beginning of each semester, and a second questionnaire that was added at the end of the Spring semester and expanded in the third semester. As part of the class assignments, students were asked to keep a weekly reflective journal about the course and their service-learning sessions, including a final reflection at the end of the semester. They also had to assess and comment on their weekly attendance and participation. After Fall 1, a two-minute video documentary about the service-learning experience was also added to the assignments.

7 Outcomes and discussion

For the purpose of this chapter, only findings related to target language interaction and social networks will be discussed.

7.1 Interaction in L2 results

The service-learning course guaranteed two to four hours of communication in Spanish outside the classroom every week for each student in a six- to eight-week period. During their visits, students had to communicate in the target language with other volunteers and the directors of each site, as well as with the students they were mentoring. The results support the findings of previous research on service-learning in study abroad contexts (Martinsen et al. 2010; Marijuan/Sanz 2018). Students reported that the service-learning experience allowed them to use Spanish with native speakers for other purposes than language study. All students also mentioned a higher confidence in their ability to communicate in the target language due to their perceived improvement in conversational skills, language gains, and higher fluency. This finding concurs with Jones (see Chapter "The Role of Languages in Transformational Internationalisation" this volume), for whom volunteering helps to develop not only personal and intercultural skills, "but also those which are highly sought by employers".

In their journals, they all reported feeling nervous and afraid during their initial solo visit to their service-learning site, regardless of their language level. A common thread to their new confidence in their language skills was that the service-learning experience forced them to overcome their fears. Beginner and intermediate low students mentioned losing the fear of communicating with speakers of different ages, not having enough vocabulary, or not being able to understand others. More advanced students wrote about the fear of making mistakes, believing they did not speak well enough or lacked a Spanish accent. Regardless of their language level and skills, they all felt insecure about their ability to effectively communicate with others in Spanish. They had to mentor students in different school subjects with vocabulary that was new to them. In order to be effective mentors, they had to find different communication strategies to get their point across (see excerpt 1). They had to learn to work around their lack of language skills as they developed them.

(1) *Me cuesta mucho hablar con los símbolos de matemática en español. He inventado maneras para explicarla. Cuando olvidé como se dice "multiplicación",*

simplemente dije "A 'con' B". Entonces fue como le ayudé a una niña en mi propia manera. Eso fue una experiencia que me pone contenta.[1]

It is hard for me to talk with mathematic symbols in Spanish. I have invented ways to explain them. When I forgot to say "multiplication" I simply said "A 'with' B". That is how I helped a girl in my own way. That was an experience that makes me happy. [My translation]

Another topic in students' reflection was learning more about the culture through their interactions in the service-learning sites. Some mentioned enjoying answering questions about their own culture during their visits. Other students wrote about the cultural differences in teaching and learning between Spain and their own countries. A few students reflected on changing their perspective about immigrants. For another student, the service-learning experience led her to revise her own beliefs about cultural differences (see excerpt 2):

(2) *Gracias a la experiencia de aprendizaje-servicio, podía conocer muchos chicos de diferentes orígenes. Pensaba que la gente de diferentes países eran muy muy diferentes y que era muy difícil hacer una amistad entre las gentes de diferente cultura, pero todo eso no son verdad. Cuando trabajando con los chicos, descubrí que los chicos de diferentes países no eran tan diferentes. Todos son iguales y similares y podemos hacer una amistad de verdad si nos llevamos con otros sinceramente.*

Because of the service-learning experience, I was able to meet many youth of different origins. I thought that people from different countries were very different and that it was very hard for people from different cultures to be friends, but that is not true. Working with the kids, I discovered that young people from different countries were not that different. All are equal and similar, and we can develop a real friendship if we treat each other with honesty. [My translation]

7.2 Social networks

Service-learning placed the students in an established host country social network, but did students form personal relationships during their

---

1 Excerpts are original and no corrections have been made.

service-learning experience? Although this question was not part of the first or second semester questionnaires, in their reflective journals five students mentioned establishing a personal relationship with the people they had worked with in their service-learning sites. Two students wrote about their relationships with the adolescents they mentored; two made friends with other volunteers; and one built a close relationship with her co-teachers as they planned lessons together for their group. They all reported that personal meaningful conversations led to these relationships and further strengthened them; thus, changing the nature of their experience. The question about making friends during the service-learning experience was added to the third semester's exit questionnaire. Three of the third semester participants mentioned making friends with the students they mentored. One participant explained that friendship developed with some of the students she mentored, and they talked about many things (see excerpt 3):

(3) *[…] con algunos niños un vínculo de amistad se crea y hablamos de todo.*

[…] with some of the children a bond of friendship is developed and we talk about everything. [My translation]

Another participant wrote about getting close to a Spanish volunteer of her same age bonding over their shared experiences working with the children (see excerpt 4 originally submitted in English):

(4) *Every volunteer was very positive and very sweet to me and the kids, you could tell they were good people, but the person I related the most was a girl who was my age, and Spanish. We would just laugh together over what some of the kids would do, and she knew a little English and was able to help me translate some words.*

As with Fall 1 and Spring semester participants, personal conversations seem to have been the key to establishing a feeling of friendship between the participants and others in the service-learning sites. This points to the need to build time and space into the service-learning experience to allow for personal social interactions.

7.3 *Individual variables and length of time considerations*

As previously discussed, service-learning helps circumvent the effect of individual variables in establishing a native speaker social network for study abroad students. However, individual variables are still very much at play during the service-learning experience and have an impact on its outcomes. The participants also have to navigate the cultural differences, attitudes, feelings, and personalities present in their service-learning site.

Although the participants felt valued, accepted, and supported in their sites, the service-learning experience was still frustrating at times. All the participants mentoring the elementary-age group struggled at some point to keep the children on task or managing their behavior (see excerpt 5 originally submitted in English):

> (5) *Every session wasn't always smooth sailing, sometimes kids refused to do their homework, some started crying and others would continually bother their classmates and could never focus on their own work.*

Some felt that the children knew they had no authority over them and took advantage of that knowledge. The participants working with adolescents experienced similar challenges. Sometimes the adolescents had no interest in completing their homework, would not pay attention, or temporarily refused assistance, making the participants feel that they were not of much help. Each participant felt elated after a successful visit and discouraged after an unproductive session. One participant observed (see excerpt 6):

> (6) *Creo que lo más importante de aprendizaje-servicio son pensar en positivo, no tener miedo de intentar y no rendirse con facilidad.*

> I believe that what is most important about service-learning is to think positive, not to be afraid of trying, and not to give up easily. [My translation]

The participants who maintained a positive attitude regardless of the situation seemed to be better able to adapt to the different weekly challenges, and smoothly navigate the idiosyncrasies of the students they were mentoring. Those who were not as flexible found it more difficult to overcome their frustration over those mentoring sessions they perceived as unsuccessful. As expected, the uniformity of the service-learning sites did not translate into uniformity of outcomes. Nevertheless, regardless of each participant's individual service-learning journey, they all considered it a worthwhile learning experience.

Length of time of the study abroad program also affects the ability of study abroad students to expand or create other native speaker social networks beyond the service-learning social network. Participants in this study mentioned that making friends with local people was not easy for international students, and that there was not a lot of time left from classes and school activities to get to know more people. Those who reported making friends in their service-learning sites also commented that the semester was too short to extend the friendship to outside social activities. As Coleman (2015: 42) points out, both locals and study abroad students "have already built close, stable bonds with family, friends and peers", making the establishment of strong ties between both groups highly unlikely due to the temporary nature of the study abroad experience. This is especially relevant in the host community context of this study. Pamplona's society is characterized by having very strong family and friend ties with firmly established closed network circles. Integrating a service-learning course allows students to join a local social network and provides them with an opportunity to feel like part of the host community. In addition, study abroad students can establish personal uniplex networks, having one-on-one contact with different native speakers (Isabelli-García 2006). This type of network can provide additional target language interactions, giving them "a broader network in order to be exposed to more varied language models" (Isabelli-García 2006: 253). Even though making friends in the host country would be ideal, establishing "weak ties" with locals (Coleman 2015: 42) can also bring about positive results. Coleman (2015: 42) observes that:

> Meeting new people can nurture new activities and new attitudes. This is the fundamental basis of learning through mobility. The new perspectives of new acquaintances allow and prompt you to re-invent yourself.

Access to different types of native speaker networks needs to be taken into account when revising host institution study abroad curricula. Service-learning can offer study abroad students meaningful target language interaction with native speakers and allow them to enter established host country social networks. It should be clear that service-learning is not the miracle solution that will erase the current challenges that study abroad programs face. It is a successful initiative to include in a host institution curriculum designed to maximize student interaction in the target language and participation in native speaker social networks. Every course offering should be designed with these two objectives in mind. Current literature shows other successful initiatives (Jackson 2018; Knight/Schmidt-Rinehart 2010; Kinginger 2011; Cadd 2012; Dewey/Ring/Gardner/Belnap 2013) that combined with service-learning can strengthen and enrich the host-country study abroad course offerings, giving all study abroad students the opportunity for a successful study abroad experience.

8 Conclusions

A study abroad experience does not guarantee linguistic or cultural gains since students can have a limited immersion experience during their stay abroad. Current research shows that an automatic language and culture immersion while abroad is part of the past. And yet, meaningful target language interaction and participation in social networks while abroad are as crucial to today's study abroad student success as in the past. Study abroad programs need to pay more attention to what happens abroad. Host institutions receiving international students need to take into account research findings and revise their target language offerings to ensure native speaker interaction and involvement in local social networks. Sending institutions who have an established relationship with a receiving institution should work closely together to revise the host institution curriculum to incorporate successful initiatives. Even though as Collentine (2009: 228) observes, it may be "difficult for a home institution to have a strong effect on a host's institution's syllabi and methodological approaches", there is an urgent need for close cooperation on both sides to meet today's students' needs and challenges abroad.

This study confirms that engaging study abroad students in the host communities is crucial to their success and proposes that service-learning should be added to host country institutions course offerings for international students. Service-learning offers every student the opportunity to be part of a native speaker social network soon after their arrival abroad. Service-learning can lead to linguistic gains, expansion of cultural understandings, and development of intercultural communication through meaningful target language interactions. Service-learning allows students to feel part of the community, as they are welcomed into established native speaker multiplex social networks. It gives them the opportunity to engage in meaningful interactions in the target language and become better intercultural communicators as they learn about themselves. As one of the participants puts it (excerpt 7):

> (7) *El aprendizaje-servicio es una experiencia enriquecedora en la que aprendes sobre ti (a tener confianza en ti misma, a ser paciente, a compartir, a ser creativa, a adaptarte, a sentirte más cómoda con el español...). Una experiencia que no podrás olvidar.*

> Service-learning is an enriching experience in which you learn about yourself (to be more confident, to be patient, to share, to be creative, to adapt, to feel more comfortable with Spanish...). It is an experience that you will never forget. [My translation]

Both service-learning and study abroad experiences are highly variable experiences, unique, and particular to each individual. There is a need for study abroad programs to develop host country curricula that offer every student, regardless of individual and contextual variables, the opportunity to have a successful study abroad experience.

References

Cadd, Mark 2012. Encouraging Students to Engage with Native Speakers during Study Abroad. *Foreign Language Annals* 45/2, 229–245.

Campus Compact 2003. *Campus Compact's Introduction to Service-Learning Toolkit* (2nd ed.). Providence, RI: Brown University.

Coleman, James A. 2013. Researching Whole People and Whole Lives. In Kinginger, Celeste (ed.) *Social and Cultural Aspects of Language Learning in Study Abroad.* Amsterdam/Philadelphia: John Benjamins, 17–44.

Coleman, James A. 2015. Social Circles During Residence Abroad: What Students Do, and Who With. In Mitchell, Rosamond/Tracy-Ventura, Nicole/McManus, Kevin (eds.) *Social Interaction, Identity and Language Learning During Residence Abroad*. Amsterdam: Eurosla Monographs Series 4, 33–52.

Coleman, James A./Chafer, Tony 2010. Study Abroad and the Internet: Physical and Virtual Context in an Era of Expanding Telecommunications. *Frontiers: The Interdisciplinary Journal of Study Abroad* 19/Fall, 151–167.

Collentine, Joseph 2009. Study Abroad Research: Findings, Implications, and Future Directions. In Long, Michael H./Doughty, Catherine J. (eds.) *The Handbook of Language Teaching*. New York: Wiley, 218–233.

Dewey, Dan P./Ring, Spencer/Gardner, Daniel/Belnap, Kirk R. 2013. Social Network Formation and Development during Study Abroad in the Middle East. *System* 41/2, 269–282.

Dwyer, Mary M. 2004. More Is Better: The Impact of Study Abroad Duration. *Frontiers: The Interdisciplinary Journal of Study Abroad* 10/Fall, 151–163.

Freed, Barbara F./Segalowitz, Norman/Dewey, Dan P. 2004. Context of Learning and Second Language Fluency in French: Comparing Regular Classroom, Study Abroad, and Intensive Domestic Immersion Programs. *Studies in Second Language Acquisition* 26/2, 275–301.

Jackson, Jane 2018. Intervening in the Intercultural Learning of L2 Study Abroad Students: From Research to Practice. *Language Teaching* 51/3, 1–18.

Jones, Elspeth 2018. Internationalisation, Employability and the Role of Languages. Opening Keynote Lecture. *36th AESLA International Conference*. University of Cadiz (Spain), 19 April.

Isabelli-Garcia, Christina 2006. Study Abroad Social Networks, Motivation and Attitudes: Implications for Second Language Acquisition. In Churchill, Eton/DuFon, Margaret A. (eds.) *Language Learners in Study Abroad Contexts*. Clevedon: Multilingual Matters, 231–258.

Kinginger, Celeste 2009. *Contemporary Study Abroad and Foreign Language Learning: An Activist's Guidebook for Foreign Language Educators*. University Park, PA: CALPER Publications.

Kinginger, Celeste 2011. Enhancing Language Learning in Study Abroad. *Annual Review of Applied Linguistics* 31/March, 58–73.

Knight, Susan M./Schmidt-Rinehart, Barbara C. 2010. Exploring Conditions to Enhance Student/Host Family Interaction Abroad. *Foreign Language Annals* 43/1, 64–71.

Lafford, Barbara A. 2006. The Effects of Study Abroad vs. Classroom Contexts on Spanish SLA: Old Assumptions, New Insights and Future Research Directions. In Klee, Carol A./Face, Timothy L. (eds.) *Selected Proceedings of the 7th Conference on the Acquisition of Spanish and Portuguese as First and Second Languages*. Sommerville, MA: Cascadilla Press, 1–25.

Magnan, Sally S./Lafford, Barbara A. 2012. Learning Through Immersion During Study Abroad. In Gass, Susan/Mackey, Alison (eds.) *The Routledge Handbook of Second Language Acquisition*. New York: Routledge, 525–540.

Marijuan, Silvia/Sanz, Cristina 2018. Expanding Boundaries: Current and New Directions in Study Abroad Research and Practice. *Foreign Language Annals* 51/1, 185–204.

Martinsen, Rob A./Baker, Wendy/Dewey, Dan P./Bown, Jennifer/Johnson, Cary 2010. Exploring Diverse Settings for Language Acquisition and Use: Comparing Study Abroad, Service Learning Abroad, and Foreign Language Housing. *Applied Language Learning* 20/1–2, 45–69.

Moreno Bruna, Ana M. 2018. Language and Intercultural Learning During Study Abroad: Maximizing Language Use Intensity and Intercultural Contacts. Paper presented at the *36th AESLA International Conference*. University of Cadiz (Spain), 19–21 April.

Pinar, Alex 2016. Second Language Acquisition in a Study Abroad Context: Findings and Research Directions. *Colombian Applied Linguistic Journal* 18/2, 83–94.

Segalowitz, Norman/Freed, Barbara/Collentine, Joe/Lafford, Barbara/Lazar, Nicole/Díaz-Campos, Manuel 2004. A Comparison of Spanish Second Language Acquisition in Two Different Learning Contexts: Study Abroad and the Domestic Classroom. *Frontiers: The Interdisciplinary Journal of Study Abroad* 10/Fall, 1–18.

Vasi Mocanu/Enric Llurda

Constructing and Reconstructing Attitudes towards Language Learning in Study Abroad

1 Introduction

Study abroad has been defined by Kinginger (2009: 11) as "a temporary sojourn of pre-defined duration, undertaken for educational purposes". In this chapter, *study abroad* refers to a period of time spent at a foreign university, which can last for one or two semesters and where the study of or studying through a second language is implied, even though it might not always be the main purpose of the sojourn.

Study abroad has consolidated as an attractive initiative for those who want to learn an additional language (Allen 2002; Isabelli-Garcia 2006; Kinginger 2011; Llanes/Muñoz 2009; Segalowitz/Freed 2004). A considerable amount of research on the topic has focused on its impact upon the acquisition of a foreign or second language, and in spite of the fact that the results are far from pointing to a single clear direction, some voices have claimed that study abroad provides a good environment for language learning. For instance, Kinginger (2013: 341) notes that:

> […] particularly in areas related to social interaction, such as awareness and use of sociolinguistic variants or command of pragmatics, the research has provided concrete and convincing evidence to substantiate the claim that students learn languages while abroad.

However, Kinginger (2011) also points to the fact that study abroad is not a magic formula for language learning *per se* and recommends programs that foster observation, participation, and reflection by the students about the sociolinguistic context. Similarly, DuFon and Churchill (2006) affirm that feelings of being rejected by the host culture or a certain degree of superficiality in the relationship with the host members can lead to withdrawal and reduce success in second language acquisition. And yet, these authors put the finger on the fact that the positions learners adopt when encountering sociocultural and linguistic differences may also play a role in restricting or facilitating their access to the target communities. Consequently, investigating language learning in study abroad contexts can be an ambitious endeavor, since there are many factors to be taken into account, such as the identities, motives, or desires of the learners, as well as the opportunities to learn and the ways they position themselves under these circumstances.

Besides language learning, which seems to be one of the highest assets of the experience (e.g. Kinginger 2013), study abroad might also be seen as a way to raise world citizens who are able to deal with cultural, linguistic and other social issues in a cross-cultural way. In this respect, a period studying abroad could give the participants the chance to see the world through a different lens provided by a different language, which might increase their opportunities on the global market. For instance, de Courtivron (2000), as cited in Brockington and Wiedenhoeft (2009: 121–122), affirms that:

> We are told that technical proficiency will one day become the only real passport needed by a citizen of the world. But such a passport will not be enough to flourish in the cultures to which it gives access. Communication skills, the ability to interact with others, historical awareness, analytical abilities, the mastery of several languages, and the cross-cultural knowledge to hear our polyphonic planet are some of the most important tools that we can provide students. And it is equally important, in my view, that we teach them how to think about, and through, this new fluidity.

In connection to the *passport* that gives access to different cultures, supranational institutions such as the European Union have been working for a few years on training European citizens to become agents in different sociocultural and linguistic environments. However, Brockington and Wiedenhoeft (2009) remark that while study abroad is perceived as the climax of intercultural experience, this is often not the case due to a lack of tools of the students to engage and learn from their sojourn, as well as to a lack of structured reflection after the stay abroad experience.

This chapter draws from a research project in which a mixed-methods longitudinal framework was adopted to approach the issue of identity, investment, and language learning in study abroad. It did so by examining the sense of belonging, imagined identities, attitudes towards languages and cultural differences, expectations, and degree of investment in both personal and professional learning among European higher education students. The general aim of the project was to investigate the impact of the participation in the Erasmus study abroad program on the identities, language attitudes and uses, and employability, as reported by international university students in three different contexts: Finland, Romania, and Catalonia (Spain).

The goals of this study in particular are to investigate how attitudes towards languages and language learning are constructed and reconstructed by European students during a study abroad period. Therefore, this chapter examines the attitudes of international students towards languages present in the three abovementioned contexts and towards language learning, as well as the participants' expectations in relation to language use at the beginning of their stay abroad and their linguistic practices eventually realized during their sojourn.

2 Methodology

2.1 Data and participants

The quantitative data presented in this chapter come from a project which included a total of 465 participants, all of them international students enrolled in a study abroad program for either one or two semesters in the three following locations: Oulu (Finland), Bucharest (Romania), and Lleida (Catalonia, Spain). However, the results that are presented here derive from a smaller pool of 155 participants from the total of 465, since our analysis exclusively focuses on those students who come from a European country and have participated in both phases of the data collection. Therefore, we will report on data elicited from questionnaires administered at the beginning and at the end of the stay abroad to a number of 80 European international students who studied in Oulu, 35 participants who did so in Lleida, and 40 international students in Bucharest.

The sample was composed by 87 males and 68 females from 26 different nationalities, and their average age was 22.2. The highest number of students comes from Italy (30), followed by Germany (27), France (18), Spain (18), the Czech Republic (10) and the Netherlands (10). The other 42 students represent Poland (7), Belgium (5), Austria (4), Slovakia (4), Bulgaria (2), Finland (2), Greece (2), Hungary (2), Sweden (2), Turkey (2), Bosnia (1), Lithuania (1), Moldova (1), Norway (1), Portugal (1), Romania (1), Slovenia (1), and Switzerland (1). Finally, 2 students have nationalities of countries outside the EU, namely Cameroonian and Kazak. The reason why these participants were included in the sample is that, in fact, they came from European countries where they were either living or pursuing a university degree, and so they were enrolled in their stay abroad through the Erasmus program. Finally, in relation to the length of their stay abroad, 116 participants spent one semester abroad, and the remaining 39 participants spent two semesters abroad.

2.2 *Instruments*

The instrument used in this study was a Likert-scale questionnaire, organized around three themes: identity, prospects of future mobility, and language attitudinal factors. The items consisted of a set of statements to which the participants had to express their agreement or disagreement by selecting from 1 (strongly disagree) to 5 (strongly agree). The questionnaire could be completed in approximately 25 minutes and was distributed in print to the international students in Oulu and Bucharest during the welcoming session and after an initial Catalan language and culture test to those in Lleida (PRE questionnaire), and electronically using Google Forms after having individually contacted all the available students via email or Facebook (POST questionnaire). The POST questionnaire was almost identical to the PRE questionnaire version. The only differences were (i) the addition of a few questions in the POST questionnaire, in which the participants were asked to reflect about their past experience; (ii) and the use of future verbal tenses to express aspects related to their expected experiences (PRE version) and past tenses (POST version). Questionnaires given to participants in the three different contexts also differed in the specific mentioning of the local context or the local language, which in the case of Lleida included references to both local languages: Catalan and Spanish.

The questionnaire contained items dealing with the following topics, directly linked to the specific objectives of the study:

1. Imagined identities and European citizenship (27 questions).
2. Multilingualism, language learning, and attitudes to languages (15 questions).
3. Investment, expectations and perceived outcomes of the stay at personal/academic/professional level (12 questions).
4. Language use, linguistic practices, and perceived language-related outcomes (13 questions added in the POST version).

Therefore, the only differences between the PRE and the POST versions of the questionnaire were in the different verbal tenses used to express aspects related to their expected experiences (future in the PRE version and past in the POST version), and the addition of 13 questions in the POST questionnaire, in which the participants were asked to reflect about their past experience. The questionnaire was distributed in English in the three contexts, but the participants in the Lleida group were given the option to choose between English and Spanish, according to their preference.

Given that the main goal of this paper is to understand the attitudes of the students towards the languages they encountered in the respective contexts in which their stay took place, we analyzed the answers to a set of eleven questions that were addressed in both the PRE and POST versions of the questionnaire. As stated above, the verb tenses were altered to reflect either the participants' initial expectations for what was coming ahead or their views on their experience at the end of the stay abroad period. Students were asked to give a mark (1 = not at all;

2 = not really; 3 = so-so; 4 = quite a lot; 5 = very much) to the following questions:

Question 1: To what extent did the opportunity to learn one of the following languages motivate you to take part in this mobility program? (Finnish/Catalan/Spanish/Romanian; English; Other languages)
Question 2: I want to spend/ I spent most of my stay with (local people/ other international students/people from my own country/native speakers of English).
Questions 3–11: A set of 9 questions on linguistic attitudes and expectations towards the local languages and English:

- I will never use Finnish/Romanian/Spanish/Catalan, so it is/was useless to learn it.
- We should all try/have tried to use Finnish/Romanian/Spanish/Catalan frequently.
- In my current context, learning Finnish/Romanian/Spanish/Catalan is/was more important than learning English.
- I like or I would like to speak Finnish/Romanian/Spanish/Catalan.
- I like listening to people speaking Finnish/Romanian/Spanish/Catalan.
- I will never use English, so it is/was useless to learn it.
- We should all try/have tried to use English frequently.
- I like or I would like to speak English.
- I like listening to people speaking English.

2.3 Data analysis procedure

Once all the data from the PRE and POST questionnaire were obtained, they were introduced in an SPSS spreadsheet for statistical analysis. As indicated above, only the European participants (total = 155) who had completed both questionnaires were included in the analysis. This analysis was conducted in a number of stages. First, the three contexts at both the PRE and the POST moments were compared by means of a one-way ANOVA test. When significant differences appeared in the one-way ANOVA test, a post-hoc Tukey HSD test was conducted in order to find exactly the contexts that were responsible for those differences. Once the three contexts were compared, a repeated measures ANOVA test was also conducted in order to compare each participant's results at the PRE and POST moments, and determine whether there were significant changes in their responses that could be attributed to the stay abroad experience.

3 Results and discussion

3.1 *Question 1: To what extent did the opportunity to learn one of the following languages motivate you to take part in this mobility program?*

As can be observed in Tab. 8-1, the one way ANOVA test revealed significant differences between the three settings in the PRE questionnaire with respect to two items: local languages and other languages.

Tab. 8-1: Language learning motivation: mean scores.

Language	Oulu		Lleida		Bucharest	
	PRE	POST	PRE	POST	PRE	POST
English	4.4	4.4/	4	3.7/#	4.5	4.3#
Local language (Finnish/Catalan/ Romanian)	2.9/	2.6/	3	2.6	3	2.6
Local language (Finnish/Spanish/ Romanian)	2.9/*	2.6/<	4.5*+	4.6#<	3+	2.6#
Other languages	2.*+	2.3*	2.	2.1	2.6+	2.3
*+/#< p < .05						

As both Spanish and Catalan are local languages encountered by students in Lleida, the item on local languages was analyzed twice: once comparing Finnish, Romanian, and Spanish ($F (2, 152)=22.63$, $p<.05$), and then comparing Finnish, Romanian, and Catalan (no significant difference). Post-hoc Tukey HSD comparisons revealed significant differences between the mean score in the Lleida group – with regard to Spanish – (M=4.5, SD=.98) and both the Oulu (M=2.9, SD=1.18) and the Bucharest group (M=3, SD=1.34). This points to the fact that, right from the beginning, the importance of the local language Spanish is a considerably more significant determinant for the choice of the stay abroad than both Finnish in Oulu and Romanian in Bucharest.

The second item with respect to which significant differences between the three groups were found in the PRE test was "other languages" (F (2, 129)=4.22, p<.05). The Tukey HSD post-hoc test signaled that the mean score for the Bucharest group (M=2.6, SD=1.26) was significantly higher than the mean score for the Oulu group (M=2, SD=1.12) and almost significantly higher than the one in the Lleida group (M=2, SD=1.13). Worth mentioning is also the fact that the mean score for the item "English" in the Lleida group was clearly lower than the mean scores for the same item in the Bucharest and Oulu groups, but no significant difference was found, possibly due to the limited number of participants in the Lleida and Bucharest groups. Were all groups made up of the same number of participants as in Oulu, no doubt more significant results would have been obtained, as means appear to be different enough as to indicate so. Finally, the lack of significant differences when the local languages Catalan, Finnish, and Romanian were compared could be regarded as an indicator of the fact that the motivation for learning the three local languages at the beginning of the stay was similar. Considering this together with the significant differences between the contexts when Spanish is taken into account, we may get some clues about language commodification and the economic value of languages in study abroad, and how Spanish is one of the most internationally marketable languages with a strong appeal to prospective learners, whereas Finnish, Romanian, and Catalan are regarded as much less valuable languages.

At the end of the sojourn, when the same ANOVA test was run, the language motivations from the beginning appeared to be regarded by the participants in a different way. In the first place, there were significant differences between the groups concerning the first item, "English" (F (2, 154)=5.06, p<.05), as the mean score for the Lleida group (M=3.7, SD=1.3) was significantly lower than the mean score for both the Bucharest (M=4.3, SD=1.07) and the Oulu group (M=4.4, SD=1.05). The second significant difference was found with respect to the item "local language" comparing Finnish, Romanian, and Spanish (F (2, 154)=41.64, p<.05). In this case, there was a coincidence of results in the PRE and POST questionnaires. Once more, the mean score assigned to Spanish (M=4.6, SD=.77) was significantly higher than the mean scores assigned to both Finnish (M=2.6, SD=1.29) and Romanian (M=2.6, SD=1.15). Furthermore, at the end of the stay, the perceived motivation for learning other languages had been homogenized among the three groups.

When a Repeated Measures ANOVA test was implemented to compare the answers given at the two moments of observation (PRE and POST), significant differences were also revealed with regard to two items. The first one was the motivation to learn Finnish in Oulu (Wilks' Lambda=.91, F (1, 78)=7.6, p<.05), which had significantly decreased by the end of the stay. In fact, a similar trend is observed concerning all local languages (Catalan, Romanian, and Finnish) with the exception of Spanish, but in the case of Romanian and Catalan, differences are not significant, probably due to the limited number of participants in those two groups. The second item that produced significant differences was the motivation to learn other languages in the Oulu group, which is perceived as significantly higher at the end of the study abroad sojourn (Wilks' Lambda=.92, F (1, 63)=5.15, p<.05).

The above results show that international students hold similar perceptions towards the local languages encountered in their settings with the exception of Spanish, which seems to be playing in a league of its own. Whereas Finnish, Romanian, and Catalan are perceived in the low-middle range of the 1–5 scale, Spanish stands out from the rest with very high scores significantly different from the scores of the other local languages both at the beginning and at the end of the stay abroad. This clearly speaks of the high international prominence of Spanish as one of the most valued world languages, in opposition to the clearly more modest roles of the other local languages in this study. Noteworthy is the lack of differences between Catalan and either Finnish or Romanian. Being the former a language without full international recognition as a national language and having no official status in the European Union, there would be ground to assume that international students would more enthusiastically embrace Finnish or Romanian than Catalan, but this is not the case. The perception of Catalan is also particular in that it shares its space with Spanish, and this clearly brings certain tensions and conflicts as international students mostly aim at increasing their proficiency in Spanish but have no specific desire to learn Catalan.

Another finding that is worth discussing is the decrease in the value attached to all local languages (with the exception of Spanish) after the sojourn. From an initial mean of 3 or 2.9, the score goes down to 2.6 for the three languages at the end of the sojourn. Finnish, Catalan, and Romanian were all rated lower at the end of the stay, though only in the case of Finnish the difference was significant.

The motivation to learn languages other than English and the local one was significantly higher among students in Bucharest than in Oulu at the beginning of the stay. Yet, no significant difference appeared at the end of the period abroad. Instead, what we see is a homogenizing trend across contexts at the end of the stay abroad. This may be so because the experience with English and the possibility of using languages that are different from English and the local one/s is rather similar in the three contexts. This question was identical in both versions of the questionnaire. They were asked to reflect on the relative importance they had allocated to the opportunity to learn different languages in their choice of place of destination. The most important outcomes here were, first, the low importance generally given to the opportunity to establish contact with speakers of other languages, and the slightly higher score in Bucharest; and second, the increase in the appreciation of other languages in Oulu after the stay abroad. All in all, a coherent pattern may be observed in the decrease of appreciation of Finnish and the increase in the value given to other languages in Finland after having experienced the study abroad life.

Students in Lleida had a very obvious goal to learn Spanish as well as English. In the other two contexts, English was the language that was profiled as the main linguistic motivation. It appears that all students had a clear awareness of the role of English as an international lingua franca. Yet, those in Lleida at the end of the stay abroad displayed significantly lower scores with regard to English than those in the other two contexts, thus reinforcing the perception that learning Spanish was a prominent factor in the choice of Lleida, at the expense of a lower prominence of English.

3.2 Question 2: I want to spend/I spent most of my stay with (local people/other international students/people from my own country/ native speakers of English)

With respect to the people the participants would like to spend most of their time with, as presented in Tab. 8-2, it seems that, by far, the students wish to spend most of their time with other international students, followed by local people, and native speakers of English. The lowest score is obtained by people from their own country of origin. On the whole, there was a contrast between the desire to spend their stay with local people, which was considerably high, and the desire to learn the local languages (Finnish, Romanian, and Catalan), which was lower (see Tab. 8-1 again). Furthermore, the willingness to spend their stay with people from their own countries is low, an indicator of a rather negative predisposition to it. In fact, the wish of the participants to spend their time abroad with native speakers of English was higher than the one with people from their own countries, even though none of the host institutions were in a country where English is the native language. Significant differences were found in the PRE test only with respect to the second item: "other international students" (ANOVA: $F(2, 152)=6.93$, $p<.05$). The Tukey post-hoc comparison showed that the mean score in Oulu (M=4.2, SD=.74) was significantly lower than both in Lleida (M=4.6, SD=.55) and in Bucharest (M=4.6, SD=.67).

Tab. 8-2: Motivation to spend time with/time actually spent with different groups of people.

Motivation to spend time with…	Oulu		Lleida		Bucharest	
	PRE	POST	PRE	POST	PRE	POST
Local people	3.9*	3*	3.8-	3.2-	4.1+	3.1+
Other international students	4.2*+	4.4	4.6*	4.5	4.6+	4.6
People from my own country	2.6*	3.1*	2.6-	3.3-	2.4+	3.5+
Native speakers of English	3.4*	2.2#*	3.3+	2.5#+	3.6-	1.3#-

-*+/# p < .05

When we compared the outcomes of the students' actual experience expressed in the POST questionnaire, we found significant differences only with regard to the last item: "native speakers of English" (F (2, 152)=16.46, p<.05). The post-hoc Tukey HSD test indicated that the mean score for Bucharest (M=1.3, SD=.60) was significantly lower than the mean score for both Oulu (M=2.2, SD=.97) and Lleida (M=2.5, SD=1.26), which points to a significantly lower contact with native speakers of English in Bucharest than in Oulu and Lleida.

In relation to differences between their initial expectations and their reported experiences at the end of the sojourn, significant differences were revealed by the Repeated Measures ANOVA test. With regard to the item "local people", the actual outcomes were significantly lower than previous expectations in the three groups: Oulu (Wilks' Lambda=.71, F (1, 79)=31.03, p<.05), Lleida (Wilks' Lambda=.78, F (1, 34)=9.57, p<.05), and Bucharest (Wilks' Lambda=.57, F (1, 39)= 29.09, p<.05). Significant differences were also found in the three groups concerning the item "people from my own country", where the final outcomes were significantly higher than the initial expectations: Oulu (Wilks'Lambda=.85, F (1, 79)=13.60, p<.05), Lleida (Wilks' Lambda=.79, F (1,34)=8.87, p<.05), and Bucharest (Wilks'Lambda=.71, F (1, 39)=15.27, p<.05). Furthermore, the outcomes regarding time expected to be spent with "native speakers of English" were significantly lower than the expectations in the three groups: Oulu (Wilks' Lambda=.63, F (1, 79)=46.38), Lleida (Wilks' Lambda=.79, F (1, 34)=8.89) and Bucharest (Wilks' Lambda=.22, F (1, 39)=134.33). These results indicate a considerable disparity between expectations and reality.

It is clear from the above results that international students initially desired to spend most of their time with other international students, and to a lesser extent with local students, followed by native speakers of English. Desire to spend time with co-nationals was by far the lowest, with scores that range from 2.4 to 2.6 in the 1–5 scale. The high score obtained by the desire to spend time with local students (3.9/3.8/4.1) is in stark contrast with the low score obtained in question 1 by the local language as a motivating factor in the choice of context (2.9/3/3).[1]

---

1 The value given for the Lleida context corresponds to Catalan (Spanish score was much higher: 4.5).

In fact, it is interesting to note that the high value given to Spanish does not correspond to a higher desire to interact with local people in Lleida than in the other two contexts. When we look at the results at the end of the stay abroad, these reflect the participants' perception of the actual time spent with different people, and so it may be considered a kind of reality check of their expectations vis-à-vis their actual experiences. What we see here is that the time spent with locals is lower than expected in all three contexts, and that is consistent with the result in question 1, in which a decrease in the motivation to learn the local languages is made evident.

Another result that deserves further comment is the difference between the low desire to spend time with co-nationals at the beginning (2.6/2.6/2.4) and the not so low score (3.1/3.3/3.5) given to the actual time spent with them. At the end of the sojourn, the participants declared that the group they spent most time with was international students, which is consistent with their initial desire. For all the other groups, significant differences appear: upward in the case of co-nationals and downward in the case of locals and native speakers of English.

3.3 Questions 3–11: Linguistic attitudes and language expectations

Concerning expectations and attitudes with regard to languages (see Tab. 8-3), there are very positive attitudes in general terms towards English across the three contexts, both at the beginning and at the end of the sojourn. Attitudes and expectations regarding three of the local languages (Finnish, Romanian, and Catalan) seem to be kept at a moderate level, and clearly lower than the remaining local language (Spanish) and English. This tendency is maintained throughout the stay. The Spanish language clearly stands out from the rest of local languages. The one-way ANOVA test revealed significant differences among the groups with respect to five of the nine items, and the sole language that accounts for such differences is Spanish.

Tab. 8-3: Linguistic attitudes and language expectations (I).

Linguistic attitudes and language expectations	Oulu		Lleida		Bucharest	
	PRE	POST	pre	POST	PRE	POST
I'll never use Finnish/Spanish/Romanian, so it's/ it was useless to learn it. (REVERSED SCORES)	3.9*	3.4/	4.7*+	4.7/#	4.2+	3.7#
… Catalan			3.6	3.2		
We should all use/have used Finnish/Spanish/Romanian frequently.	3.1*	3/%	4.1*+	4.1/#	3.4+	3.5#%
… Catalan			2.9	2.9		
Learning Finnish/Spanish/ Romanian is/ was more important than learning English.	2*	1.9/	3.1*+	3.4/	2.2+	1.9#
… Catalan			1.5/	2		
I like or I would like to speak Finnish/Spanish/Romanian.	3.9*	3.5#	4.8*+	4.8#%	4.2+	3.9 %-
… Catalan			3.4/	2.9-		
I like listening to people speaking Finnish/Spanish/Romanian.	3.8*	3.7/%	4.6*+	4.9/#	3.9+	3.8#-
… Catalan			3.3/	2.8 %-		
I will never use English, so it's/was useless to learn it. (REVERSED)	4.9	4.8	4.9	4.9	4.8	5
We should all try/ have tried to use English frequently.	4.5	4.6*	4.5	4.1*+	4.4	4.9+
I like or I would like to speak English.	4.6	4.7*	4.7	4.6*/	4.6	4.9/
I like listening to people speaking English.	4.5	4.4*	4.4	4.3*/	4.5	4.7/

*+#%- p<.05

The main differences found among the three contexts in the PRE test are listed below:

- I'll never use Finnish/Spanish/Romanian, so it's useless to learn it: ($F(2, 152)=9.96$, $p<.05$). The reversed mean score[2] in Lleida ($M=4.7$, $SD=.61$) is significantly higher than in both Oulu ($M=3.9$, $SD=1.04$) and Bucharest ($M=4.2$, $SD=1.12$).
- We should all use Finnish/Spanish/Romanian frequently: ($F(2, 151)=11.37$, $p<.05$). Mean score in Lleida ($M=4.1$, $SD=.99$) is significantly higher than in both Oulu ($M=3.1$, $SD=1.00$) and Bucharest ($M=3.4$, $SD=1.03$).
- Learning Finnish/Spanish/Romanian is more important than learning English: ($F(2, 152)=11.56$, $p<.05$). Mean score in Lleida ($M=3.1$, $SD=1.07$) is significantly higher than in both Oulu ($M=2$, $SD=1.20$) and Bucharest ($M=2.2$, $SD=1.24$).
- Learning Finnish/Catalan/Romanian is more important than learning English: ($F(2, 152)=3.72$, $p<.05$). Mean score in Lleida ($M=1.5$, $SD=.88$) is significantly lower than in Bucharest ($M=2.2$, $SD=1.24$). This indicates that the interest to learn Catalan in Lleida is not just low, but significantly lower than the interest to learn Romanian in Bucharest.
- I like or I would like to speak Finnish/Spanish/Romanian: ($F(2, 152)=11.73$, $p<.05$). Mean score in Lleida ($M=4.8$, $SD=.77$) is significantly higher than in both Bucharest ($M=4.2$, $SD=.86$) and Oulu ($M=3.9$, $SD=.99$).
- I like or I would like to speak Finnish/Catalan/Romanian $F(2, 152)=6.28$, $p<.05$). Mean score in Lleida ($M=3.4$, $SD=1.16$) is significantly lower than in Bucharest ($M=4.2$, $SD=.86$).
- I like listening to people speaking Finnish/Spanish/Romanian: ($F(2, 151)=10.11$, $p<.05$). Mean score for Spanish ($M=4.6$, $SD=.84$) is significantly higher than for both Finnish ($M=3.8$, $SD=.95$) and Romanian ($M=3.9$, $SD=.94$).

---

2 The reason why we have reversed the results obtained in questions that were formulated in a negative way is to reflect more intuitively the attitudes behind them, as higher scores are typically associated to positive attitudes and lower scores normally convey a negative value.

- I like listening to people speaking Finnish/Spanish/Romanian: (F (2, 152)=4.15, p<.05). Significantly lower mean score for pleasure listening to people speaking Catalan (M=3.3, SD=1.25) than Finnish (M=3.8, SD=.95) and Romanian (M=3.9, SD=.94).

Finally, as mentioned previously, the participants showed very positive attitudes and rather ambitious expectations with regard to the English language. No significant differences were encountered among the three contexts concerning English in the PRE test. In the POST test, the following significant differences among the groups were revealed by the one-way ANOVA test:

- I will never use Finnish/Spanish/Romanian, so it was useless to learn it: (F (2, 151)=17.82, p<.05). Mean score in Lleida (M=4.7, SD=.65) significantly higher than in both Oulu (M=3.4, SD=1.33) and Bucharest (M=3.7, SD=1.05).
- We should all have used Finnish/Spanish/Romanian frequently: (F (2, 151)=15.34, p<.05). Mean score in Lleida (M=4.1, SD=.87) significantly higher than in both Oulu (M=3, SD=1.14) and Bucharest (M=3.5, SD=1.12). Also, mean score in Bucharest (M=3.5, SD=1.12) significantly higher in Oulu (M=3, SD=1.14).
- Learning Finnish/Spanish/Romanian was more important than English: (F (2, 151)=20.77, p<.05). Mean score in Lleida (M=3.4, SD=1.46) significantly higher than in both Oulu (M=1.9, SD=1.15) and Bucharest (M=1.9, SD=1.25).
- I would like to speak Finnish/Spanish/Romanian: (F (2, 151)=18.65, p<.05). Mean score in Lleida (M=4.8, SD=.45) significantly higher than in both Oulu (M=3.5, SD=1.22) and Bucharest (M=3.9, SD=1.20).
- I would like to speak Finnish/Catalan/Romanian: (F (2, 151)=5.44, p<.05). Mean score in Lleida (M=2.9, SD=1.32) significantly lower than in Bucharest (M=3.9, SD=1.2).
- I like listening to people speaking Finnish/Catalan/Romanian: (F (2, 150)=7.33, p<.05). Mean score in Lleida (M=2.8, SD=1.38) significantly lower than in both Oulu (M=3.7, SD=1.20) and Bucharest (M=3.8, SD=1.07).
- We should all have tried to use English frequently: (F (2, 150)=11.72, p<.05). Mean score in Lleida (M=4.1, SD=1.01) significantly lower than in both Oulu (M=4.6, SD=.72) and Bucharest (M=4.9, SD=.30).

Overall, Spanish appears to play a role that is substantially different from the role played by any other local language. In fact, the power and attraction of Spanish seems to equal the power and attraction of English in the Lleida group. We may argue that this might be the reason why Catalan is assigned significantly lower scores than Finnish and Romanian in some cases. This adversity can be perceived most especially when it comes to a possible wish to learn Catalan, and even the mere fact of listening to people speaking Catalan.

Table 8-4 includes the same items as in Tab. 8-3 incorporating a symbol to indicate the cases where the Repeated Measures ANOVA test showed significant differences between the PRE and the POST questionnaires. Significant differences between the initial and final moments of the stay abroad are listed below:

- I'll never use Finnish/Spanish/Romanian, so it's/it was useless to learn it: Decrease in Oulu (Wilks' Lambda=.89, $F (1, 79)=9.38$, $p<.05$), and also decrease in Bucharest (Wilks' Lambda=.87, $F (1, 38)=5.47$, $p<.05$).
- Learning Catalan was more important than English: Increase in Lleida (Wilks' Lambda=.84, $F(1, 34)=6.45$, $p<.05$).
- I like or I would like to speak Finnish/Spanish/Romanian: Decrease in Oulu (Wilks' Lambda=.86, $F (1, 79)=11.86$, $p<.05$), and decrease in Bucharest (Wilks' Lambda= .88, $F (1, 38)=5.16$, $p<.05$).
- I like listening to people speaking Catalan: Decrease in Lleida (Wilks' Lambda=.84, $F (1, 34)=6.11$, $p<.05$).
- We should all try/have tried to use English frequently: Decrease in Lleida (Wilks' Lambda=.87, $F (1, 34)=4.95$, $p<.05$), and increase in Bucharest (Wilks' Lambda=.76, $F (1, 38)=11.63$, $p<.05$).

Therefore, we can say that, in fact, with regard to the first question: "I'll never use Finnish/Spanish/Romanian, so it's/it was useless to learn it", at the end of the stay, significantly more negative attitudes are reported by the students in Oulu towards Finnish, and by the students in Bucharest towards Romanian. A similar trend can be observed in relation to Catalan in Lleida, even though the difference is not significant. Spanish, on the other hand, maintains the same high score. Interestingly, when it comes to the relative importance of learning Catalan vs. English, and despite the fact that the score is still very low in the POST test, it is significantly

Tab. 8-4: Linguistic attitudes and language expectations (II).

Linguistic attitudes and language expectations	Oulu		Lleida		Bucharest	
	PRE	POST	PRE	POST	PRE	POST
I'll never use Finnish/ Spanish/Romanian, so it's/ was useless to learn it. (REVERSED SCORES) … Catalan	3.9*	3.4*	4.7 3.6	4.7 3.2	4.2/	3.7/
We should all use/ have used Finnish/Spanish/Romanian frequently. … Catalan	3.1	3	4.1 2.9	4.1 2.9	3.4	3.5
Learning Finnish/Spanish/ Romanian is/ was more important than learning English. … Catalan	2	1.9	3.1 1.5#	3.4 2#	2.2	1.9
I like or I would like to speak Finnish/Spanish/ Romanian. … Catalan	3.9#	3.5#	4.8 3.4	4.8 2.9	4.2 %	3.9 %
I like listening to people speaking Finnish/Spanish/ Romanian.	3.8	3.7	4.6	4.9	3.9	3.8
… Catalan			3.3/	2.8/		
I will never use English, so it's useless to learn it.(RE-VERSED)	4.9	4.8	4.9	4.9	4.8	5
We should all try/ have tried to use English frequently.	4.5	4.6	4.5+	4.1+	4.4-	4.9-
I like or I would like to speak English.	4.6	4.7	4.7	4.6	4.6	4.9
I like listening to people speaking English.	4.5	4.4	4.4	4.3	4.5*	4.7*

*+#%- p<.05

higher than in the PRE test. However, if we take into account also the results of the first item with regard to Catalan, and the significantly lower score to the item "I like listening to people speaking Catalan", we might interpret the higher importance allocated to the need to learn Catalan as an outcome of the realization that the Catalan language had a considerable weight for the local people in Lleida, and therefore, the participants might have realized it was certainly more important to learn it than they had imagined at the beginning of their sojourn. Yet, it seems that this situation did actually lead to an increased animosity towards the Catalan language. In fact, more negative feelings towards the local languages (Finnish, Catalan and Romanian) are revealed in the POST test, where the participants assign significantly lower scores to those three languages.

Finally, with regard to English, the students in Lleida assign a significantly lower score to the item "We should all have tried to use English frequently in the POST test", while the ones in Bucharest do the opposite, assigning a significantly higher score to the same item. A possible interpretation could be that the Lleida group might perceive they did not learn as much Spanish as they expected to, and using English might have interfered with their use of Spanish. On the other hand, the students in Bucharest might also perceive that their English level may not have improved to the extent they expected. If we take into account the reported time the students spent with people from their own countries, using one's first language might be understood as a factor limiting the use of English, which the participants could regret at the end of their stay abroad.

4 Conclusions

The results of this study show that, straight from the beginning, the roles of different languages in study abroad are perceived to be different. The clearest example of this is the considerably higher importance assigned to English and to the local language Spanish, when compared to all the other local languages considered in this study. Therefore, the motivation and degree of investment of the participants in each language might be correlated to the perceived economic value of the languages more than to anything else. The similar value assigned to Finnish, Romanian, and Catalan at the beginning of the stay points to the same direction. However, it is worth mentioning that despite not holding the same status as Finnish and Romanian, Catalan is embraced in a similar way.

The stay abroad sojourn seems to have a homogenizing effect among the three groups with regard to the motivation to learn languages other than the local ones and English: while at the beginning of the sojourn, the participants appear to be significantly more motivated to learn other languages in Bucharest than in Oulu, at the end of their stay, these differences have disappeared, and we can observe a decrease in the appreciation of Finnish, as well as an increase in the interest for other languages in the Oulu group – all of it as a result of the study abroad experience.

The prominent role of English is considerably visible both at the beginning and at the end of the stay. However, the scores assigned to English in the Lleida group at the end of the sojourn are significantly lower, which points to the fact that Spanish was the language in which the participants were willing to invest in, even if it was at the expense of not investing so much in the global lingua franca – that is, English.

With respect to the desire to spend their time with local/international/co-national/native speakers of English, it seems that initially, spending time with other international students is the most highly preferred option, followed by local people, and native speakers of English. Spending time with co-nationals receives the lowest scores. The high degree of willingness to spend time with locals contrasts with the rather low degree of investment in the local languages. The contrast is also found in the case of Spanish: a high motivation for learning this language does not seem to trigger a higher motivation to spend time with local people.

At the end of the stay, expectations and reality are different in the three groups. Time reported to have been spent with locals is significantly lower in all three contexts, which correlates with the decrease in motivation to learn the local languages. Time expected to be spent with co-nationals is also significantly different from time reported being spent with this group of people–participants report having spent much more time with their co-nationals than expected or desired. The opposite pattern is observed in the case of time expected to be spent and time actually spent with native speakers of English.

As we have already mentioned, Spanish seems to play a considerably different role than the other local languages. This might have triggered some of the significantly lower scores attributed to Catalan when compared to Finnish and Romanian with respect to willingness to learn the language and a liking for listening to people speaking Catalan. This fact, together with the perceived need to speak Catalan in Lleida after the sojourn, might have led to an increased negative feeling towards Catalan. However, this trend can also be appreciated in the case of Romanian and Finnish, and significantly lower scores are assigned to the three languages at the end of the stay.

All in all, the above findings indicate a certain disparity between expectations and reality in these three study abroad contexts. This concerns both social aspects, like the groups of people in the company of whom the stay is expected to be spent or reported to have been spent, and language-related aspects. In the first place, a certain *fetichisation* of English appears straight from the beginning, which is observable through the high expectations to learn English and spend time with native speakers of English in contexts where English is not spoken as a native language. Secondly, what we can observe is a clear *hierarchisation* of languages and a resulting different degree of investment in each of the encountered languages according to their economic value. Finally, the results also indicate a rather unexpected effect of the stay abroad experience which is an increased adversity towards the local languages in all three contexts. As explained above, this study is part of a wider project in which qualitative interview data were also collected. We expect that the analysis of such interviews will shed more light onto the deep reasons that inspire the participants' attitudinal responses to the different languages present in their respective environments.

Acknowledgements

This research was supported by Ministerio de Economía y Competitividad (grant number FFI2015-67769-P) and Agència de Gestió d'Ajuts Universitaris i de Recerca (grant number 2017 SGR 1522).

References

Allen, Heather Willis 2002. Does Study Abroad Make a Difference? An Investigation of Linguistic and Motivational Outcomes. PhD thesis, Emory University 2002. *Dissertation Abstracts International-A* 63/4, 1279. <https://works.bepress.com/heatherwillisallen/50/>.

Brockington, Joseph L./Wiedenhoeft, Margaret D. 2009. The Liberal Arts and Global Citizenship: Fostering Intercultural Engagement through Integrative Experiences and Structured Reflection. In Lewin, Ross (ed.) *The Handbook of Practice and Research in Study Abroad*. London/New York: Routledge, 117–132.

De Courtivron, Isabelle 2000. Educating the Global Student, Whose Identity Is Always a Matter of Choice. *Chronicle of Higher Education* 46/45, B4. <https://www.chronicle.com/article/Educating-the-Global-Student/22400>.

DuFon, Margaret A./Churchill, Eton (eds.) 2006. *Language Learners in Study Abroad Contexts*. Clevedon: Multilingual Matters.

Isabelli-García, Christina 2006. Study Abroad Social Networks, Motivation and Attitudes: Implications for Second Language Acquisition. In DuFon, Margaret A./Churchill, Eton (eds.) *Language Learners in Study Abroad Contexts*. Clevedon: Multilingual Matters, 231–258.

Kinginger, Celeste 2009. *Language Learning and Study Abroad. A Critical Reading of the Research*. London/New York: Palgrave Macmillan.

Kinginger, Celeste 2011. Enhancing Language Learning in Study Abroad. *Annual Review of Applied Linguistics* 31/1, 58–73.

Kinginger, Celeste (ed.) 2013. *Social and Cultural Aspects of Language Learning in Study Abroad*. Amsterdam: John Benjamins.

Llanes, Àngels/Muñoz, Carmen 2009. A Short Stay Abroad: Does It Make a Difference? *System* 37/3, 353–365.

Segalowitz, Norman/Freed, Barbara 2004. Context, Contact, and Cognition in Oral Fluency Acquisition: Learning Spanish in at Home and Study Abroad Contexts. *Studies in Second Language Acquisition* 26/2, 173–199.

Oana Maria Carciu/Laura-Mihaela Muresan

"There Are So Many Dimensions of Internationalization": Exploring Academics' Views on Internationalization in Higher Education

1 Introduction

At European level, the Bologna Declaration encouraged scholarly dialogue on internationalization in teaching, learning, and research for the success of its reforms, knowledge transfer and, as a result, social change (Sin 2015). There is an increasing body of research on the phenomenon of internationalization in higher education, with topics ranging from actions such as student and staff mobility to internationalization plans at curriculum or institutional level (see Knight 2004, 2013; Altbach/Knight 2007; Leask 2008, 2013; Childress 2009; Dewey/Duff 2009; Bardi/Muresan 2014; Muresan/Pérez-Llantada 2014; Jones 2013; de Wit/Leask 2015; Jones/Coelen/Beelen/de Wit 2016; Bocanegra-Valle 2018, to cite just a few). While these actions facilitate knowledge transfer – defined as an instance of academics' teaching, research, and administration activities or as an extra to these activities (Francis-Smythe/Haase/Steele/Jellis 2007), at their core there is a fundamentally simple question, that of communication of knowledge and the language in which it is transmitted.

As shown in a recent comprehensive systematic review (Yemini/Sagie 2016), the most frequently recurring themes found in the literature on internationalization seem to share a clear focus on teaching, learning and research priorities with the operationalization of English as the language of these knowledge transfer activities in an internationalized higher education environment; that is, top scores were obtained for the following themes: English as a lingua franca (12.05 %), multicultural issues (11.86 %), ICT/online learning (9.95 %), while life-long/adult learning (7.68 %), although present, did not attract the same attention from researchers. However, the key emerging themes in the literature also revealed institution-wide policy goals for internationalization, such as student mobility (11.48 %), competition (9.78 %), internationalization abroad (9.77 %), internationalization policies (9.69 %), internationalization at home (9.14 %), and quality assurance (8.17 %). Although these two overarching groups of themes seem to be underpinned by different agendas – a focus on knowledge creation and flow, on the one hand, and knowledge economy and globalization, on the other – it is important to emphasize not only their interrelatedness (cf. Knight 2015), but also the centrality of communication, especially in English as the medium of teaching, learning and research. More specifically, English as a lingua franca is mediating the production of academic knowledge, is the main vehicle for knowledge transfer activities, and has become central to the process of internationalization at tertiary level.

Given that knowledge transfer is a significant instrument of social change, the objective of this chapter is to contribute to understanding how academics perceive the impact of internationalization on the three dimensions of the first overarching group of themes, that is, the triangle of teaching, learning and research activities. This is a salient and still under-researched aspect. Therefore, gaining insights into internationalization processes at grassroots level could inform future policy-making, institution-level decision-taking, and research on higher education management. We conducted semi-structured interviews with academics at one institution engaged in the process of internationalization to inquire into the following aspects: (i) What are the main features that faculty associate with internationalization? (ii) What internationalization-related activities do faculty observe occurring at their university? (iii) Are these linked to any major concerns about the impact of internationalization on teaching, learning and research activities? These three aspects were the main focus of the interviews and are discussed in the chapter in light of the respondents' perception of opportunities and challenges related to internationalization, as well as its impact on the triangle teaching–learning–research. In examining faculty views at one institution only, it is not possible to generalize the findings; however, we hope that they can shed light on the complexity of multi-layered internationalization endeavours.

2 Methodology

To reveal faculty perspectives on the process of internationalization, we conducted a qualitative, single-case study research. The case studied was The Bucharest University of Economic Studies (Romania), a university which met pre-determined sampling criteria that could be indicative of demonstrated commitment to internationalization such as being adherent to and signatory of the Bologna process, presence of degree programmes in English and other *lingua francas* (both at undergraduate and at postgraduate levels), academics involved in English, French or German-medium teaching and research, and interest in the recruitment of international students, among others. The institution was in the process of designing its internationalization strategy at the time when we were conducting the interviews. The approach taken to sampling was to select a small number of individuals for in-depth or "thick description" of the case (Duff 2008). The selection of participants was based on the opportunistic convenience sampling criterion (available academics, but all involved in teaching, research, and administration activities with an international focus). A total of 10 interviews were recorded and transcribed. The data were collected over one week in February, 2016. Interviewed respondents are referenced in this study individually from R01 to R10. All interviews were conducted in Romanian, the respondents' native language, and transcribed in the language of the interview. Both the coding and analysis were done on the original transcripts, and only the 23 quoted excerpts chosen for inclusion in this chapter were translated into English by the authors.

Traditional qualitative research methods were used, that is, semi-structured interviews and document analysis (Yin 2003). The analysis of the transcribed interviews was conducted using Computer-Aided Qualitative Data Analysis Software (CAQDAS), *ATLAS.ti 8.2.0*. The interviews explored the academics' views on several aspects that were the focus of the interview prompt "What is an international campus?" Theming the Data was the type of coding performed on the data (Saldaña 2009). The emergent themes were triangulated between the authors of this study, so as to strengthen the dependability and trustworthiness of the findings. We also used the techniques of corpus linguistics, that is, the transcripts (electronic format documents) were processed by the *#LancsBox v. 4.0* (Brezina/McEnery/Wattam 2015) software package. First, we searched for frequent words as they can reveal information about the main themes prevalent within the texts. Second, we looked at concordances, that is, stretches of text which show the linguistic environment of target words and allow the identification of patterns, that is repeated meanings in the transcripts which are not easily uncovered by merely reading the texts (Hunston 2008).

3 Findings and discussion

Interview analysis identified themes and sub-themes, related to the following aspects: academics' perspectives on internationalization, in general, and their perceptions on internationalization-related dimensions in their own academic context. Their views in relation to teaching, learning and research will be detailed below.

3.1 Faculty views on the concept of internationalization

The analysis of the interview data revealed the respondents' complex and nuanced understanding of an "international campus" as a multi-faceted reality. The main dimensions mentioned could be grouped as shown in Tab. 9-1.

A prominent category in the interviews is that of human resources, with two subcategories, academic staff and students. Our respondents highlighted academic staff mobility as a process that would allow institutions to draw staff from various locations of the world either through exchange programmes or hiring. Interestingly, one of the respondents noted the need of a change in hiring practices to recruit academic staff with diverse language and cultural competences, from a variety of

Tab. 9-1: Dimensions of an international campus in respondents' perspective.

Focus area	*Examples of pre-requisites for internationalization*
Human resources: Academics	"human resources with diverse language and cultural competences" (R01); "teacher exchanges" (R05)
Human resources: Students (undergraduate and graduate)	"flexibility regarding incoming and outgoing student mobility" (R03) (beyond ERASMUS+); opportunities for international and local students to exchange experience, to socialize (R09)
Resources: Material and information	"access to information" (R02) "free access to specialized literature" (R07)
Teaching	"a considerable exchange of experience with teachers from other universities in Europe" (R03)
Research	"joint research programmes" [with universities from all over the world] (R04) "international research teams" (R06); "research centres" [for facilitating work on international projects] (R08)
Academic programmes	"joint academic programmes" (R04)
Institutional management	"having a long-term internationalization strategy" (R05, R10); "partnerships with universities from abroad" (R04); "exchange of experience among universities" (R08)

geographical regions (see excerpt 1). An alternative human resources plan is that of exchange programmes which, according to our respondents, contribute to training and development of both teaching and research skills and, as a result, to multi-skilling of outgoing academics and widening horizons (see excerpt 2). International practitioners invited to speak at workshops or conferences are another category of human resources that the university can capitalise on (see excerpt 3). Further adoption of this practice, which seeks to bridge the world of work and study, is likely to enhance employability. All three actions, that is, hiring procedures, exchange programmes and inviting professionals from abroad, can also be considered practices that contribute towards a particular type of internationalization, that is, internationalization at home (cf. Beelen/Jones 2015).

(1) For a campus to be international [...] the main prerequisite, in my opinion, is that related to human resources. I mean having teachers from diverse cultures, diverse geographical areas, who have a diversity of linguistic and cultural competences (...) (R01)

(2) In concrete terms, this would mean having more, inviting more professors from abroad to teach here. And secondly, to send [teaching staff] abroad. A Romanian professor who teaches a semester in China and comes back here has another approach, also the case studies s/he introduces stand out from this horizon which makes us feel comfortable and self-sufficient (...) (R05)

(3) I'm thinking of international speakers who could come to hold lectures – not necessarily theoreticians, academics, but rather practitioners. For instance, at our Faculty (...) we have recently had two guests from the US – a theoretician, Assistant Professor in Illinois, Northern Illinois University, who talked to students about transparency and corruption, and then, later on, we had a practitioner who came to talk on the same topics, a gentleman who was working at an anti-corruption agency in the States, yes, and this contributes a lot to internationalization. (R04)

Human resources development for internationalization touches not only on recruitment of academic staff but also on recruitment of students. However, although student mobility at undergraduate level was discussed in terms of incoming students (R05), being proactive and valorising internal human resources was considered strategically important in order to maximise opportunities for internationalization (i.e. internationalization at home). As one respondent mentioned, the institution should involve the home student body returning from exchange or study abroad programmes in the organization of informal activities and events, in order to obtain feedback from them and, at the same time, to build on their experience for a better integration of international students on campus (see excerpt 4). The respondents also considered that the institution should aim to explore the views of international students on a regular basis, and should create more opportunities for local and international students to engage in dialogue (see excerpts 4–5). These processes were seen as aspects likely to increase the impact that mobility may have on local and international students. For example, organising summer schools at home would be a way to manage human resources, to enhance capacity building, competitiveness and, subsequently, employability (see excerpt 5). Once again, postgraduate incoming students were seen as human capital that could be involved in teaching and research activities at the host institution (see excerpt 6).

(4) There is a preoccupation for organising events and for helping those who come from different cultures to get to know each other [...] Well, I have realised that the perspective one has on various developments can be complemented by the points of view of those who come and spend some time here [...] There is also a further aspect that we should take into account, for internationalization to become reality people should spend more time together. What we have noticed over the last few years is that students stay at university only for the course schedule, and there is only little availability for joint activities, for having a coffee or going to a film together, or for a discussion. (R09)

(5) [international summer schools at home] can foster our students' ability to relate to their international peers, and this would help them become more competitive. (R10)

(6) (...) attracting not only students who come through the Erasmus programme but also masters' and doctoral students, and their involvement in research activities and even in teaching. (R01)

Apart from human resources, the respondents underlined the educational dimension of internationalization, a theme which included the categories of teaching and academic programmes. They mentioned that teaching activities reflected the shift to multilingualism, with academic staff embarking on teaching content subjects in other languages, especially in English, but also in French or German. One of our respondents discussed this change in terms of knowledge transfer – that is, reaching out and imparting knowledge from one country context to students from other geographic regions through teaching and learning via the medium of a *lingua franca* (see excerpt 7). In addition, these teaching practices, reflected in the commitment to use a greater variety of multilingual teaching materials for learning, as mentioned by one of the respondents, posed a challenge to academic staff who have to keep up with the pace of developments in the field and, at the same time, to upskill their language competences (see excerpt 8). Again, it was felt that courses should cater for future professional needs (see excerpt 9), with plans to implement foreign language learning programmes in more languages of geopolitical interest, such as Russian or Arabic.

(7) Regarding the institutional level, I have noticed that more and more universities implement a curriculum strand in a foreign language, including universities that traditionally did not have them [...] To have a British student in the group, and also a Chinese student, was for me extraordinary, even if I was

very nervous in the beginning about teaching in English, but this means that we are opening up and local knowledge becomes available and part of the global knowledge flow [...]. (R02)

(8) To take into account also the teaching materials for students in all these languages. So there is a need to use materials in foreign languages in class on a regular basis. (R10)

(9) The internationalization of universities has become a necessity, because the professional world is already engaged in this process and, therefore, experiencing internationalization during university studies we create favourable premises/conditions for successful adjustment/better adaptability in the profession. (R09)

A common thread running through the "Academic programmes" category is that of joint academic programmes (see excerpt 10). It was considered that summer schools and other extracurricular activities also offered opportunities for learning which may result in knowledge that is pivotal to social and economic progress. As one respondent succinctly put it (see excerpt 11), summer schools might be a practical approach to enhance competitiveness of the regional or national workforce, but also to train human resources for the workplace of the future (employability) in which the competitive edge would be based on human capital with skills of "a person comfortable with themselves as well as flexible enough to collaborate and negotiate with others who are different from themselves in order to forge a common interest" (Cope/Kalantzis 2009: 174).

(10) And, of course, the programmes unfolded in cooperation with universities from abroad are very interesting. I remember an example from the Faculty of Accounting, [...] they have an agreement with the University of Amsterdam, for the masters' programme – the MA at ASE is a two-year programme, in Amsterdam only one year. So how does this work: you do your first year in Romania and, if you are accepted, you do the second year in Amsterdam, and you obtain a double diploma, that is also from the University of Amsterdam, and the exams you have taken in Amsterdam are recognised as the equivalent of the second year in Romania. In my view this is very interesting and very useful for students and also for universities. (R04)

(11) A very important instrument, frequently used by universities abroad consists in summer schools. I contributed to several at ASE, and this is a very good start, but they need to be used on a regular basis as an opportunity for making foreign students aware of the potential we have and also for enhancing our students' capacity of rapid integration in an [international]

environment in our country, with their colleagues from abroad. This way they can become more competitive, they overcome inhibition, and develop communication competences. This is a plus for their future job, whether in-country or abroad. (R10)

Another thematic thread is that of research as a dimension of internalization. This theme frames matters of collaboration in joint research programmes and projects (see excerpt 12), participation in international research teams, or research planning measures such as setting up research centres (see excerpt 13) and, as one respondent underlined (see excerpt 14), formalised strategic alliances in research. All these were considered practices that would help to build an international community of researchers, but also lead to professional development in the areas of teaching and transfer to learning. One of the respondents (R06) identified conference participation and another one the joint publication of research outcomes by international teams (R07) as central to networking and cooperation beyond national borders, thus contributing to internationalization in the area of research.

(12) I don't know, I'm thinking of research programmes, or training and development programmes jointly organised with universities from different parts of the world, or between our university and other universities in the world. [...] I am also thinking of international research projects – Horizon 2020 – where the requirements include international teams, with participants from different EU member states and not only. (R04)

(13) If we refer to research, I would think of research centres or exchange of experience with universities, so as to facilitate the access of professors to Visiting Professorships, this could mean a lot. [...] But I think there is not enough cooperation, not enough research centres, so as to have proper interdisciplinary cooperation, or mixed international research teams involved in international research projects, I think there aren't many. It [internationalization] would be easy to implement through participation in conferences and by creating robust networking. (R08)

(14) Considering the contacts with universities from abroad, yes, there is a need for more effort and an extremely well targeted strategy, one that is aggressive and active, for circulating the human resources from our own context and for bringing in colleagues from abroad, who should get involved in what we are doing here, to teach, to do research, to create mixed research teams [...] There is also a need for a more assertive presence in important international associations, that would open up new contacts and collaboration opportunities. (R01)

Material resources and information is a theme that runs across the educational dimension as reference to access to information (see excerpt 15); however, it can also be found in the research dimension in relation to funding for projects and participation in conferences (see excerpts 16–17).

(15) I think that an important component of internationalization is access to information, that is access to information that everyone should have, irrespective of citizenship, and then, if information or the majority of information is available in a language of international circulation, this would contribute to internationalization. I've had groups of students from Arab countries, also students from China, so from Asia, and access to information is most important. It is up to you what you do with information, but first of all, it is important to have access to it. (R02)

(16) A lot depends on European funding, and then there are certain predefined and pre-established trajectories. We cannot simply participate with a project we have designed within our university, we have to align [the project] to certain priorities associated with these financing sources. I would say that this is, of course, a great opportunity, and we should develop such projects, but at the same time we have to be aware that there are certain restrictions regarding themes we would be interested in but for which there is currently no funding. In concrete terms, there are a lot of research projects on policies at European level but we don't have resources for studies on the Middle East or the Eastern partnership, and I'm not referring necessarily to neighbouring countries but, for instance, countries around the Caspian Sea. (R07)

(17) Yes, there are some projects we would like to develop and carry out but they don't depend only on our Faculty, there are several factors involved, and it depends heavily on whether the necessary funding can be obtained or not. [...] In terms of research, it seems to me that there is not enough support for academics at our university, and especially for the young ones, to help them become good researchers. (R04)

All these internationalization activities seem to be initiated by academic staff in a bottom-up approach (see excerpts 18–19). At the same time, as another respondent pointed out, a long-term institutional strategy would need to be formulated. Of note, in the years following our interviews the institution worked on and designed such a plan, formulating a clear mission statement and strategy.

(18) Everything is centralised at personal level, as it were, but there is no coherent institutional policy regarding this. (R01)

(19) Interestingly, there are a lot of scholars who do this individually, from their own funds, their own resources, their own connections; sometimes you would be surprised how many do this on a personal level; just as the colleague you mentioned, from the Language Department. But institutionally, there is a lack of strategy. There are the Eramus programmes but, in my view, they are not part of a logic, they are simply there [...] so one goes [on a mobility abroad], one comes, there are some incoming students, some outgoing students, ok, but without an internal consistency, without the internal coherence of the endeavour. (R05)

There was a certain degree of overlap among the responses and a general agreement that institutional involvement and strategy was crucial for the existence of a truly international campus, as R10 stated (see excerpt 20).

(20) I don't know if our university has a strategy, so I think it should design one for several years, with the aim of becoming truly international. So there should be a strategy for the university in order to address this international issue (...) long-term thinking. (R10)

The differences in the responses were more in terms of weighting given to the various focus areas associated with internationalization. A recurrent element in the interview material was the value attached to human resources and, in close connection to it, the relevance of academic staff mobility. Arguments supporting this view included the manifold effect of mobility on professional development, e.g. for upgrading teaching, research and publication related competences. For example, research stays and international research partnerships were likely to lead to participation in joint research projects or organization of international events, as well as co-authoring of research papers published in international journals, but also to invitations to teach. Given that mobile staff integrated all the expertise acquired abroad into their daily teaching and research practices, academics' international mobility resulted in benefits for the entire student body, not only those who are mobile. Of note, all these activities contribute to knowledge transfer and are favourable to a particular type of internalization, that is, internationalization at home (cf. Beelen/Jones 2015: 12; Korka 2018).

3.2 Factors influencing internationalization

When reflecting on internationalization in their own academic environment, staff mobility was cited once again as promoting both international teaching and research activities; however, it is important to note that in the respondents' view, these were all individually initiated activities. Significantly, some respondents reflected on the "decentralized nature of internationalization initiatives" (R01, R03, R05, among others), with its pluses and minuses, while others mentioned that there was not enough transparency and clarity of direction regarding the recruiting of international students and of attracting professors from abroad.

Recurrent topics were the necessity to ensure funding and the need to improve "tedious administrative procedures" (R06). The participants also mentioned the impact of professional development on teacher and researcher knowledge. The inter-disciplinary masters' programme, "Research and Teacher Education for Business & Economics" (EDU-RES), was cited as an example. This programme was aimed at academic staff at all levels and had a facilitating role for professional development and provided the opportunity for refining their skills for both teaching and research communication in English (Bardi/Muresan 2014). It is noteworthy that the respondents, who had graduated from the programme some years ago, underlined the importance of creating more such development opportunities at institutional level, for continuously improving the quality of teaching, research and international publishing. Examples of such facilitating, still developing, support measures included pedagogic training (short-term workshops), material infrastructure and motivation strategies, such as awards and recognition (cf. Cardoso/Tavares/Sin 2015). These findings reveal the respondents' interest in lifelong learning and an increased awareness of how their own development may contribute to better student learning.

Just as mobility was considered an enabling factor in the exchange of best practice for the teaching dimension, international partnerships together with the creation of research centres and membership in international associations were seen as facilitating factors for enhancing the internationalization of academic research; in contrast, lack of funding, the necessity to ensure access to specialized literature, international visibility of published research, integration of research centres into international networks were found as main challenges for the internationalization of research. In addition, interview findings pointed to the need to develop mechanisms for structuring the involvement of faculty and administrators in the development of a strategic internationalization plan (cf. Childress 2009; Korka 2018).

Interestingly, one of the participants cited teaching in English as an international language as a factor that could impede learning, given the lack of linguistic and academic study skills of some of the incoming foreign students. In order to internationalize the curricula and minimize the threat of having to lower academic standards, academic English-language courses could be offered to students who take English medium instruction (Korka 2018). This could also help counter the concern expressed in interviews with reference to the internationalization of the curricula.

Along the same lines, communication and use of language for communication reflect another enabling factor. To explore this theme, a simple search of the term "language" (*limba*, in Romanian) was performed using corpus software (*#LancsBox v.4.0*, Brezina/McEnery/Wattam 2015). The search term was entered in a form that would allow to pick up all the variations of the word (i.e. *limb**) and concordance lines were sorted alphabetically to the right of the node word so as to allow for the identification of patterns of meaning. All texts were run on *#LancsBox v.4.0,* and frequency and dispersion calculation per interview file of the word "language" (*limb**) showed that explicit reference to communication as knowledge of other languages was a recurrent theme in seven out of the ten interviews conducted for this study. In a total number of 9,546 tokens of text, the relative frequency was 43.99 occurrences (normalised to the basis of 10,000 tokens). The set of concordance lines obtained for the search word "language" (*limb**) revealed the complexity of language-related issues and their relevance for communication as a factor influencing internationalization.

First, languages of communication were Arabic, Russian, German, English, and the most generic term "foreign" (*străine*). These languages serve as languages of communication, that is knowledge is disseminated through them, but also as languages for communication, that is they facilitate contact and serve as a common language that scholars need when communicating with their peers or with students. Of note, multilingualism seemed to be key for communication and intercultural understanding, that is, being able to speak one or two other languages, besides English, thus confirming also previously published research outcomes (Muresan/Pérez-Llantada 2014).

Once again, English seems to play a prominent role in communication in all fields of knowledge transfer. It maintains its position as the primary lingua franca of courses taught at home or abroad, of exchange programmes or double degree academic programmes, of communication with students in the classroom and mediation in intercultural events organized for Erasmus students, as well as in communication of research in conferences or of published papers. For areas such as conducting research as a member of an international research team, networking with peers at conferences, communication with students outside class, and accessing required bibliographical references, in addition to English other languages were mentioned as useful. The examples given included French, German, Spanish and Russian (R05, R09, R10).

Therefore, increasing internationalization favours knowledge of other languages, not only English. In our interviews, language learning programmes or international double degree programmes were channels to provide multilingual education. One of the respondents (see excerpt 21) mentioned initiatives to introduce language tuition (not in English, but Arabic or Russian) at graduate level.

> (21) […] we have a couple of projects, a centre for Middle East studies, and through the Language Department there are courses of Arabic […], and we are exploring how to formalise this, in the attempt to establish closer links and to have exchanges of ideas, of experiences with the Middle East, which is very diverse and politically challenging but, at the same time, very close and with a major impact now and in the future. (R05)

However, when construed as reactions to perceived student needs, internationalization was operationalized mainly as English-medium degree programmes (see excerpt 22). This was considered a practical choice associated with the prominent role of English in the world (cf. Saarinen/Taalas 2017).

> (22) (…) for instance, at a certain moment we had a French-medium programme […] a bachelor level programme in cooperation with the University of Toulouse, and the teachers from France were coming to hold their modules (it was

held in modular format); the Romanian students enrolled in the programme were attending two study programmes in parallel, the classical/usual one in Romanian, held at our Faculty, and, in parallel, the one in French, conducted by professors from France in modular format. This was a double degree programme, but eventually there was a drop in demand because our students know mainly English (…) so at a certain moment there was no demand anymore, because in Romania the main focus is on English. (R04)

The discussion of the position of multilingualism in general or languages other than English was done as an explicit recommendation to promote languages other than English in teaching, learning and research activities (see excerpt 23). Other statements made reference to the need to encourage multilingualism, where the context implied that multilingualism was not limited to the use of English but included other languages as well.

(23) It is mandatory that those who teach know at least English for communication purposes, for documentation, for presentations to be delivered both in-country and abroad, so this is what needs to be in place for the teachers. For the students, both the Romanians and those from abroad, there is the need for knowing several languages, in addition to English, and during their university study they should learn one or two languages, even if they don't achieve fantastic fluency. (R10)

Communicative competence in other languages was another language-related issue which was thematized by several respondents. While they considered internationalization of academic staff recruitment as an implicit starting point, the teaching, learning and research activities required academic communication skills (i.e. reading, listening, writing, speaking and oral interaction in academic settings) also in other languages for knowledge production and dissemination. It was considered that staff and students alike were under the pressure of academic language competence development.

4 Conclusions

The current study sought to capture the respondents' (academic staff) experiences of higher education internationalization with a clear focus on how it can be operationalized and what factors are likely to influence it. Academics' perceptions revealed that internationalization is a multi-dimensional phenomenon – as one of our respondents stated "there are so many dimensions of internationalization" (R04).

The themes identified share a clear focus on teaching, learning and research, and on the pre-eminence of English as the lingua franca of these knowledge transfer activities in an internationalized higher education environment. The main challenges tend to fall into categories that run along themes pertaining to human resources (academics and students), material resources and information, and teaching and research with an international dimension, academic programmes and institutional management. Key aspects that were problematized as challenges in relation to these themes ranged from English and other *lingua francas*, multicultural issues, and lifelong learning in teaching and research activities, to staff hiring practices, recruiting students, competition, employability, internationalization at home and internationalization plans at curriculum or institutional level (cf. Yemini/Sagie 2016; Korka 2018).

Among practices with a positive impact on local and international human capital we could count hiring procedures, cross-border mobility of academic staff and students, and exchange programmes, inviting professionals from abroad, being proactive in valorising internal human resources, multicultural activities on campus, the shift to multilingualism in teaching and research, joint double degree academic programmes, collaboration in joint research programmes and projects, participation in international research teams and international conferences, research planning measures and strategic alliances (partnerships), as well as institutional and financial support. Of note, in this study internationalization was found to be a process of developing academic values rather than branding – a finding which aligns with Knight's (2013) call for careful monitoring of the values and purposes of internationalization. Given the evolution of the concept of internationalization from the first student mobility exchange initiatives to the current complex phenomena and processes, which include cross-border education, global citizenship, cross-border academic networking (Knight 2013), a focus on academic values is meant to ensure the sustainable development of the university (Korka 2018).

Teaching, learning and research are the main activities higher education is engaged in. These have undergone changes during the implementation of the Bologna process (Sin 2015) to accommodate the realities of work and social needs in the 21st century (Cope/Kalantzis 2009). An interesting feature in our interviews is that internationalization is motivated by social changes. That is, the references to teaching and learning activities reflect a great concern for employability or higher education's contribution to help students develop skills and competencies that employers value, and become competitive on the international labour market, at home and abroad. This is in line with a concern for academic values and promotion of good learning practices. Enhancing employability implies enhancing the quality of teaching, learning and research, as one respondent stated (R09).

The interview data revealed that, at that point in time and at the institution under study, the process of internationalization was considered mainly a bottom-up initiative, as a result of the academics' own interest and involvement in internationalization activities. Another noteworthy finding was that whether the partnership begins "bottom-up" or "top down", it was felt that some degree of institutional leadership and management was necessary. According to Korka (2018), "top down" and "bottom-up" initiatives have to go hand in hand in an integrative approach if the quality of higher education is to be enhanced.

It appears that academics' perceptions revealed that internationalization is a multi-dimensional phenomenon, which underscores the need for a multi-sited and multi-layered approach when studying it (Knight 2013, 2015). Given that this study examined faculty views at one institution only, it is not possible to generalize the findings. Therefore, it would be useful for future research to replicate this study in different countries and world regions to make the study findings generalizable (cf. de Wit/Leask 2015). Also, since an internationalization strategic plan was adopted immediately after this study was completed, it would be important to follow up on this study findings to examine the relationship between faculty perceptions and the strategic plan implemented by the institution.

Acknowledgements

We wish to thank the participants in this study, academics at the Bucharest University of Economic Studies, Romania, for generously sharing their views. We are also grateful to the editor of this volume for her insightful comments and valuable feedback. This work is a contribution to the research project "Ecologies of genres, ecologies of languages: an analysis of the dynamics of local, cross-border and international scientific communication" (FFI2015-68638-R MINECO/FEDER, EU), funded by the Spanish Ministry of Economy and Competitiveness, and the project *Comunicación Internacional y Retos Sociales* (CIRES, code H16_17R), funded by the Government of Aragon.

References

Altbach, Philip G./Knight, Jane 2007. The Internationalization of Higher Education: Motivations and Realities. *Journal of Studies in International Education* 11/3–4, 290–305.

Bardi, Mirela/Muresan, Laura-Mihaela 2014. Changing Research Writing Practices in Romania: Perceptions and Attitudes. In Bennett, Karen (ed.) *The Semiperiphery of Academic Writing*. Basingstoke: Palgrave Macmillan, 121–147.

Beelen, Jos/Jones, Elspeth 2015. Europe Calling: A New Definition for Internationalization at Home. *International Higher Education* 83/ Special issue, 12–13.

Bocanegra-Valle, Ana 2018. English as a Lingua Franca on the International Campus of Excellence: Initiatives and Outcomes. In Curado, Alejandro (ed.) *EPiC Series in Language and Linguistics. LSP in Multi-disciplinary Contexts of Teaching and Research* 3, 12–18.

Brezina, Vaclav/McEnery, Tony/Wattam, Stephen 2015. Collocations in Context: A New Perspective on Collocation Networks. *International Journal of Corpus Linguistics* 20/2, 139–173.

Cardoso, Sónia/Tavares, Orlanda/Sin, Cristina 2015. The Quality of Teaching Staff: Higher Education Institutions' Compliance with the European Standards and Guidelines for Quality Assurance — The Case of Portugal. *Educational Assessment, Evaluation and Accountability* 27/3, 205–222.

Childress, Lisa K. 2009. Internationalization Plans for Higher Education Institutions. *Journal of Studies in International Education* 13/3, 289–309.

Cope, Bill/Kalantzis, Mary 2009. 'Multiliteracies': New Literacies, New Learning. *Pedagogies: An International Journal* 4/3, 164–195.

Dewey, Patricia/Duff, Stephen 2009. Reason Before Passion: Faculty Views on Internationalization in Higher Education. *Higher Education* 58/4, 491–504.

de Wit, Hans/Leask, Betty 2015. Internationalization, the Curriculum, and the Disciplines. *International Higher Education* 83/Special Issue, 10–12.

Duff, Patricia 2008. *Case Study Research in Applied Linguistics*. New York and London: Routledge.

Francis-Smythe, Jan/Haase, S./Steele, C./Jellis, M. 2007. Competencies for Academics in Knowledge Transfer (KT) Activity. In *Proceedings of the British Sociological Society's 2007 Occupational Psychology Conference, Bristol, England*. URL: https://eprints.worc.ac.uk/id/eprint/278.

Hunston, Susan 2008. Starting with the Small Words: Patterns, Lexis and Semantic Sequences. *International Journal of Corpus Linguistics* 13/3, 271–295.

Jones, Elspeth 2013. Internationalization and Employability: The Role of Intercultural Experiences in the Development of Transferable Skills. *Public Money & Management* 33/2, 95–104.

Jones, Elspeth/Coelen, Robert/Beelen, Jos/de Wit, Hans (eds.) 2016. *Global and Local Internationalization*. Rotterdam/Boston/Taipei: Sense Publishers.

Knight, Jane 2004. Internationalization Remodelled: Definition, Approaches, and Rationales. *Journal of Studies in International Education* 8/1, 5–31.

Knight, Jane 2013. The Changing Landscape of Higher Education Internationalization – For Better or Worse? *Perspectives: Policy and Practice in Higher Education* 17/3, 84–90.

Knight, Jane 2015. New Rationales Driving Internationalization. *International Higher Education* 34/1, 3–5.

Korka, Mihai 2018. Challenges of True Internationalization in Higher Education. Paper presented at the *7th International Conference: Synergies in Communication*, 22–23 November 2018, Bucharest, Romania.

Leask, Betty 2008. Internationalisation, Globalisation and Curriculum innovation. In Hellstén, Meeri/Reid, Anna (eds.) *Researching International Pedagogies*. Dordrecht: Springer, 9–26.

Leask, Betty 2013. Internationalizing the Curriculum in the Disciplines – Imagining New Possibilities. *Journal of Studies in International Education* 17/2, 103–118.

Muresan, Laura-Mihaela/Pérez-Llantada, Carmen 2014. English for Research Publication and Dissemination in Bi-/multiliterate Environments: The Case of Romanian Academics. *Journal of English for Academic Purposes* 13/1, 53–64.

Saarinen, Taina/Taalas, Peppi 2017. Nordic Language Policies for Higher Education and Their Multi-layered Motivations. *Higher Education* 73/4, 597–612.

Saldaña, Johnny 2009. *The Coding Manual for Qualitative Researchers*. London: Sage.

Sin, Cristina 2015. Teaching and Learning: A Journey from the Margins to the Core in European Higher Education Policy. In Curaj, Andrei/Matei, Liviu/Pricopie, Remus/Salmi, Jamil/Scott, Peter (eds.) *The European Higher Education Area*. Cham: Springer, 325–341.

Yemini, Miri/Sagie, Netta 2016. Research on Internationalization in Higher Education – Exploratory Analysis. *Perspectives: Policy and Practice in Higher Education* 20/2–3, 90–98.

Yin, Robert K. 2003. *Case Study Research: Design and Methods*. London: Sage.

Part 3: Employability and Social Challenges

Martha C. Pennington

Pronunciation and International Employability[1]

1 Introduction

People judge each other, in part, not only by what they say but also how they speak, including accent and voice quality, the articulation of individual words and sounds, fluency and phrasing in running speech, and the contouring of speech by pitch and stress to convey different kinds of meaning and feeling. A person's pronunciation in all of these dimensions is a rich and complex surface characteristic of speech that listeners use to judge deeper level characteristics such as intelligence, education, and social class as well as such qualities as friendliness, openness, and trustworthiness, or their opposites. Features of pronunciation, especially outside the context of any visual indicators (as when talking to someone on the phone), may also be used by listeners to socially profile a person in terms of country of origin, ethnicity, race, age, state of health, and gender. In addition to these global judgments of a person's character and characteristics, pronunciation is crucial to intelligibility and comprehensibility – that is, to a listener's ability to perceive linguistic components and structure within the stream of speech as a basis for understanding what a speaker says. In these different ways, pronunciation communicates many types of information tied to utterance meaning and speaker identity. Fig. 10-1 summarizes the different kinds of meaning communicated by a person's pronunciation.

---

1 This chapter is a revised version of the paper by the same title presented on 20 April 2018 at the 26th AESLA (Spanish Association of Applied Linguistics) Conference in Cadiz, Spain. I wish to thank the conference facilitators and organizers, especially Ana Bocanegra-Valle and David Levey, for their wonderful hospitality and kind assistance in helping me manage a badly sprained ankle and ensuring that I had an enjoyable and memorable time at the conference in spite of my extremely limited mobility. I also thank David for useful comments on a draft of this written version.

Fig. 10-1: What pronunciation communicates (adapted from Fig. 1.1. Dimensions of pronunciation, Pennington/Rogerson-Revell 2019: 7)

What Pronunciation Communicates: Message Features

Pronunciation is the initial layer of talk through which speakers construct and listeners decode and interpret linguistic signals as a meaningful message, using features of pronunciation as indicators of:

Linguistic Units

- sounds (phonemes), syllables, words, phrases, clauses, multi-clause units

Types of Information

- known/new information, key/non-key information, turn continuation/transition, statement/question/command

What Else Pronunciation Communicates:

Speaker Characteristics

Pronunciation is also a major ingredient in first impressions and in the interpretation of people's background and intentions, using pronunciation features as indicators of:

Nature

- inherent characteristics (sex and age)

Nurture

- place of origin, education level, communal identity (e.g., race, ethnicity, social class)

Situational Positioning

- communicative role/position, attitude towards the audience and topic

The importance of pronunciation is especially relevant for the near quarter of all the people on earth who find themselves using English in their lives, "as the language of global business [...] and the most commonly used lingua franca in multilingual professional contexts such as diplomacy, research, and education" (Pennington/Rogerson-Revell 2019: 344). English is also a widely used medium of instruction in universities in Europe (Marsh/Laitinen 2005; Jenkins 2014) and other parts of the world where the majority of students have a different mother tongue (L1) and speak English as an additional or second language (L2). Although linguists and applied linguists argue for the value and legitimacy of all accents and varieties of language, it is nonetheless a fact of life that pronunciation is a factor in employability in international contexts and can impede a person's ability to work successfully in some fields under some circumstances.

2 How pronunciation can negatively affect communication and listener perceptions

2.1 Segmental level and fluency

A certain level of practiced and routine articulation skill is required for intelligibility and also for fluency. Pronunciation difficulties can impede the production of understandable linguistic units as well as interrupt the flow of speech, creating disfluencies. A speaker's lack of pronunciation skill impacts the listener's process of comprehension, making it more effortful and slowing it down. Listeners may find it hard to listen to and interact with such speakers, and as a result may lose attention and patience. In addition, listeners for whom specific pronunciation features or a certain accent are negatively valued or especially salient may find these distracting or annoying.

Some errors or features of pronunciation or accent, while not impeding understanding, can draw a listener's attention to *language form*, and away from a focus on *communicative content*. When language form becomes salient, this alters the processing of speech to focus on how speakers sound, which is a value judgment, rather than on what they are saying. This can distract from the processing of speech, especially if the value judgment of pronunciation or accent is negative, and may cause listeners to become annoyed. Negative judgments of pronunciation or accent features may be the result of their frequency or of the listener's assessment of them as errors or nonstandard features. They may also be the result of linguistic stereotyping.

For example, some Spanish speakers of English may pronounce words that have the vowel /ɪ/ (e.g., *sit* and *sister*) as [i] and may pronounce English /r/ words with a Spanish-influenced tap or trill. Some listeners may find it hard to listen to a speaker whose speech is full of such sound substitutions, even if they have minimal effect on intelligibility or comprehensibility. The degree of tolerance is often connected to linguistic stereotyping and pronunciation features functioning as "identity markers" (Zuengler 1988) – such as the different ways that the letter *r* is pronounced in Spanish, French, American English, and British English. Beinhoff's (2013) research highlights the fact that negative perceptions of accent are often due to specific sounds and how these are pronounced by different speaker groups, such as the pronunciation of English /r/ by German and Greek speakers.

As another example for L1 Spanish speakers, a study of attitudes to the speech of Puerto Rican learners of English by Fayer and Krasinski (1987) showed that listeners judged pronunciation errors and nonstandard features, along with hesitations, to be annoying and to distract from their message more than other aspects of their speech, such as grammar or wrong words.[2] It is noteworthy that native Spanish speakers were far less tolerant toward Puerto Rican English than were native English speakers.

2.2 Suprasegmental level: Intonation

Variations in the conventions for intonation can result in misinterpretation of a speaker's intention, that is, in a misreading of the *metamessage* – "how you mean what you say" (Tannen 2014: 358) – framing and contextualizing speech. A falling pitch contour, though considered to be the unmarked norm for statements, is being used less by English speakers around the world (Pennington 1996; Pennington/Lau/Sachdev 2011), in a style of communication that makes less definitive statements by using rising contours to signal attention to and inclusion of audience perspective. This phenomenon, which has been termed *Uptalk* or *Upspeak* (Bradford 1997), is a trend among young people in the L1 English-speaking world that is being adopted by L2 speakers worldwide. The fact that the conventions for use of falling and rising pitch are different in the younger and older generations is the source

2 To get a sense of some Puerto Rican speakers' English pronunciation and hesitations, you can listen to a selection of Puerto Rican speakers in the Spanish section of the Speech Accent Archive at George Mason University, such as the female speaker labeled *Spanish81* (<http://accent.gmu.edu/browse_language.php?function=detail&speakerid=1347>). Note that in all of the samples in the Speech Accent Archive the requirement to read a diagnostic passage affects a person's speech performance – pronunciation and fluency, in particular.

of negative reactions and misunderstandings on both sides, as older speakers hear rising pitch as questioning and consider it to be incorrectly applied when what is said is not intended to be a question, while younger speakers hear falling pitch as being overly assertive and insufficiently collaborative, thus indicative of dominance and exclusionary communication.[3]

The relative height or level of pitch is also a factor in how messages are framed by speakers and interpreted by listeners, as Estebas-Vilaplana (2014) demonstrated in a study in which pitch was mechanically manipulated in recordings of question and answer sequences as produced in Spanish and English versions by a bilingual speaker. While the low-pitched Spanish question-and-answer sequences were judged by L1 Spanish listeners as polite, the English listeners judged most of the English question-and-answer sequences spoken with low pitch as unexpected and rude in comparison to the high-pitched English sequences, which were judged as natural and polite.

3 How pronunciation can impede job-related intelligibility in international and second-language contexts

Pronunciation can impede communication in terms of intelligibility, that is, pronouncing speech in such a way that listeners cannot recognize linguistic units and so experience difficulties in comprehending what a speaker is saying. While intelligibility problems can arise in any context, including between speakers of the same language, they are often noted in job-related communication in international or L2 contexts, when speaker and listener have different mother tongues or first languages.

For example, many researchers on pronunciation have noted communication difficulties in these contexts based on the stress difference

3 Examples and discussions of Uptalk can be found on the internet (e.g. <https://www.youtube.com/watch?v=pPZMy_JWsOU>).

between the tens and teens numbers, like *forty* and *fourteen*.[4] A business-related example is this transaction between a Filipino service representative in an overseas call center and a caller from the United Kingdom:

Customer: How much is the ticket?
Representative: FOURteen pounds.
Customer: FORTy pounds! That's too expensive. (Tomalin 2010: 175)

This distinction in number words is obviously important in sales. Getting the number words right can be even more important than this – in some cases, literally a matter of life or death.

Imagine an air traffic controller, speaking to the pilot of a jumbo passenger jet which is coming in for a landing, who reports the wind speed at ground level as *fifteen* versus *fifty* miles per hour (Pennington/Rogerson-Revell 2019: 15). This may be a critical difference for the pilot in deciding the final speed of descent of the aircraft. Another type of life-or-death case is the example of a doctor's ability to clearly differentiate in pronunciation between a *15 mg* vs. a *50 mg* dosage of a medication (Wilner 2007) when giving instructions to a nurse in a medical emergency. A study at a U.S. university hospital training international medical graduates as doctors (Labov/Hanau 2011) found that the international trainees' pronunciation interfered with understanding their descriptions of samples taken in a pathology lab. The descriptions were recorded and then transcribed by experienced medical secretaries, who misunderstood and so mistranscribed many words, such as *patch* misheard and transcribed as *plaque*, *ascending* as *descending*, *infarction* as *infection*, and *firm* as *full*. The number and the severity of the misunderstandings were considered by the hospital staff to be alarming, leading the hospital to require pronunciation instruction for a number of their international medical trainees.[5]

---

4 As Mompean (2014) has noted, the possibility of misunderstanding related to stress is compounded by the fact that the final /n/ in *-teen* words is not always fully articulated.

5 For further discussion of pronunciation problems in health communication, see Pennington/Rogerson-Revell (2019: 352–358).

Beyond problems in comprehension, listeners may have other kinds of negative responses to pronunciation difficulties that impede speech processing. Not only may unclear or nonstandard pronunciation cause some listeners to become annoyed and distracted from a speaker's message (Fayer/Krasinski 1987), pronunciation problems may cause them to stop paying attention and to avoid communicating with the speaker in future (Singleton 1995). There is a fine line in the processing of speech between not understanding and not wanting to make the effort needed to understand.

Difficulties in understanding foreign-accented speech may also cause listeners to evaluate a speaker as less credible. Research by Lev-Ari/Keysar (2010) demonstrated that the reduction in "processing fluency" which listeners experienced in listening to a "heavy" foreign accent made them perceive the speaker's statements as less truthful than statements made by native speakers or those with a "mild" foreign accent. How hard someone is to understand is causally related to how strong their accent is perceived to be. Yet a listener's familiarity with an accent will enhance a speaker's intelligibility, as will the listener's attitude towards and tolerance for specific speakers, speaker groups, and accents. Thus, intelligibility is affected by individual listeners' experience and their attitudes and beliefs.

All of these factors impacting intelligibility can affect speakers' employability in specific countries and types of work.

4 How pronunciation can impede other aspects of job-related performance in international and second-language communication

Features of pronunciation besides the way linguistic units are articulated can impact job-related performance. For example, research on communication problems in an offshore call center in India that was doing contract work outsourced from the United Kingdom (Tomalin 2010) found that a number of pronunciation features that were not strictly matters of intelligibility caused difficulties, including pitch and intonation and the speed and pacing with which information was given to callers. The Indian representatives often had a relatively "sing-song" intonation and highly varied pitch contour and spoke at a relatively fast pace that customers found irritating and difficult to listen to. In the words of Tomalin (2010: 178):

> One of the key features in training therefore is to teach a more relaxed speed and pacing and also to help the more "emotional sounding" representatives to adopt a slightly flatter intonation, without losing the lively and welcoming quality of their voices [...]. Our observations of calls, especially where sales calls were concerned, affected both comprehension and willingness to listen. Where a call centre representative was delivering a sales pitch, for example offering the financial benefits to the customer of a new credit card, the speed of delivery appeared to come at the listener like an express train, making it almost impossible to take in the relevant information and make a judgment about the value of what was on offer. The result is that the British customers sometimes complained of "machine gun" delivery.

As a contrasting example, Yau's (2010) investigation of problematic telephone conversations between American customers and Filipino customer service representatives (CSRs) revealed that a "plain", rather monotone voice, conveying limited positive emotion, can downgrade the level of interpersonal interaction between CSR and customer. Thus, a "thank you very much" said with minimal intonation downgrades the gratitude expressed and can be "seen as a superficial and insincere construal of the speaker's viewpoint. This is seen as a sarcastic phrase, what the speaker really means is that the CSR has not provided real help and really does not deserve to be thanked" (Yau 2010: 119). Tannen (2014) refers to this type of misunderstanding as a failure to understand the metamessage conveyed by intonation, such as whether the message is serious or light-hearted, friendly or distant, polite or impolite, or is to be taken literally or not. The ability to communicate in international business transactions and customer service interactions is particularly challenging when talking by phone, without the support of eye contact, facial expressions, and gestures.

In addition to the effects of the way information is delivered in terms of pacing, intonation, and voice quality, a person's accent has an impact that goes beyond intelligibility per se in giving an impression of the speaker's social background and personal qualities. In professional and business contexts, such as sales or advertising, customers' evaluation of staff based on accent may shape their attitudes towards a company and its products or services. According to a review of the literature on the effects of accent in business transactions by Hoffman/Mai (2014: 152):

> The extant studies predominantly demonstrate that foreign accented advertising spokespersons, job applicants or salespersons are evaluated, and often discriminated against, in terms of competence, social attractiveness and integrity.
>
> Furthermore, a foreign accent decreases comprehensibility and therefore hampers message processing. In consequence, consumers express lower intentions to purchase and are less willing to recommend a product, service or brand than when interacting with a standard accented person.

Hoffman/Mai (2014: 152) advise employers to recognize the potential for accent to create customer bias and to offer speech training for employees with "very strong regional and foreign accents". However, as they also observe, a foreign accent can sometimes be an asset in business communication, for example, if the customer is fond of or identifies with the salesperson's accent.

5 Attitudes to accent

5.1 Perceptions of accent

People tend to perceive accent or accentedness in relation to a certain kind of pronunciation, which may be that of their own reference group or that of a standard language, as being the *normal* – that is, the common or expected – pronunciation or the *correct* pronunciation. When considered against the listener's concept of a pronunciation baseline or model, other pronunciations will be perceived as more or less divergent or marked, or more or less accented, in comparison to the baseline, which appears to be unaccented or less accented. As Beinhoff (2013: 42–43) points out:

> The idea of a 'neutral' or 'standard' accent seems to be well established in the general public and the remark that somebody [...] speaks 'without an accent' or with 'hardly any accent' are often used when referring to non-regional accents. These remarks indicate that the accents in question are perceived as 'neutral'. However, the concept of a 'neutral' or 'standard' accent does not really exist in sociolinguistics since every accent carries some form of additional social information about the speaker [...].

There are in fact multiple standards for the same language, such as standard British, Australian, New Zealand, South African, American or North American varieties of English, and the many varieties of standard Spanish that are associated with all of the different countries where Spanish is a native language. Each country's standard variety is distinctive in many ways, including pronunciation.

The goal of *plurilingualism* promoted by the Language Policy Division of the Council of Europe (Council of Europe 2001) is to develop the ability to use several languages to varying degrees, with different levels and types of competence, such as in speaking and writing, and for distinct purposes. The primary objectives are being able to participate in intercultural interaction and developing *linguistic tolerance* towards different languages and accents (Coste/Moore/Zarata 2009/1997). Under the goal of promoting linguistic tolerance, the relatively open attitude of the Council of Europe Language Policy Division towards different accents contrasts sharply with the negative attitude towards speaking with a country-specific, regional, ethnically, or racially identified, or non-standard accent in many locales, such as the United States (Finegan/Rickford 2004) and China (Liang 2015).

5.2 Stereotyping based on accent

An accent which is accepted in one setting or for certain kinds of work can make a person unemployable in another setting or for other kinds of work, even if the person is understandable and highly qualified, for the fact that the accent is unfamiliar or is negatively valued, stereotyped or stigmatized. For example, Lowe (2000) has documented how negative stereotyping of Filipino English in Hong Kong supports the marginalized status of Filipinos, the majority of whom are young women employed as live-in housekeepers and child-minders, in that locale. Although most Filipinos in Hong Kong are fluent in English, considered a requirement or an asset for this type of work as well as for many other types of work in Hong Kong, and although many hold professional certificates or college degrees, stereotyping makes it very difficult for them to find employment other than in domestic service.

In the process of *linguistic stereotyping*, listeners assign certain attributes or characteristics to speakers based on their language variety, including specific pronunciation features or overall accent, such as social class, education level, and intelligence. Tannen (2014: 372) points out that "negative stereotypes can have important social consequences, affecting decisions about educational advancement, job hiring, and even social policies on a national scale". Baugh (2003: 155) uses the term *linguistic profiling*, which he describes as "the auditory equivalent of visual 'racial profiling,' " and documents how profiling based on language variety has resulted in both positive and negative discrimination in housing and employment, such as the advantaging of White Americans who speak standard English and the disadvantaging of Black Americans who speak the non-standard variety of African-American Vernacular English (AAVE).

Some linguistic stereotypes may be positive, such as a typical American response to English spoken with a French accent as sounding romantic or sexy, while others may be less positive, such as a typical American response to a German accent as sounding unemotional or distant. The value judgments underlying linguistic stereotyping are unpredictable and may differ from one group of listeners to another, based on differing historical and social factors. The standard British or RP accent, for example, which is considered "posh" or "high-class", is generally positively evaluated by Americans but negatively valued by many in the United Kingdom and Australia as symbolizing undeserved status and privilege based on increasingly irrelevant class distinctions.

Two notable cases of employment-related negative linguistic stereotyping or profiling for specific ethnic groups involved accent and employment as teachers in U.S. schools. In the 1980s, I witnessed negative and discriminatory linguistic stereotyping in Hawaii, where well-qualified teachers of Filipino background who were fluent English speakers were excluded from teaching in local schools based on "accent discrimination against Filipinos" (Chang 1996: 139) and the potentially contributing effects of interviewer bias and the prejudices of school principals.[6] The rationale given by school principals and members of the state Department of Education was that the majority of local students would not be able to understand or relate to the Filipino teachers.[7] More recently in Arizona, where many teachers are Hispanic bilinguals, there was an attempt to implement accent testing as a requirement for being qualified as an English teacher. The required accent assessment was, however, discontinued when it was legally challenged on the grounds of violating teachers' civil rights (Ballard/Winke 2017: 122).

5.3 Considering employability based on accents of Spanish

Based on how intelligible they are, in combination with other factors of speaker evaluation and stereotyping, speakers with Spanish accents characteristic of different Latin American countries might make different impressions on native speakers of European Spanish or of other languages, in terms of whether the accent, and the person speaking it, sounds nice or pleasant and in terms of such characteristics as the speaker's education, social class, and intelligence. Assessments based on accent are often deemed relevant when considering whether the speaker would be suitable for different kinds of employment in a specific country or region,[8] for example, as:

---

6 I testified as a pronunciation specialist and professor employed at the University of Hawaii in front of the Hawaii state legislature during hearings on this issue. I made a case that there were no employment-related grounds for excluding Filipino teachers from teaching in Hawaii schools based on accent and that doing so was based on negative bias comparable to that attached to speakers of African American Vernacular English (AAVE).

7 As counterevidence to this claim, Mikey Busto's entertaining You Tube "Filipino Accent Tutorial", which is intentionally done with a strong Filipino accent, can arguably be considered to represent a strong teaching performance (<https://www.youtube.com/watch?v=3BBtS1ir4tA>).

8 A selection of Latin American Spanish accents (Mexican, Puerto Rican, Cuban, Venezuelan, Colombian, Ecuadorian, Peruvian, Chilean, Argentinian,

1 Television news announcer
Based on a person's accent, some listeners may judge that the person might be hard to understand or might give the wrong impression (e.g., of status or competence) and so could not or should not be hired as a television news announcer.
2 University lecturer
Accent may be seen as less important for a university lecturer, given the assumption of high scholarly qualifications and achievements, although some listeners might consider that a university lecturer would benefit by cultivating the accent which is standard for the country or region where the university is located.
3 Elementary school teacher
Some employers might judge a certain accent as not representing a good model for children's language and on this basis not hire a person who speaks with that accent as an elementary teacher. Others might consider that a person with a certain accent might not relate well to children who speak with a different accent, or, conversely, that the children might not relate well to the teacher. On the other hand, some might think that it could be good for children to experience a teacher with a heritage different from that of the students. There may also be some who believe that accent would not be a factor for a good teacher, though it could be for a poor teacher.
4 Person who answers the phone in an office
In the case of a person who is responsible for answering the phone in an office, accent may be important depending on how much the person needs to talk and how complex the content of talk is (e.g., beyond greeting and directing the caller to another person).

Even while individual speakers are evaluated as representatives of their country or region of origin, its history and its culture, based on accent, they are also evaluated based on their personal characteristics and situation-specific performance, which can override negative stereotyping to a greater or lesser degree. Negative stereotyping can also be reduced through experience and familiarity with people who are the target of such stereotyping. It can be expected that increasing exposure to people of different cultural and linguistic backgrounds can increase appreciation and tolerance for different accents. There are, however, some counteracting forces that can adversely impact people's attitudes to different

---

and Uruguayan) illustrate that there are ample differences which might affect listeners' perceptions of speaker characteristics and their employability, especially in nonlocal or international contexts (<https://www.youtube.com/watch?v=-F2mkQALAt4>).

groups and how they speak, and it seems that accent-based discrimination may be on the rise in both the United States and the United Kingdom (Moyer 2013: 172) – a reflection perhaps of current negative sentiment toward immigrants on both sides of the Atlantic.

6 Compensatory strategies

6.1 Aiming for pronunciation as a value-added factor

Fortunately, there are some strategies that can make a difference in the reaction one gets from listeners and so ensure that pronunciation will be "a value-added factor" (Pennington/Rogerson-Revell 2019: 22) and not a value-subtracted factor in communication. They involve focusing on sound in context, attending to intonation, and eliminating stereotyped features. These strategies can be especially helpful in contexts of L2 communication and international employment.

6.2 Focusing on sound in context

The first point is to move away from idealized or spelling-based pronunciation and pay attention to how people really sound when they speak. This strategic orientation involves noticing how pronunciation changes in context and varies from one speaker, variety, and language to the next. Once you learn to focus on sound, you can try to imitate the pronunciation of those whom you want to sound like, as a way to acquire the language variety that you want to speak.

As discussed by Pennington/Rogerson-Revell (2019: 14), "[p]aying attention to details of pronunciation and learning to imitate well can pay off". I had this experience in learning Turkish in relation to words spelled with *e* and with final *r*. In the first weeks of lessons, I noticed that my Turkish tutor and teacher, both of whom were L1 Turkish speakers, pronounced the word for *I* in Turkish (*ben*) with a vowel that sounded much closer to English /æ/, as in *ban*, than English /ɛ/, as in the name *Ben*. Soon I had adjusted my pronunciation of Turkish *ben* to rhyme not with

English *Ben* but with English *ban*. I also noticed that the final /r/ in the Turkish word for *a* or *one* (*bir*) was pronounced by the teacher and the tutor as devoiced and breathy, as if forcefully whispering the /r/, while also trilling it – like a whispered yet forcefully articulated Spanish trilled /r/ in *burro* ("donkey"). Based on my observations and reflections on pronunciation of this final /r/, I aimed to produce the final /r/ in *bir* as a whispered trill every time that word came up. These adjustments influenced my pronunciation of Turkish significantly, both because *ben* and *bir* are very frequent words and because my sound-based pronunciation of those two words led to making similar adjustments away from pronunciation based on English spelling conventions in other words. Even though I had been learning Turkish for only a few weeks, my Turkish teacher and tutor commented on how good my Turkish was, and other L1 Turkish speakers were ready to talk to me and help me with my Turkish.

By mastering what are considered difficult sounds in another language – such as, for an English speaker, the French, Spanish, or Turkish *r* or, for a French, Spanish, or Turkish speaker, the English *r* – an L2 speaker can receive a positive impression from those who speak in the way that has been practiced. Speakers might be prepared to spend more attention, time, and effort in communicating with a learner who shows skill in the pronunciation features or overall accent of their language variety, thus aiding the learner's process of language acquisition and potentially making good social and professional connections as well. "Thus, paying attention to pronunciation can have a significant communicative payoff that aids language learning" (Pennington/Rogerson-Revell 2019: 14) and also employability.

6.3 Attending to intonation

The second compensatory strategy, which goes hand in hand with focusing on sound in context, is to pay attention to intonation, which is important in making a good first impression and connection to the audience, in maintaining audience attention and interest, and in framing a message so that it conveys the intended metamessage signifying the function of the utterance and the context in which it is to be received. A speaker can often make up for limited knowledge of a language by using intonation well. People will be more likely to interact with a speaker who sounds pleasant or nice and seems to connect to them, and they will be less likely to misread a speaker's intentions given appropriate intonation. Setting up and maintaining a good basis for communication through intonation can also make people less likely to give up on a speaker who is having trouble being understood.

The phenomenon and worldwide spread of Uptalk as a way to signal attention to and inclusion of audience perspective suggests that a strategy for attending to intonation in L2 and international contexts is to use more rising and less falling intonation. Using frequent pitch rises and limiting the use of pitch falls can make a person sound upbeat, friendly, and listener-inclusive, and can avoid the potentially negative connotations of monotone pitch and of frequent pitch falls. Using frequent pitch rises and limiting the use of pitch falls can therefore make a speaker sound enthusiastic toward a product or service being offered and client- or customer-oriented, and in general make the speaker sound more engaged with the people – including colleagues – and tasks of the workplace. An Uptalk orientation to intonation may, therefore, increase effectiveness in many types of work interactions and transactions as a means of soliciting and maintaining active engagement with clients, customers, and/or colleagues.

In attending to intonation, it is nonetheless important to consider audience expectations and context factors. Americans are accustomed to overt signs of enthusiasm, and so are comfortable with relatively emotive intonation containing ample rising contours and relatively high pitch overall, and may perceive low and falling pitch negatively, as indicating disinterest or unfriendliness. Some British people, on the other hand, especially in the older generation, are accustomed to more understated forms of expression, and so will consider emotive intonation negatively, as insincere; they can be more like Spaniards in being comfortable with lower-pitched speech. Since the younger generation in Britain and elsewhere seems to be adopting the worldwide Uptalk convention of more high pitch and rising contours as a more audience-oriented and collaborative style of interaction, if speaking to people in those countries – with the possible exception of older speakers who grew up with different conventions and expectations as regards the meaning of high vs. low and rising vs. falling pitch – one piece of advice is to use more high and rising pitch, to seem not just polite but friendly and open.

6.4 *Eliminating stereotyped features*

For speakers of a second language, pronunciation gives an impression of language competence, and may also give a generally positive or negative impression of a speaker in other ways. In recognition of this reality of speaker evaluation, a third point is to work on those features of accent that are stereotyped. If you are a native Spanish speaker, for English these might be trilled /r/, substitution of /i/ for /ɪ/, or a generally nasal voice quality. Reducing or eliminating stereotyped features can help to make a generally positive impression on listeners and keep them focused on what the speaker is saying and not on the speaker's pronunciation.

7 Conclusion

Those who will be working internationally in English can benefit by paying attention to pronunciation and trying to imitate speakers with whom they will be interacting. Mastery of even just two or three key features of pronunciation can make listeners evaluate a speaker positively, and adjusting one's speech to align pronunciation more closely to those with whom one communicates on the job can increase communicative and job-related effectiveness and opportunities. Those working internationally in L1 and L2 English environments can seek to project friendliness and listener orientation through intonation, which can attract communication partners and deflect attention away from details of pronunciation while also ensuring that intended messages and metamessages are projected to specific audiences. They can also seek to reduce or eliminate stereotyped features from their speech to counter the potentially negative attitudes and frustrations of listeners. Through use of these strategies, pronunciation can be not a hindrance but a resource for effective communication and employment in international contexts.

At the same time, all of us must also try to develop in ourselves – and perhaps also demand from others – linguistic tolerance, that is, appreciation and respect for speakers of different languages and different accents and the positive contributions they can make to specific employment situations and our lives more generally.

References

Ballard, Laura/Winke, Paula 2017. Students' Attitudes towards English Teachers' Accents: The Interplay of Accent Familiarity, Comprehensibility, Intelligibility, Perceived Native Speaker Status, and Acceptability as a Teacher. In Isaacs, Talia/Trofimovich, Pavel (eds.) *Second Language Pronunciation Assessment: Interdisciplinary Perspectives*. Bristol: Multilingual Matters, 121–140.

Baugh, John 2003. Linguistic Profiling. In Makoni, Sinfree/Smitherman, Geneva/Ball, Arnetha F./Spears, Arthur K. (eds.) *Black Linguistics: Language, Society and Politics in Africa and the Americas*. New York: Cambridge University Press, 155–168.

Beinhoff, Bettina 2013. *Perceiving Identity through Accent: Attitudes towards Non-native Speakers and Their Accents in English*. Bern: Peter Lang.

Bradford, Barbara 1997. Upspeak in British English. *English Today* 13/3(51), 33–36.

Chang, Jeff 1996. Lessons of Tolerance: Americanism and the Filipino Affirmative Action Movement in Hawaii. *Social Processes in Hawaii* 37, 112–146. <http://www.efilarchives.org/pdf/social%20process%20vol%2037/sp37_chang_tolerance.pdf>.

Coste, Daniel/Moore, Danièle/Zarate, Geneviève (2009/1997). *Plurilingual and Pluricultural Competence*. Strasbourg: Council of Europe, Language Policy Division. Studies towards a Common European Framework of Reference for language learning and teaching. Revised from original version that appeared in French, 1997. <https://www.coe.int/t/dg4/linguistic/Source/SourcePublications/CompetencePlurilingue09web_en.pdf>.

Council of Europe 2001. *Common European Framework of Reference for Languages: Learning, Teaching, Assessment*. Strasbourg: Council of Europe, Language Policy Division. <https://rm.coe.int/1680459f97>.

Estebas-Vilaplana, Eva 2014. The Evaluation of Intonation: Pitch Range Differences in English and in Spanish. In Thompson, Geoff/Alba-Juez, Laura (eds.) *Evaluation in Context*. Amsterdam/Philadelphia: John Benjamins, 179–194.

Fayer, Joan M./Krasinski, Emily 1987. Native and Nonnative Judgments of Intelligibility and Irritation. *Language Learning* 37/3, 313–326.

Finegan, Edward/Rickford, John R. (eds.) 2004. *Language in the USA: Themes for the Twenty-first Century*. New York: Cambridge University Press.

Hoffman, Stefan/Mai, Robert 2014. Accents in Business Communication: An Integrative Model and Propositions for Future Research. *Journal of Consumer Psychology* 24/1, 137–158.

Jenkins, Jennifer 2014. *English as a Lingua Franca in the International University: The Politics of Academic English Language Policy*. Abingdon: Routledge.

Labov, Joanna/Hanau, Cheryl 2011. Pronunciation as Life and Death: Improving the Communication Skills of Non-native English Speaking Pathologists. In Hoekje, Barbara J./Tipton, Sara M. (eds.) *English Language and the Medical Profession: Instructing and Assessing the Communication Skills of International Physicians*. Leiden/Boston: Brill, 261–285.

Lev-Ari, Shiri/Keysar, Boaz 2010. Why Don't We Believe Non-native Speakers? The Influence of Accent on Credibility. *Journal of Experimental Social Psychology* 46/6, 1093–1096.

Liang, Sihua 2015. *Language Attitudes and Identities in Multilingual China: A Linguistic Ethnography*. Heidelberg: Springer.

Lowe, Cecile T. 2000. *The Outsider's Voice; Discourse and Identity among Filipina Domestic Workers in Hong Kong*. PhD thesis. City University of Hong Kong. <https://www.cityu.edu.hk/lib/eres/ethesis.htm>.

Marsh, David/Laitinen, Jim 2005. *Medium of Instruction in European Higher Education: Summary of Research Outcomes of European Network for Language Learning amongst Undergraduates*

(ENLU) Task Group 4. Jyväskylä, Finland: UniCOM, University of Jyväskylä.
Mompean, José 2014. Stress Shift in English: The Case of Teen Numbers. In Monroy-Casas, Rafael/Arboleda-Guirao, Immaculada (eds.) *Readings in English Phonetics and Phonology*. Valencia, Spain: IULMA/Universidad de Valencia, 149–169.
Moyer, Alene 2013. *Foreign Accent: The Phenomenon of Non-native Speech*. Cambridge: Cambridge University Press.
Pennington, Martha C. 1996. *Phonology in English Language Teaching: An International Approach*. London: Longman.
Pennington, Martha C./Lau, Lawrence/Sachdev, Itesh 2011. Diversity in Adoption of Linguistic Features of London English by Chinese and Bangladeshi Adolescents. *Language Learning Journal* 39/2, 177–199.
Pennington, Martha C./Rogerson-Revell, Pamela 2019. *English Pronunciation Teaching and Research: Contemporary Perspectives*. London: Palgrave Macmillan.
Singleton, David 1995. Introduction: A Critical Look at the Critical Period Hypothesis in Second Language Acquisition Research. In Singleton, David/Lengyel, Zsolt (eds.) *The Age Factor in Second Language Acquisition*. Clevedon: Multilingual Matters, 1–29.
Tannen, Deborah 2014. Language and Culture. In Fasold, Ralph/Connor-Linton, Jeff (eds.) *Introduction to Language and Linguistics* (2nd ed.). Cambridge: Cambridge University Press, 353–381.
Tomalin, Barry 2010. India Rising: The Need for Two Way Training. In Forey, Gail/Lockwood, Jane (eds.) *Globalization, Communication and the Workplace*. London: Continuum, 172–189.
Wilner, Lynda K. 2007. Communication Skills Training Programs for Doctors. *Academic Internal Medicine Insight* 5/3, 14–15.
Yau, Jenny N. W. 2010. Call Centre Discourse: Graduation in Relation to Voice Quality and Attitudinal Profile. In Forey, Gail/Lockwood, Jane (eds.) *Globalization, Communication and the Workplace*. London: Continuum, 107–124.
Zuengler, Jane 1988. Identity Markers and L2 Pronunciation. *Studies in Second Language Acquisition* 33/1, 10–49.

Troy B. Wiwczaroski/Mária Czellér

Disparities between Foreign Language Skills Taught in Higher Education and Job Market Needs

1 Second language (L2) knowledge and jobs

As higher education functions to provide students with marketable skills for future employment, in developing course materials taught to students, the needs of locally operating businesses – large and small – must be identified and met, in order to assist graduates with job placement, to help companies be able to maintain new hires and to close gaps in key communication skills. Social changes, including the very ways many choose to live their daily lives are impacting the kinds of skills necessary to access many workplaces, whether in customer service industries or auxiliary services provided to manufacturers and logistics services. These changes are seen, by way of example, in the virtual world of social media, internet chatting applications or online audio-visual software. In the globalised business world, the ability to move in and out of Information Technology (IT)-based or virtual workspaces and face-to-face communication with customers, clients, service providers and vendors is coupled with the need for honed foreign language skills in specific areas of competence.

As part of their human resource developmental or overall corporate strategies, businesses may choose to invest substantial budgets on the foreign language development of their employees. These strategies, and the money spent to pursue them, demonstrate the prominence of the roles business activities performed using foreign languages have in the daily operations of these businesses. In relation to this, business management is also communicating to government, educators and potential employees, through statistics provided by public news channels, government publications, professional/sectoral publications and university research findings that need the help of educators to be successful. Moreover, companies invest in the further training of their employees, which often presume that the participating employees already possess an adequate foundation of foreign language competences. Seen against this background, one may recognise the significance of companies choosing to spend an average 300 Euros per employee for them to attend two-day workshops in the development of soft skills in business communication, public speaking or international negotiations. (IIR Hungary 2019)

Indeed, a growing number of job advertisements are targeting individuals with such capabilities. Almost half (43 %) of all listings on Randstad's website include the term *communication*, with almost half (48 %) of all listings on the Randstad Financial & Professional website including references to *excellent communication* and *listening skills*. 97 % of employers queried by Randstad (2015) regarded soft skills as important to their current business success, with more than half ranking them as more important than academic qualifications.

Recent research by the Development Economics group estimated that soft skills are worth £88bn per year to businesses (Faragher 2015). Soft skills not only help individuals thrive at work and become assets to their employers, but can also improve their abilities to enhance their careers. What such workshops have in common is the understanding of the fact that the prerequisite for being considered employable at the contracting company and, therefore, being able to be developed further in professional soft skill areas, is a working knowledge of business English.

Seen within the context of how many foreign language programmes have been imperilled by budget cuts and staff reductions at universities across Europe, perhaps the time has come for such programmes to undergo reform in how these are positioned in university curricula. In seeking this change, educators working in such programmes need to ask business for their support with decision makers. In order to be able to make such requests, however, we educators must be able to demonstrate a willingness and capability to address and meet business needs in a targeted manner. This means putting our educational programmes into the right contexts: we in higher education are mindful of how foreign language knowledge alone is not enough to qualify an applicant for a position. Professional communication skills, combined with the proper attitudes towards communicating with diverse cultures and attitudes, are just as vital as a sound command of grammar. Below, we discuss the disparities between foreign language skills taught in higher education and job market needs and offer suggestions for remedying them through cooperation, based on the example of the changes in the job market our city of Debrecen (Hungary) has undergone in the past years and is continuing to experience.

2 Some pertinent facts and figures

There is much opportunity for jobs and growth in the modern world. Where once manufacturing was the key to mass employment, we now live and work in what is known as the Digital Age, a world in which employment is often based in all types of service industries. This does not mean that manufacturing has gone for good, but rather that it has been revolutionised and found support in digital technologies. Indeed, many of the activities that inform, shape and make our modern lives have simply become impossible without computer skills. Modern companies would be unthinkable without digital technologies. Globalization is also nothing new. In fact, international trade has been around since Neolithic times, a fact which countless archaeological finds attest. Throughout time, as now, the use of foreign languages was often indispensable for ensuring one's livelihood – if not one's survival. In today's Europe, human resources managers, headhunting companies and managers from across business sectors are telling us in education what many of us have long known: the job search for the graduates of today and tomorrow will be harder than ever if those graduates are not equipped with solid IT and foreign language skills (Grosse 2004; Swaffar/Urlaub 2014). Even our students realize this, but strangely often lack the courage and/or the disposition to actually pursue the honing of these essential skill sets. While European digital economy is growing seven times faster than any other sector (Jobline 2014), the lack of IT skills in job applicants is leaving vacant posts unfilled across the continent (Eurostat 2015). In Hungary, we see this as well. Whether in the capital of Budapest, in Debrecen, Pécs, Győr, Szeged, Miskolc or Székesfehérvár – wherever one looks in a city of any notable size – the IT sector is developing dynamically, huge business centres are being built to house companies that are active in IT-related sectors and seeking to employ thousands. Conversely, the lack of the critical competences of IT skills and foreign language skills prevents many job applicants from making it to the first round of interviews. Where is higher education and why have the statistics released by such companies about their inabilities to fill open positions gone unheard?

For any employer or employee in a role requiring business communication with foreign partners, customers or even suppliers, the ability to communicate clearly and convincingly in English is a necessity. Obviously, time is money and miscommunication can be an expensive error. Moreover, and even more onerous for the businessperson, there is the weight of the first impression on one's ability to persuade new business contacts. The importance of a proper first impression cannot be understated. Potential investors, purchasers or customers meeting new business partners who are not confident when expressing themselves in English will be viewed as being less reliable partners than self-confident English communicators with a good command of the jargon of the economic sector in which business is being conducted.

3 Jobseekers and L2

We have examined the requirements of businesses, but what do those people seeking work, or even those already employed, have to say about required foreign language skills and how they see their own abilities? One-third of workers polled last year in France felt that their lack of English language skills had left them unqualified to apply for valuable job opportunities (The Local 2017). However, focusing only on those French workers between the ages of 20 and 45 and as applies to a lack of knowledge of any foreign language, then that number rises to a full 55 % – a significant change from the 73 % of French baby boomers who argue that they did not require foreign languages to find work when they were younger (The Local 2017). Results from a recent study of the correlation between foreign language knowledge and the job market of the Visegrad countries Hungary, Poland, Slovakia and the Czech Republic, showed that foreign languages are required in one-third to three-fourths of all job advertisements in those countries, with English required for 52 % of the jobs being advertised, followed by German with 12 % and French, Italian, Spanish and Russian coming in at around 3 % (Beblavý/Fabo/Lenaerts 2016). Research focused solely on the significance of foreign language skills in specific occupations is also prevalent. At the start of the current decade, Maxwell (2010) analysed the role of English language skills in low-skilled positions, finding that workers with a limited knowledge of the English language had fewer employment opportunities and lower wages than their more proficient counterparts.

Even in the United States, a nation traditionally disparaged for its lack of foreign language knowledge, a recent study published by *New American Economy* highlighted that the demand for bilingual workers is growing (n.a. 2017). Figures mentioned in the report indicate American employers seeking to fill almost a quarter million jobs with bilingual workers in 2010, with that number rising to over 630,000 within five years. In addition to the customary Spanish-speaking positions, the study showed employers needing workers conversant with Chinese, Spanish and Arabic. The study noted that the number of employers seeking Chinese speakers in 2015 had tripled since 2010. During the same time period, job advertisements listing Spanish and Arabic as a desired foreign language soared by a remarkable 150 percent. The study also noted the growing need for workers who can speak at least one foreign language, and this was for jobs at both the lower and higher ends of the pay scale. Additionally, 15 of the 25 occupations (60 %) with the highest demand for workers proficient in a foreign language in 2015 were open to individuals with only a high school or two-year college diploma. These jobs included work as tax preparers, customer service representatives and medical assistants. On the other end of the pay and professional level, requiring at least a university Bachelor's degree, were job listings seeking financial managers, editors and industrial engineers who were proficient in a foreign language.

In Hungary, which we can speak for, foreign language skills not only remain far behind the averages for Europe, but for Central and Eastern Europe as a whole. The 2014 Eurobarometer survey revealed that one in five Hungarians was able to have a conversation in English with 40 % of those prepared for only the most rudimentary situations, such as understanding if a customer wants coffee or tea (European Commission 2014). Moreover, only 12 % of the Hungarian population could understand English language news – whether from TV or a newspaper. In contrast, the populations of every other Member State joining the EU in 2004 had higher percentages of their citizens able to communicate in English. As the best example, the Eurobarometer survey results showed that Slovenia boasts an admirable 59 %.

The Eurobarometer figures (European Commission 2014) showed that this is not only a problem of the older generation of Hungarians, as even youths are severely lacking English language skills. Only one in four Hungarians aged 15–34 speaks "good" English. This dismal result does not bode well for the future of business, much less for job prospects for these individuals. According to the Eurobarometer report (European Commission 2014), this problem is even more striking when comparing Hungary to its neighbours: except for the Czech Republic, every country shows a higher percentage of young English speakers, with 32 % in Romania and Poland. However, just under one-third is hardly a good performance, either. While the younger generation is clearly behind its – still – underperforming regional competition for jobs on the EU market, the crisis in English language learning is even more abysmal for middle-aged Hungarians. Because it is exactly this generation of citizens who make up the majority of the workforce, one might expect that companies have looked after their employees' language skills in order to remain competitive. Unfortunately, this is definitely not the case. The Eurobarometer figures revealed that only 11 % of those aged 35–54 possess a higher than basic level (B1) of English, while only a shocking 3 % of those over 55 even reach B1 level.

Now, under the present government, there have been some signs of change: the latest survey by Education First (EF) published in 2014 indicates that Hungary's English proficiency index (EPI) measuring the level of English language skills increased by 15 % between 2007 and 2013, at least among those who filled out the online test of the global language school network. Yet, even with this improvement, Hungary still ranks only sixth among the eight Central European EU members surveyed. In comparison, the Czech Republic and Slovakia had somewhat lower scores (for more detail see Education First 2014).

4 Employees, education and authenticity

Foreign language education at colleges and universities offers a unique opportunity to prepare future employees in a range of competences, all within a single classroom and subject environment. It should be noted here that any competence is more than simply what one understands to be knowledge and skills. Rather, a competence encompasses one's ability to live up to complex demands by utilizing and activating a set of known/learned resources (i.e. skills and attitudes) in a specific context. Seen within the context of communication, as only one example, one's ability to communicate effectively is a competence that may require an individual's knowledge of a specific (L2) language, even requiring the simultaneous use of applied IT skills, as well as one's attitudes towards those with whom communication is taking place (i.e., the application of interpersonal or even intercultural communication skills).

This raises the question of what the difference between a competence and a skill is. In short, seen within today's economy, which emphasizes employee flexibility, there is practically no difference. The concept of what a skill may be has changed from the definition of a skill as – by way of example, the technical knowledge and skills required by a particular job or occupation, to an understanding that includes a variety of wide-ranging, as well as personal, aptitudes and attitudes. Within communication, a competence is viewed as a necessity for accessing and staying in the job market. This ability is neither determined by level of education, nor type of work. Defined, communication may be understood as an effective use of spoken and written (foreign) language skills in various demanding situations. Indeed, communication is an essential tool for functioning appropriately in society, in an educational setting, in a workplace or even in doing business with an administrative office or in doing one's shopping. In other words, communication involves our actually participating in effective dialogue with others.

In today's European job market, communication skills are seen as crucial to the success of the growing service sector. Communication manifests in both the ability of a worker to interact with customers and how they communicate with their fellow employees from other areas of the same company – that is, what is known as the internal customer. In the service sector, communication and L2 competences may even precede technical qualifications in hiring of new staff. This is because service sector work requires more than just technical skills, but effective social skills – forcing workers to look and sound right. In other words, the worker in the service sector is a professional communicator first, and then, for instance, an IT expert, a salesperson or a hotel receptionist.

Should a job applicant not possess the right communication competences, especially as related to the job sector skills required to actually carry out job-specific tasks, then this lack may have direct and negative economic consequences for the company who decides to hire him/her. Although communication skills are equally vital to the effective operation within knowledge-based manufacturing enterprises, whether in various automotive industries, telecommunications industries or the travel industry, employers face the problem that, while such skills are of ever-increasing importance in the workplace, the so-called soft skills are more difficult to train. Applied skills in foreign and, particularly, special purpose languages – that is, public speaking, negotiating, assertive communication, customer care and communication – as well as intercultural communication, all involve intensive, expensive and rigorous training over time.

Individual employees simply need to be able to engage with others on their own. Furthermore, they will invariably encounter people from a range of backgrounds, depending on the company and sector they work in, so it is also imperative that they are able to interact in heterogeneous groups. At many multinational companies, group work is indeed the preferred option utilized for the development of oral communication, problem-solving, leadership training, assigning responsibility and decision-making.

Research shows that less than 10 % of IT sector posts can be filled without solid foreign language skills (Jobline 2014). Knowledge of two foreign languages or proficiency in so-called smaller European languages are a tremendous advantage. The site further reports that without knowledge of foreign languages and computer skills, the ability of graduates from across the higher education curriculum to find full time employment will be even more difficult than ever from next year, with companies now willing to import new workers or relocate current employees from other countries, if necessary.

4.1 Misguided goals in authenticity

How are universities to respond? English language learning at Hungarian colleges and universities is largely focused on the requirement that students in the majority of degree programs pass one of a total of 22 accredited, formal, foreign language examinations, in order to receive a diploma at the completion of their studies. Currently, some 50,000 Hungarian university graduates cannot get their diplomas because they lack language exams certificates. Equally unfortunate, the test-focused system of foreign language teaching means that students are often taught to pass a specific test. By over-focusing learning on passing a specific test, students are left to their own devices when it comes to their actually reaching a level of foreign language proficiency in their chosen field that would make them hireable. ESP courses exist, but these are not always available to students in a manner that is degree-specific. Moreover, many ESP courses are, as mentioned, test-focused in nature.

Indeed, the methods of foreign language testing in use at any time tend to reflect the view that a generic certificate awarded for foreign language knowledge might somehow in itself qualify a student for employment using that foreign language. However, this view is still seen through a prism of devising and running a testing programme, which inherently means that a potential corpus of necessary vocabulary and expressions must be pared down to small portions of content. What is considered to possess value worthy of being tested from the huge range of *Englishes* and the kind of task or item type chosen as a means of testing a particular type of English are all highly subjective choices made by the test item writer. The problem is that while highly experienced teachers of general English are hired to write test items, these teachers may not have any experience of the usage of the English language as pertains to any particular job sector. They do not know jargon, contexts of use or the related technical terminologies. For example, they might know how to test reported speech, but know nothing about the Englishes used in upselling/tiering in sales departments, logistics management terms or the jargon of SAP tools for accounting. In other words, the tests the Hungarian students are taking do not necessarily reflect the needs of the job market pertaining to specialised English knowledge they will need to know for their chosen fields of work after graduation.

How did this happen? As we know, communicative language testing evolved out of a shift in language teaching/learning theory and methodology, away from a predominantly structural focus, towards one that emphasized the importance of language in use. Numerous textbook series were published with just this subheading: *Language in Use*. Language departments worldwide jumped on board and their intentions were good. However, no running dialogue was established with domestic commerce and industry to check the applicability of the English being taught to students for the jobs they were to seek.

Presently, the Common European Framework of Reference for Languages (CEFR) (Council of Europe 2001) contains a model of language ability. Essentially, this model may be understood as being a European policy statement defining communicative competence: communicative competence (sociolinguistic, linguistic, pragmatic) is a form of general competence that leads to language activity (interaction, production, reception, mediation) using tasks, texts and strategies in four principal domains (public, occupational, educational, personal) in which situations arise, consisting of locations, containing organizations that structure interaction, persons with definite roles, objects (animate and inanimate) that constitute an environment, events that take place in it, and operations that are performed (see Chapter 4 of the CEFR).

Authenticity is a criterion which, by definition, requires continual updating. The notion of authenticity is not new in language teaching theory and methodology. Since the late 1970s, the notion of authenticity has been extensively researched, in order to devise a principled approach to using authentic documents and texts in both the teaching and testing of language skills. Widdowson (1978) and Bachman (1990) conceptualized authenticity as existing at two levels, the situational level and the interactional level.

Situational authenticity refers to the degree to which the test method characteristics of a language task reflect the characteristics of a real life situation where the language will be used; in other words, the extent to which the task is an accurate representation of some language activity which occurs naturally in everyday life. In designing a situationally authentic task, it is necessary first to identify the critical features that define the task in the target language use domain. It is then possible to design test tasks which have these critical features.

Interactional authenticity denotes the interface between test task and test taker; it entails test writers and developers utilizing texts, situational contexts and tasks which simulate *real life*, without attempting to replicate life exactly; it also means the attempt to use situations and tasks which are likely to be familiar and relevant to the intended test taker at the given level, and it clarifies the purpose for doing a particular task, together with the intended audience, by providing appropriate contextualization and making clear the criterion for success in completing the task.

When selecting texts and designing items to accompany them, it is therefore important to give some thought to whether the tasks are situationally authentic and whether the processes candidates are being asked to think through and then perform on the basis of the selected texts represent the kinds of processes that actually reflect what will be expected from them later in their careers. Nonetheless, the discussion is still only focused on testing, and the over-focus on testing is one of the chief disconnects between educational goals and job market needs.

5 What education must do

Moving away, therefore, from testing-based L2 education, we will now focus on what needs to be considered if education is to supply the job market with suitable candidates with relevant English language competences. The following problems appear to be common and therefore require rethinking of curricula, syllabi and taught subject matter. First, primary and secondary education programmes do not, in the view of jobseekers, prepare students for a future of using foreign languages to do work-related tasks. Focus is rather on general and everyday language, which is necessary to provide a basis for actual use, but there is a lack of focused guidance and preparation of students for the actual expectations of their future employers.

Additionally, in countries such as Hungary, those who earn their state accredited language examination certificates at a younger age are either not motivated to maintain their language knowledge or even shut out of foreign language education altogether, leaving them to forget the foreign language long before they actually need to use it in their careers. The irony of this situation is that Hungarian state–accredited language exams are not accepted by foreign educational institutes and employers. Moreover, employers have no sources to get relevant information about the applicants' language skills, except to use their own resources to test and assess these themselves. Some employers use the services of headhunters to do this for them, but the fact is that most headhunters do not have professionals to evaluate language skills properly.

Enlightening is to see these issues in contrast, from the employer's point of view, as they feel that the following problems are common and require action. First, job portals, Europass and EURES are all valuable resources for employers to gain information about applicants; however, they do not contain up-to-date, electronic language portfolios on applicants. Second, even if an applicant is in possession of a language examination certificate, if this was obtained years ago, then it simply cannot provide prospective employers with relevant information about an applicant's actual language skills. Third, headhunters use pre-filtration techniques that are not always reliable and professional, as they are not experts in the fields for which they are trying to find employees and also do not have the relevant experience or necessary insight to choose a candidate who would have the matching foreign language and related soft skills in that foreign language. Fourth, too much time is wasted on first round job interviews, which a proper database of relevant information on applicants could remedy. Fifth, and this is a chief concern of any employer, deficiencies in employees' foreign language knowledge may lead to significant business losses. Finally, like it or not, employers know that employee foreign language knowledge has to be developed from the companies' own resources in order to ensure progress and the meeting of targets.

6 The local job market and L2 education

There is abundant research on the connection between L2 knowledge and career opportunities on the job market, as well as impact on businesses and economies. There is disagreement on how that connection should best be studied. For example, Zhang and Grenier (2013) contend that traditional research on the relationship between economics and languages can be divided into three strands: language and economic status, dynamic development of languages (from an economic perspective), and language policy and planning (also from an economic perspective). Globalisation and its impacts have demonstrated not only how economies worldwide have become interconnected. Events such as the illegal immigration crisis affecting Europe in this decade or the Brexit vote and its aftermath highlight to what degree countries are consistently confronted with the effects of national politics and local conditions on international trade and foreign direct investment. For all such phenomena, language undoubtedly plays a role.

Other researchers, such as Kim, Liu, Tuxhorn, Brown and Leblang (2015), focus on the strong relationship between foreign language knowledge and foreign direct investment (FDI). Stöhr (2015) proposes that workers earn substantially higher wages due to their foreign language skills in Europe, and discusses how particularly English knowledge means larger pay packets for German workers. Kureková, Beblavý and Haita (2012) explored the demand for a range of skills in the case of 23 low- to medium-skilled occupations in Slovakia and concluded that communication skills and foreign language knowledge were ranked among the three most requested skills for an astounding 87 % of jobs.

The research we examined demonstrates that L2 knowledge is a highly demanded skill on a par with, for instance, a degree in economics, management science or marketing. However, the L2 communication skills demanded by employers are worthless without an employee's possessing intercultural and professional communication skills, such as presentation, negotiation and customer communication skills. All three of these skill sets are areas in which reputable companies invest thousands of Euros per employee to hire external trainers to hold workshops for their employees. Yet, L2 classrooms in higher education can go far in ensuring that graduating students have these skills. The question is, how?

6.1 Debrecen, Hungary

Following the discussion in the previous section, we would now like to provide a specific example of the disparities between foreign language skills taught in higher education and local job market needs. Afterwards, we will offer suggestions for remedying them through cooperation between our higher education institution and locally-running businesses needing our graduates.

Since the changes that swept Europe in 1989–1990 with the collapse of the Eastern Bloc's Soviet-run totalitarian regimes, the city in which our university is located, Debrecen, Hungary, has seen demand for foreign languages and relevant sociocultural and communication skills skyrocket. The opening of our markets to foreign businesses and the general effects of globalization have brought companies from a variety of sectors here, with some taking over failing Hungarian companies and transforming them into profitable enterprises while others opening local branches of their multinational ventures. The companies include Texas-based engineering and technical manufacturer National Instruments, as well as fluid motion and control manufacturer Flowserve's auditing and accounting branch; the British corporation BT, which provides a wide variety of IT and communication support services worldwide; Israel's largest employer TEVA Pharmaceuticals, which took over the former Hungarian Biogal pharmaceutical manufacturer; American-based software engineering and development company EPAM; German IT giant T-Systems; German automotive and aerospace manufacturer Schaeffler group; as well as the Irish airlines Ryan Air customer and sales support team, to name but a few. These companies operating in a variety of capacities in Debrecen are now being joined by a series of German manufacturing giants, all announcing moves to Debrecen in the last two years: a new BMW Automobile manufacturing plant, ThyssenKrupp is opening a new plant to produce automotive parts, a new Continental automotive components manufacturing plant, a factory for bottles, cans and containers being opened by Krones AG.

The list above is incomplete, but it serves to provide a feel for the needs of locally operating businesses. Obviously, with all of these companies to be found in Debrecen, a city of only 300,000 inhabitants, the role of foreign language skills in the local labour market is unquestionable. Both for our graduates and for prospective employers here, knowledge of foreign languages matters, whether one considers daily business operational reasons or the ability to compete with competitors in the sectors in which the companies mentioned above are engaged. Additionally, our locally hiring businesses need employees with foreign languages and relevant sociocultural and communication skills to enhance sales figures, to advance the impacts of their marketing activities and to accomplish logistical and managerial goals regarding cross-border (Schengen and otherwise) supply chains. The import and export of raw materials, manufactured goods, the preparation and obtaining of certification, permits and licenses, the negotiation of delivery dates, prices, payment dates, the rescheduling of delayed shipments and the holding of employee meetings online are only a few examples of the purposes for which these companies will need these foreign language–based skills – not only to be met, but to be practised and honed.

As seen above, foreign languages are more than just a means in which to communicate with fellow employees located in other countries. More importantly, they provide access to those individuals and organizations most often required for key externally focused business activities, such as attending business meetings with potential clients and customers, maintaining relations with already contracted partners or presenting the company, its products and services in venues as wide-ranging as industrial fairs, events held by chambers of commerce abroad, conducting public relations activities or meeting foreign dignitaries and trade delegations.

And yet, as we have examined above, foreign language education in Hungarian higher education is not focused on its true goal: providing businesses with job applicants who can meet their specific needs for foreign languages and are equipped with relevant sociocultural and communication skills.

6.2 Making the connection

Based on the example of Debrecen, below we provide a list of suggestions of changes that would be required in our university to meet the foreign language skills needs of businesses on a local or regional level. These changes could be adapted for use by others at universities across Europe, as and wherever applicable:

First, the general conditions for teaching should be remedied, wherever necessary. While we are lucky in our Faculty of Economic Sciences and Business to be able to provide students in several Bachelor's degree programmes with six hours/week of training in up to two foreign languages, this is neither standard for all faculties or degree programmes – even within our own faculty. In view of the list of potential employers in town, and particularly of the list of business activities we provided during our discussion above – which is only partial – it would seem evident that students enrolled in degree programmes across the curricula of the Faculty of Economic Sciences and Business, the Faculty of Engineering, the Faculty of Agricultural and Food Sciences and Environmental Management, the Faculty of Pharmacy, the Faculty of Science and Technology and the Faculty of Informatics should benefit from foreign language skills and relevant communication skills development classes in every semester of their studies. After careful consultations and needs analysis work involving locally operating businesses with foreign language needs, the university faculties involved should – in cooperation with their foreign language teaching staff – devise sets of core LSP courses to address the established needs for each faculty's students.

Depending on their L2 knowledge levels and the expectations of the pool of potential employers in the region, an adequate number of mandatory hours per week and semester should be offered to these students. Should a student not enter university with a proper L2 foundation of intermediate knowledge in all four L2 skills, then that student should have to pay for and take mandatory update classes until their deficits in L2 knowledge have been addressed.

Teaching aids and materials are another crucial area: Textbooks are often out of date, with instructors having to purchase their own materials or devise their own materials for ever-changing educational needs. In other words, instructors are offering different courses to different levels of students in different LSP courses from semester to semester. Rather, in revising the curricula and syllabi, new, comprehensive materials should be developed for each core LSP study focus area, for each involved faculty. External funding sources, such as grants, donations from the businesses to be assisted by these changes in curricula, EU and national funds should be applied for in order to pay for these materials to be purchased and/or developed. Time should also be given for proper creation, development, quality and content review by experts and piloting.

Moreover, the contributions of the students themselves are worth addressing. Unfortunately, students often produce work which is unsatisfactory. Not only do teachers face indifference among students, but an overall lack of diligence and rigour are key problems to be addressed. Departments involved in foreign language teaching need to invite Human Resource managers and business leaders into the classroom to speak to the students in the target language of study. These experts are necessary to rattle them into understanding the absolute requirement and necessity of L2 skills, in order to even gain an invitation for a job interview – much less to be actually employed. These invited guests are required to collaborate with the university teachers to confront students with real life tasks and activities to be done in class in the target language, so the students can understand what challenges await them upon graduation. This cooperation is key for ensuring that the bridge between higher education and the business world is properly built and functioning.

Most crucially, multi-semester courses in soft skills, offered in the target language, should be accessible to all students in minimally their last year of study. These subjects may range from public speaking to customer communication, from assertive communication to negotiation skills, from problem-based learning in a specific area of business, engineering or IT (as three such examples, depending on the student's field of study) to holding meetings or handling complaints. The list of possibilities is long, but relying only on intermediate level Business English courses to supply the job market with potential employees does not go far enough. As educators in higher education, our classes are often the last opportunity our students will have to develop the foreign language study skills they will need to stay relevant in a job market dominated by multinational business organizations functioning in multilingual business environments. Therefore, we need to ensure that our students understand that foreign language learning is not something one can stop dealing with when issued a university diploma. Rather, knowledge of a foreign language requires dedication to investing one's time in maintaining proficiency throughout one's career.

7 Conclusion

In providing students with marketable skills for future employment, the needs of locally operating businesses – large and small – must be identified and met, in order to assist graduates with job placement, to help companies be able to maintain new hires and to close gaps in key communication skills. Foreign language knowledge alone is not enough to qualify an applicant for a position. Without the relevant professional communication skills, combined with the proper aptitudes towards communicating with diverse cultures and attitudes, students will find it difficult to progress in their careers, and companies will lose a valuable competitive edge. Therefore, universities have to forge connections with local and regional employers, encourage dialogue, conduct needs assessments and then follow through on them. Universities need to replace foreign language requirements based solely on ministerial and institutional educational requirements, and focus on the real needs of the graduating students to find and maintain gainful employment, by matching the skills they are being taught with those expected by prospective employers.

References

Bachman, Lyle F. 1990. *Fundamental Considerations in Language Testing*. Oxford: Oxford University Press.

Beblavý, Miroslav/Fabo, Brian/Lenaerts, Karolean. January 2016. *The Importance of Foreign Language Skills in the Labour Markets of Central and Eastern Europe. An Assessment Based on Data from Online Job Portals*, *CEPS Special Report*, 129, 1–44.

Council of Europe 2001. *Common European Framework of Reference for Languages: Learning, Teaching, Assessment.* Cambridge: Cambridge University Press.

Education First 2014. *English Proficiency Index*. <www.ef.com/epi>.

European Commission 2014. *European Area of Skills and Qualifications.* No. 417. <ec.europa.eu/commfrontoffice/publicopinion/archives/ebs/ebs_417_en.pdf>.

Eurostat 2015. *Job Vacancy Trends*. <http://ec.europa.eu/eurostat/statistics-explained/index.php/Job_vacancy_trends>.

Faragher, Jo. 1 July 2015. Soft Skills "worth £88 billion" to UK Economy. *Personnel Today*. <https://www.personneltoday.com/hr/soft-skills-worth-88bn-to-uk-economy/>.

Grosse, Christine U. 2004. The Competitive Advantage of Foreign Languages and Cultural Knowledge. *Modern Language Journal* 88/3, 351–373.

IIR Hungary 2019. *Rendezvénynaptár*. January 2019. <https://www.iir-hungary.hu/rendezvenynaptar.html>.

Jobline 2014. *Ki Talál Munkát Jövőre?* <http://www.piacesprofit.hu/kkv_cegblog/piac/ki-talal-munkat-jovore/>.

Kim, Moonhawk/Liu, Amy H./Tuxhorn, Kim-Lee/Brown, David S./Leblang, David 2015. Lingua Mercatoria: Language and Foreign Direct Investment. *International Studies Quarterly* 59/2, 330–343.

Kureková, Lucia Mytna/Beblavý, Miroslav/Haita, Corina 2012. Qualifications or Soft Skills? Studying Job Advertisements for Demand for Low-Skilled Staff in Slovakia. *NEUJOBS Working Paper* D.4.3.3, 1–32. <https://www.researchgate.net/publication/311451661_Skills_Requirements_for_the_30_Most-Frequently_Advertised_Occu-

pations_in_the_United_States_An_analysis_based_on_online_vacancy_data>.
Maxwell, Nan L. 2010. English Language and Low-Skilled Jobs: The Structure of Employment. *Industrial Relations* 49/3, 457–465.
n.a. 2017. Not Lost in Translation: The Growing Importance of Foreign Language Skills in the U.S. Job Market. *A New American Economy Report.* 33 pp. <https://research.newamericaneconomy.org/report/not-lost-in-translation-the-growing-importance-of-foreign-language-skills-in-the-u-s-job-market/>.
Randstad 2015. *Ranstad Financial & Professional Website.* <https://www.randstad.co.uk/financial-professional/>.
Stöhr, Tobias. 2015. The Returns to Occupational Foreign Language Use: Evidence from Germany. *Labour Economics* 32/C, 86–98.
Swaffar Janet/Urlaub Per (eds.) 2014. *Transforming Postsecondary Foreign Language Teaching in the United States.* Dordrecht: Springer Science+Business Media.
The Local 2017. *French Workers Fear Their Poor English Is Harming Their Career Chances.* <https://www.thelocal.fr/20170428/french-workers-fear-their-poor-english-is-leaving-them-behind>.
Widdowson, Henry G. 1978. *Language Teaching as Communication.* Oxford: Oxford University Press.
Zhang, Weiguo/Grenier, Gilles 2013. How Can Language Be Linked to Economics? A Survey of Two Strands of Research. *Language Problems & Language Planning* 37/3, 203–226.

Penny MacDonald/Llum Bracho

What Do Young People Think of the Phenomenon of Immigration? A Corpus-Based Study of University Students' Ideas and Attitudes as Expressed in EFL Classes

1 Introduction

Like most countries worldwide, Spain has gone through phases of its history when its citizens have been compelled to leave the country for the sole purpose of improving their economic and social conditions or to escape from persecution in times of war and/or dictatorships. When considering Spain's migratory tendencies, the last decade of the 20th century marked a period of increased immigration to the country. From 1990 to 2012, the number of immigrants arriving in Spain rose sharply becoming a news item almost daily in the Spanish media. Spanish people's attitudes to immigration in general have been studied through research into agenda setting and framing (Igartua et al. 2004; Igartua/Muñiz/Cheng 2005; Muñiz-Muriel et al. 2008, among others); the Spanish Social Survey results (Zapata-Barrero 2009; Buades Fúster et al. 2010), and the European Social Survey (Green 2007; Hainmueller/Hiscox 2007; Sonck/Loosveldt 2010; Arikan/Bloom 2012; Bridges/Mateut 2014; Markaki/Longhi 2013; Davidov et al. 2015). However, not many studies have addressed young people's ideas and how these attitudes may have changed over time, and there are even fewer references in the literature which have looked at how these attitudes may be expressed when using a second or foreign language.

With a view to making a contribution to this issue, we present the results of a preliminary study which aims at investigating university students' attitudes to immigration when writing in English as a Foreign Language. Several hundred university students, both of Spanish mother tongue and Erasmus students, have contributed to the MiLC Corpus

(Andreu et al. 2010) which has been developed in two stages: firstly, between 2008 and 2013 (Corpus 1) and secondly during 2017 (Corpus 2). One hundred and fifty compositions written by students whose mother tongue is either Spanish or Catalan or one of several other languages spoken by incoming Erasmus exchange students are analysed. Using Atlas.ti, a qualitative-descriptive analysis of the texts is carried out and the different attitudes are categorised and analysed according to the writer's opinion on immigration.

2 Sociohistorical background: Immigration to Spain

Spain, Greece, Ireland and Portugal are among the so-called new receiving countries as regards immigration. According to figures published by the Spanish National Statistics Office (INE) in 1998, 1.6 % of the population of Spain were foreigners, just over half a million people. In 2011, this percentage had risen to 12.2 % (5.7 million people) almost ten times the figures for 1998. In 2017, there was a drop to 4.4 million, with foreigners accounting for 9.5 % of the population. With regard to European immigration among the 28 member states, 4.3 million people immigrated to one of the EU countries during 2016 (latest official data). Of these, 2.4 million had come from non-member countries. There were also 3 million emigrants who were reported to have left any one of the EU Member States.

Attitudes to immigration vary greatly, and there are many variables to be taken into account: economic situation of the receiving country, levels of unemployment, religion and identity, country of origin of migrants, and so on. According to the Migration Observatory at the University of Oxford, immigration has been ranked among the top five regarding the most pressing issues among the public interviewed in social surveys, with as much as three-quarters of the population saying they favour reducing immigration (Migration Observatory 2011). One wonders where these attitudes come from. Certainly many studies have established an association between the framing strategies found in the news media and anti-immigration attitudes (Peffley/Shields/Williams

1996; Domke/McCoy/Torres 1999; Oliver 1999; Vergeer/Lubbers/Scheepers 2000; Boomgaarden/Vliegenthart 2009, among others) and possibly one of the main reasons for the *yes* vote for Brexit in 2017 can be attributed to the public's negative attitude to immigration.

Much has been written about public opinion and how it can be influenced by different media. Much cited in the literature, Lippmann (1922: 60) carried out one of the first contemporary studies on public opinion and social stereotypes from a cognitive point of view and noted that:

> We notice a trait which marks a well-known type, and fill in the rest of the picture by means of the stereotypes we carry about in our heads. [...] The subtlest and most pervasive of all influences are those which create and maintain the repertory of stereotypes. We are told about the world before we see it. We imagine most things before we experience them.

Countries like Spain, which have less experience of newcomers arriving on their shores, often have a more ambiguous relationship with the newly arrived immigrant population, and it takes time before they become accepted as part of the "country's usual demographical make-up" (Bridges/Mateut 2014: 418). So, when did immigration become a *problem* in Spain? Immigration starts to be perceived as a *problem* with the arrival of these new migrants and, within the Spanish collective imaginary, the social construction of *the other* is introduced (Zapata-Barrero 2009) – this one being different from the historical *other* in Spain which traditionally would be the Romani people (Cachón Rodriguez 2012). With regard to the Spanish Social Survey barometer (Centro de Investigaciones Sociológicas 2018), from the year 2000, the phenomenon of immigration became a permanent question when enquiring about the three most important *problems* affecting the country, and since April 2005 immigration has been situated among the top three most important problems. In September 2006, it reached the first position for the first time (Zapata-Barrero 2009).

But how did people perceive immigration at that time? Did it really affect them personally? Did they have a realistic idea concerning the number of immigrants arriving on Spanish shores or working and living within its borders? In response to the second question, there is almost always a significant difference in the survey results between the percentage of interviewees that declare that "immigration is the most important problem" and then how much "immigration affects me personally". In the social survey carried out in Valencia, Spain, in 2007, almost 27 % claimed that immigration was the biggest problem in Spain, although this percentage dropped 10 % when asked if immigration affected them directly in a negative way (El País 2007). With regard to the perception of the numbers of immigrants in Spain, Zapata-Barrero (2009) noted that in quantitative terms, there is a difference between the real number and that perceived by the Spanish public. This author also noted that it is more the "border management-related factors and subsequent policies that impact on negative attitudes" (Zapata-Barrero 2009: 1107) rather than a general rejection by the public of the immigrant population.

In 2018, it would appear that the phenomenon of immigration is not so high on the political agenda as it has been in the past, and therefore it is not so visible in the mass media. Despite the fact that the immigrant population has only gone down by less than 3 % (figures for 2017), in the latest Spanish Social Survey (Centro de Investigaciones Sociólogicas 2018), for the month of September 2018, the most pressing problem was unemployment (39.5 % of citizens interviewed), followed at a distance by corruption (11 %) and in sixth place comes the perception of immigration as the main problem, 4.1 %, whilst those saying that it affected them on a personal level, dropped to eleventh place, only 1.4 % of the interviewees. It seems to be a contradiction that so many of those interviewed for the Social Survey find immigration to be such a problem while at the same time they admit that immigration has a minimally negative effect on their own lives and personal context. This would seem to support the idea proposed by Van Dijk (1993) that people tend to be highly influenced by different information sources which have an effect on our beliefs and our interpretation of specific social and political events even though they may not affect us directly.

3 Attitudes among young people

Some studies have highlighted the fact that adolescence is a crucial time for shaping social and political ideas and the development of intergroup attitudes (Reindes 2003; Duriez/Soenens 2009). Moreover, the attitudes formed at that time have been shown to be relatively stable and last even throughout adulthood (Hooghe 2004; Hooghe/Wilkenfeld 2008). For Stephan et al. (2005) when analysing attitudes to immigration, two different types of threats can be seen to influence attitudes. On the one hand, those which are termed *realistic threats*, that is, from the point of view of immigration threatening the economic and social stability of the in-group, and on the other, *symbolic threats* which focus on immigration threatening national identity and the values, traditions and customs of the majority. When analysing the attitudes of Italian and French secondary school children, Bergamaschi (2013) concluded that contextual factors (among others, the educational institution, the community where a child lives) explain why the adolescent Italians in the study tend to see immigration as a realistic threat, and the French adolescents see this phenomenon more as a symbolic threat. The so-called realistic threats are often voiced by politicians and cited in the press, declaring that the immigrant population takes *our* jobs, overuses *our* scarce public services, and increases crime, amongst other accusations. On the other hand, symbolic threats tend to focus on the immigrants' different style of life, values, beliefs and religions which can undermine the majority in-group way of life.

4 The study

4.1 Aims

Our main aim is to analyse the written compositions collected from students learning English at a technical university on the topic of immigration. With this main objective in mind, the more specific aims are to:

1. Code the attitudes (positive, negative, neutral) identified in the EFL compositions of all the subjects.
2. Compare the attitudes found in the compositions of different groups within Corpus 1 (Spanish females and males, and Erasmus females and males)

3. Compare the attitudes of the Spanish-speaking subjects in Corpus 1 and Corpus 2 since there had been a time lapse of over four years and there were several new variables to be taken into account when students were writing about the topic.

4.2 Hypothesis

Taking into account the increase in levels of immigration to Spain previous to, and during the period of recollection of Corpus 1, and the predominant discourse in the mass media in Spain, followed by the years of economic crisis, we hypothesise that the students would reproduce the (negative) discourses they had been exposed to at that time. Moreover, we predicted that after 2013 (Corpus 2) these attitudes would possibly change due to the fact that many immigrants resident in Spain (and many young Spaniards too) had left the country in search of work in other places. Also considering the global media attention given to refugees from 2015 onwards, we predict that students would show more tolerance, and be more open to the idea of globalization and world citizenship as being new phenomena that allow people to seek a dignified life for themselves and their families in other parts of the world.

4.3 Methodology and research tools

Several hundred university students, both of Spanish mother tongue and Erasmus students have contributed to the MiLC Corpus (Andreu et al. 2010) which originally included learner texts written in several foreign languages, but later became an exclusively English language learner corpus collected at the Universitat Politècnica de València, Spain. The corpus has been developed in two stages: firstly, between 2008 and 2013 (Corpus 1) and secondly during 2017 (Corpus 2). Of this corpus, the present study analyses 150 compositions which have been extracted randomly, but in equal numbers from both Corpus 1 and

Corpus 2. Thus, from Corpus 1 there are 25 compositions from Spanish females and 25 from Spanish males; 25 from Erasmus females and 25 from Erasmus males. And from Corpus 2, there are 25 compositions from Spanish females and 25 from Spanish males (see Tab. 12-1 for details of corpus sizes). The subjects were aged between 18 and 25. The mother tongue of the Spanish subjects contributing to Corpus 1 and 2 is either Spanish or Catalan, and in the case of the Erasmus exchange students, the native languages listed are: Polish (10), German (5), Hungarian (5), Czech (8), Dutch (3), Latvian (3), French (7), Taiwanese (1) Slovenian (1) Slovakian (1) Estonian (2) Arabic (1) Italian (1) Lithuanian (1) and Rumanian (1).

Tab. 12-1: Learner corpora.

CORPUS SIZE (Corpus 1 + Corpus 2)	CORPUS 1 (2008–2013) Number of words per student group	CORPUS 2 (2017) Number of words per student group
	Spanish females 6,623	Spanish females 5,621
38,609 words	Spanish males 6,304	Spanish males 5,841
	Erasmus females 7,559	
	Erasmus males 6,661	

As it was not possible to collect Erasmus students' data for 2017, we will be investigating attitudes comparing the following groups:

- Spanish and Erasmus students (Corpus 1).
- Spanish females and Spanish males (Corpus 1).
- Erasmus females and Erasmus males (Corpus 1).
- Spanish females and Spanish males (Corpus 1 and Corpus 2).

It must be noted that although the exact number of words in each sub-corpus is not identical a normalisation test at 10,000 words was carried out and the difference was found to be irrelevant.

The students were provided with the instructions for writing the composition, and this was uploaded (with the learners' metadata) to the webpage used for collecting the corpus (and still available at <http://www.etsmre.upv.es/dla/corpus/Eng.asp>).[1]

ATLAS.ti v.8.1.30 was used for the analysis of the two corpora. Forty codes were elaborated to identify the attitudes and these are listed in Tables 12-2 to 12-4.

Tab. 12-2: Attitudes identified in corpora: Positive codes.

Positive codes
1. Beneficial for birth rate
2. Beneficial for having multicultural society
3. Beneficial for more diversity of food, drink, different ways of thinking
4. Beneficial for pensions and/or economy
5. Do the jobs we don't want, bad conditions, poor pay
6. Emigrate is not easy, leave family, go on a very difficult journey
7. Empathy
8. Escape from persecution
9. Improve economic, social, political conditions for self/family. Find work.
10. Integration: shared responsibility
11. No border controls or less control or totally free movement of people
12. World citizenship

The codes were revised several times, merged and sometimes eliminated. They were divided into three main code groups: positive (12 codes), negative (20 codes) and neutral (8 codes). These were categorised according to the criteria of the researchers, so what we may think is negative – that is, "Stricter border controls needed" may be considered positive by another person, depending on how they think, their ideology, etc.

1 Instructions: you have 50 minutes to write an essay on the following topic. You may make notes, use a dictionary, and you may check your work and make changes within the 50 minutes allowed.

- Length: Approx. 250 words.
- As we all know immigration is a pressing issue everywhere. Write about this topic, either thinking about this phenomenon in your home country, or in Spain, or just from a general point of view. You may make a definition, consider the advantages and disadvantages, give your opinion, and so on.

Tab. 12-3: Attitudes identified in corpora: Negative codes.

Negative codes
1. (Stricter) border controls needed
2. Bad influence on future generations
3. Brain drain
4. Cause overpopulation/ overcrowding (destination)
5. Cause the crime rate to go up/associated with terrorism
6. Customs and habits are different
7. Decline of birth rate in country of origin
8. Illegal or undocumented
9. Immigration is a problem or a threat
10. Immigration is a security problem
11. Integration: they don't try or it's their responsibility
12. Negative effect on culture, religion or language of destination
13. Numbers of immigrants/emigrants
14. Only high-level immigration
15. Other reasons for migrating: poverty, environmental factors (drought, etc.)
16. Take our jobs (causing higher unemployment in times of crisis)
17. They become homeless
18. They lower the wages for us
19. Use or abuse public services
20. Ways to stop migration

Tab. 12-4: Attitudes identified in corpora: Neutral codes.

Neutral codes
1. Country/area of destination
2. Country/area of origin
3. Definition
4. Due to globalisation
5. Effect of migration on country of origin
6. Emigration from Spain or writer's home country
7. Other reasons: study, travel, job promotion, know other cultures
8. Other solutions: what can be done about migration?

Among the neutral attitudes, were: Country of origin and/or destination of the immigrants; definition of immigration; other reasons for migration, among others. It was thought that these categories did not show the attitudes of the writers. Also when regarding the classifications of the positive attitudes, when referring to the code "they (the immigrants) do the jobs we don't want", researchers understand that although this is not a good thing, it does show that students are aware of the situation of the immigrant population arriving in Spain, and if they are taking *their* jobs, they are the ones not wanted by the Spanish people.

5 Results

In the first place, we present the more general results regarding the number of positive, negative and neutral codes in the two corpora, followed by some specific examples and quotes taken from the coded compositions.

Figure 12-1 shows all the codes used for describing attitudes in Corpus 1 and 2. Considering these in quantitative terms, out of a total of 880 quotations identified by the researchers, 343 were within the negative code group (40 %), 283 were positive (32 %) and 254 were considered neutral (29 %).

5.1 Comparison of attitudes between Spanish and Erasmus students (Corpus 1)

From the graph in Fig. 12-2, there appear to be some notable differences concerning the attitudes found in certain groups. The female Erasmus group shows a tendency to be much more negative towards different aspects of immigration compared with their male counterparts and in comparison to the Spanish groups (both female and male). More precisely, out of 25 texts, over 110 negative comments were made. They also made more neutral comments than the others. Turning to the positive attitudes detected, these were slightly lower than both the female and male Spanish groups but higher than their Erasmus male counterparts. The Erasmus male group used fewer positive expressions in their compositions than any other group.

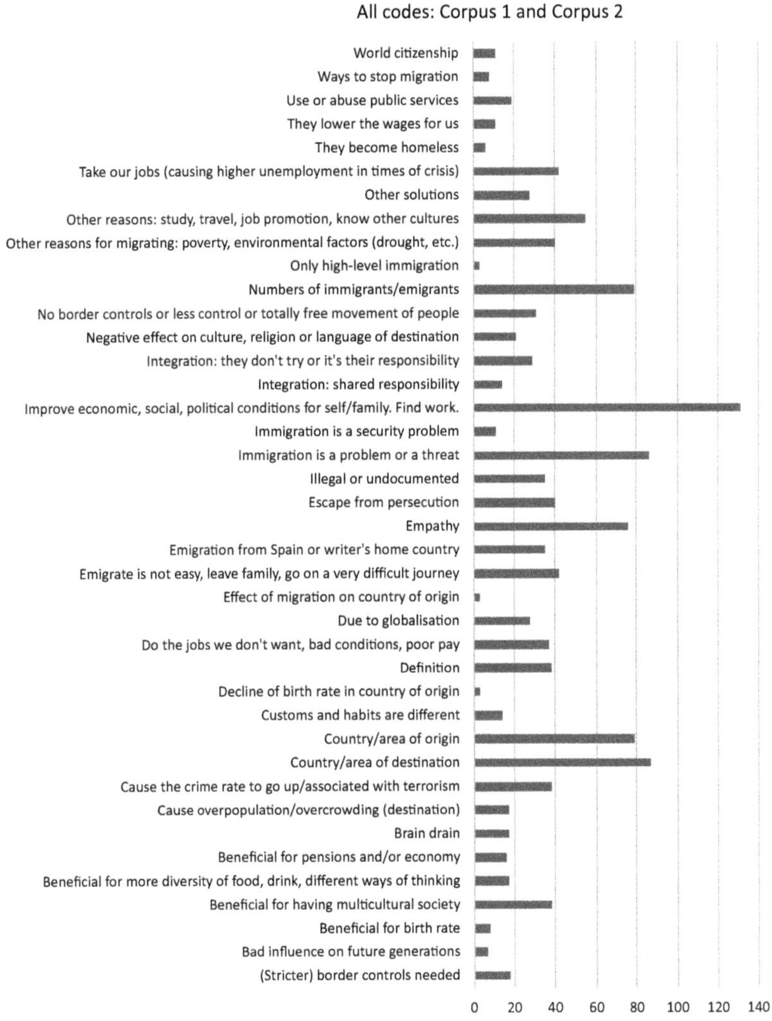

Fig. 12-1: All codes used in Corpus 1 and Corpus 2.

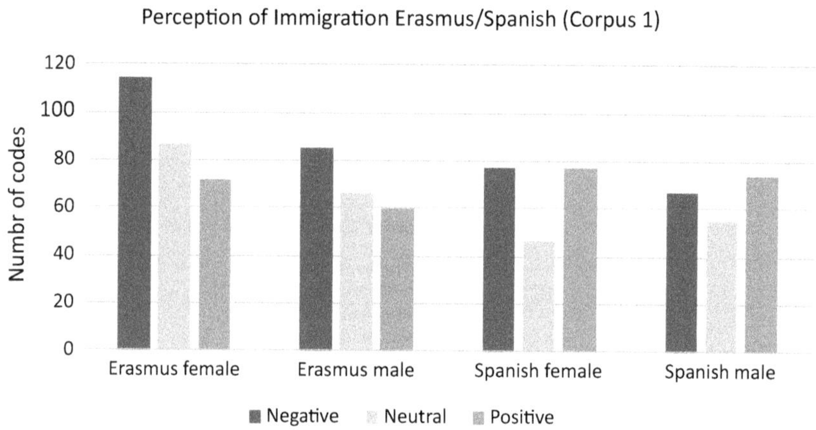

Fig. 12-2: Comparison of attitudes between Spanish and Erasmus students (Corpus 1).

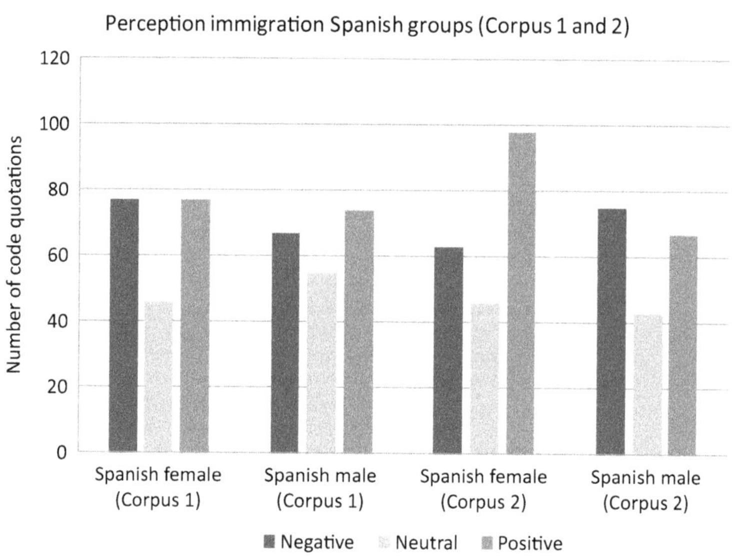

Fig. 12-3: Attitudes between Spanish groups (Corpus 1 and Corpus 2).

5.2 Comparison of attitudes between Spanish students Corpus 1 and Corpus 2

Comparing the data from Corpus 1 and Corpus 2, and looking at the Spanish groups only (Fig. 12-3), the females' positive attitudes seem to have gone up substantially, and negative attitudes have dropped in the later corpus. With the Spanish male groups, figures are similar, with a slight rise in positive comments and slight fall in negative attitudes.

5.3 Comparison of negative attitudes between Spanish and Erasmus students (Corpus 1)

Erasmus females are noted for their negative attitudes (Fig. 12-4).

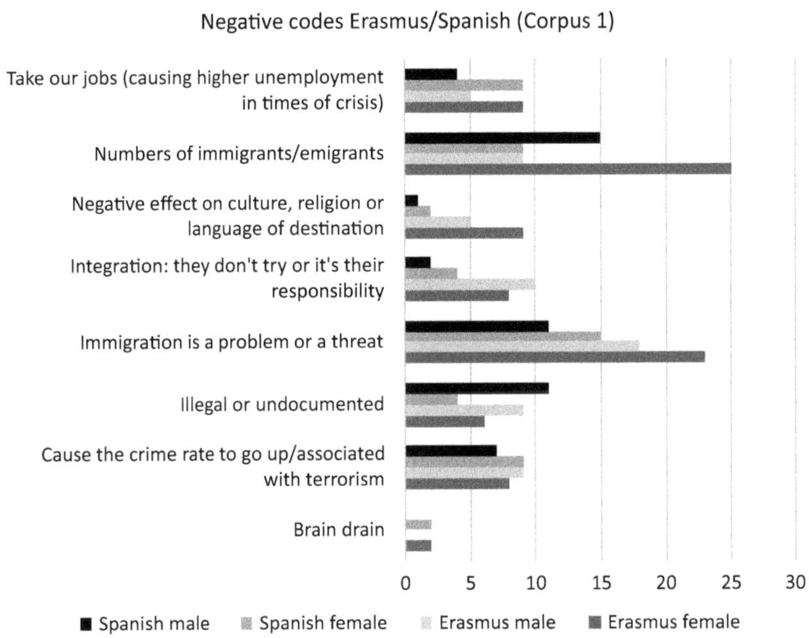

Fig. 12-4: Comparison negative codes Spanish and Erasmus students (Corpus 1).

The highest number involved two codes. First, the *numbers* of immigrants – that is, the excessive amount of immigrants arriving. Here are some examples. The language errors have not been corrected, thus all the quotes are shown as written by the students:

(1) The Czech Republic became an immigration country in 2009, two years ago and over the last twenty years the number of foreigners has increased thirteen-times [Erasmus female]
(2) France, the European country with huge rate of immigration. Some research, however it is hard to define, talks about 14 million people from other countries in France. [Spanish female]
(3) The result is that Slovenian people do not agree with such high level of immigrants [...] according to people's thinking there will be no original Slovenian population at all. [Erasmus female]
(4) Excessive flow of newcomers. [Erasmus male]

Second, almost as many comments were detected concerning the use of the terms *problem* or *threat* to describe immigration:

(5) All over the world the immigration is a big problem. [Erasmus female]
(6) Immigration causes problems. [Erasmus female]
(7) In my opinion immigration is one of the biggest problem in nowadays economy. [Erasmus male]
(8) With no doubts, immigration can be considered a threat. [Erasmus male]

However, it must be added that in nearly all the different groups in Corpus 1, negative reference was made to immigration as being a problem or threat.

Some of the other examples of negative attitudes with respect to immigration shown by the Erasmus females (although similar numbers are found for all groups) are:

a) Immigration causes the crime rate to go up/associated with terrorism:

(9) And increasing dangerous and criminality because of their nature. [Erasmus female]
(10) Crime is increasing because of the fact that the immigrants are often bad people who are criminals in their countries of origin. [Erasmus male]
(11) Nevertheless, we can see that crime increases in coordination with immigration. [Erasmus male]

b) Negative effect on culture, religion, language, and so on:

(12) The next problem is that Muslims build there mosques and thanks for it are changing habits and thinking of original French population. [Erasmus female]
(13) Specific local traditions are getting weaker. [Erasmus male]
(14) We must think about future, about saving national culture, traditions. [Erasmus male]

c) They take our jobs (similar number with Spanish females):

(15) It happens that some German people could not find any work because is ocupated by Turkish people. [Erasmus female]
(16) If immigrants stay in country, they have to start to work when want to live, so occupate our places where we can work. [Erasmus female]

d) Integration, they do not try (to integrate) or it is exclusively their responsibility:

(17) These people are inadaptable, living in own communities. [Erasmus female]
(18) So they often don't learn the German language and don't integrate into the whole society and this often lead to these more serious problems. [Erasmus female]
(19) Immigrants do not want to socialise and fail to participate in active life of the countries they live in. [Erasmus male]

Erasmus males and Spanish males have in common the following negative codes:

a) Mention of illegal or undocumented immigrants:

(20) In each country there are problems with illegal people. [Erasmus female]
(21) Illegal immigration which is really out of control. [Erasmus male]
(22) This illegal people when have arrived to their destination country they do not have nothing so is clear that they have to do something that many times are not legal. [Erasmus male]

b) The researchers had anticipated that the students would mention the idea of "brain drain" when describing the negative effect of migration. However, our results show that only 4 mentions are made by both Erasmus and Spanish groups in Corpus 1.

(23) A part of immigrants are people with formation, even with university studies, well prepared and with experience. [Erasmus female]
(24) Supply of young, active, sometimes skilled labor immigration into the country. [Erasmus female]

However, it must be said that we also notice a certain amount of empathy or understanding of the reasons that make people leave their home country to try to improve their economic conditions and that of their family, as we will see in the next section.

5.4 *Comparison of positive attitudes between Spanish and Erasmus students (Corpus 1)*

In Fig. 12-5, the positive attitudes reflected in the coding of the Spanish and Erasmus students contributing to Corpus 1 are compared. The positive codes in the compositions refer to the following concepts, dealt with below from the most to least frequent:

a) Migration is caused by the need to improve economic, social or political conditions. Female Erasmus students show the highest number, but with all the groups this is the highest:

(25) Many people in poor countries, which are adjacent to those rich leave their country with the prospect of acquiring wealth and achieving better standards of living and education. [Erasmus female]
(26) In most of cases people are immigrating for the reason of looking for better life in terms of getting a better, well-paid job. They are also seeking better social conditions. Reasons for immigrating can also be religious or political. [Erasmus female]
(27) They need to economic support for their families. [Erasmus female]
(28) Poverty and unemployment are said to be two major causes of immigration. [Erasmus female]
(29) They emigrate because of different reasons e.g. to find a job, better living conditions, more freedom to act out their religion and much more. [Erasmus female]

b) *Empathy* is shown in particular by Spanish males and to a lesser extent, Spanish females. On the contrary, there are fewer examples among Erasmus females and males. This would seem somewhat surprising since these students are on a study exchange and one would think this might broaden the mind and reduce intolerant attitudes:

(30) It seems that people who think in this way don't remember about the Spanish emigration in the 60's, when more than a million people had to moved mainly to another European countries, but also to America, looking for a job opportunity. [Spanish female]

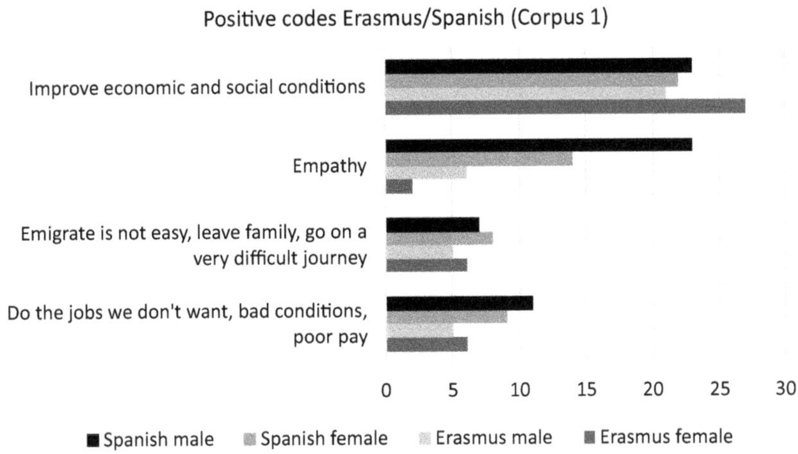

Fig. 12-5: Positive codes Spanish-Erasmus (Corpus 1).

(31) So we must bear in mind what it means to be an immigrant since we ourselves can be one of them very soon. [Spanish female]
(32) They come here and to other countries, and we have to help them like other people did in the past with us. [Spanish female]
(33) We, here in our warm home, don't have any idea about how difficult life has to be for one person to make the decision of leaving his country, leaving his home and all the things he knows, to get into an unknown country. [Spanish female]

We would add that although many of these positive codes give reasons for understanding why people actually migrate, the separate code empathy was added since this is a way of actually expressing "how would we feel if we were in their shoes" or "it could happen to us some day too".

5.5 Comparison of negative codes between Spanish groups (Corpus 1 and Corpus 2)

Turning to the data from Corpus 1 and 2 concerning the Spanish students (Fig. 12-6), the goal is to determine if there is a difference in the attitudes expressed by these groups considering the time lapse between the collection of the first corpus and the second, and taking into account the social changes that have taken place during that time, as mentioned previously.

Once more, the negative code with the highest number is "immigration as a problem or threat". However, with Spanish females there is a large drop in 2017, whilst this negative code among the Spanish males rose. Immigration being the "cause of rise in crime rate", dropped in Corpus 2 for both sexes. The idea that immigrants "take our jobs" is mentioned by Spanish females in both corpus, in fact, the number actually increases in Corpus 2 for this code, as it does in the case of the Spanish males too. Spanish females write more about illegal or undocumented migrants in 2017, Spanish males hardly mention this in Corpus 2. Regarding the "Brain drain" phenomenon, although hardly mentioned in Corpus 1, it appears more in Corpus 2 among both sexes:

(34) The case of emigrants from Spain, most of them have a high level of education, like masters or degrees, but they do not find a job that fits with their profiles or these jobs are not well paid. [Spanish female]

(35) Lot of good Spanish scientist and engineers has immigrated to other countries of the European Union looking for a job or better labor conditions. We are investing a lot of money to form a scientist, for example, and then he will migrate to other country, this is very harmful for Spain. [Spanish male]

(36) Spanish people living and working in other countries is also dangerous if we see it with other view, there are a lot of them that probably will live there for the rest of their lives and we will have loosed a worker in Spain, this is happening at this moment and politics don't know how to fix it. [Spanish male]

It is clear from these extracts that in 2017 young Spanish university students are seeing this phenomenon from a new angle; that is, they and their peers are now enduring what many other countries have been experiencing for decades with the mass emigration of their university graduates, researchers and skilled workers forced to migrate in order to seek a salary that would allow them to live in a dignified way or keep them away from long queues at unemployment offices.

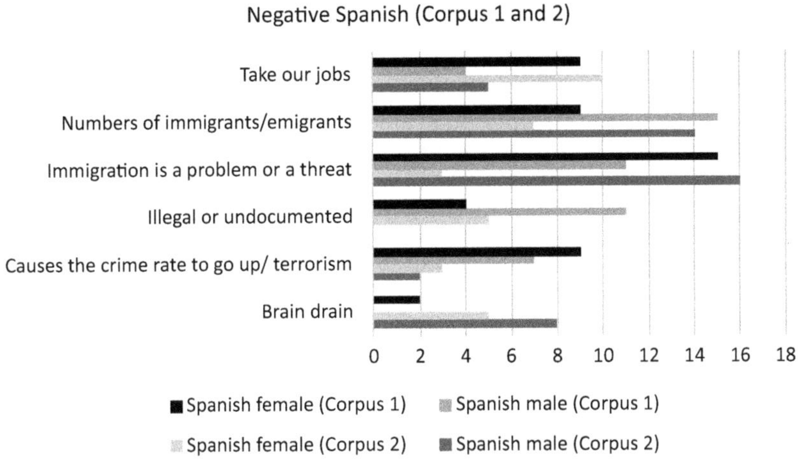

Fig. 12-6: Negative codes Spanish (Corpus 1 and Corpus 2).

5.6 Comparison of positive codes between Spanish groups (Corpus 1 and Corpus 2)

There are some notable differences when comparing positive attitudes among the Spanish students from Corpus 1 and 2 (Fig. 12-7).

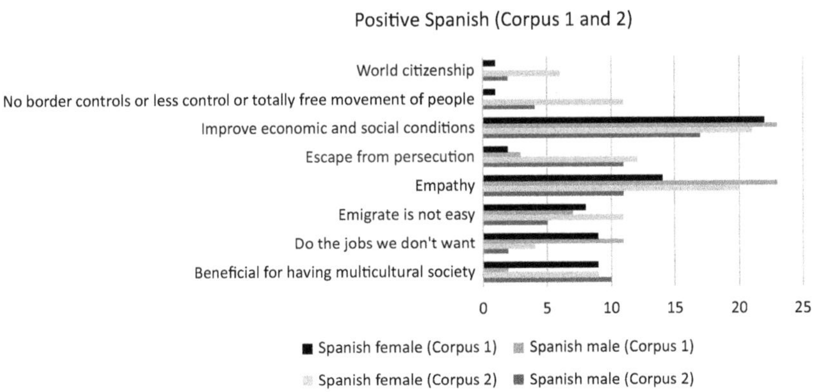

Fig. 12-7: Positive codes Spanish groups (Corpus 1 and Corpus 2).

To begin with, in Corpus 1, we see more empathy shown among the Spanish males, but when looking at the results from Corpus 2, it is the Spanish females who show much more empathy than the males and more than their female counterparts who contributed to Corpus 1. This includes thinking that "emigrating is not easy".

(37) If they left their country of birth, they will have not got much time to see their family and they can feel alone. Furthermore, they have to start new habits and it could be difficult because they should know the country's habits. [Spanish female]
(38) This people risk their lives in order to if they're lucky live normally on Spain, others are sold as slaves, returned to their countries with inhuman conditions or sometimes killed on the journey to Spain. [Spanish male]
(39) In general no one wants to abandon his home and restart his life, because, it implicates to know new people, cultures, style of life, food and a lot of new things. [Spanish female]

Both females and males understand that one of the main reasons for migrating is to improve economic and social conditions, although the figure drops in Corpus 2. Also, both males and females declare immigration is beneficial for having a multicultural society (not the case of the males in Corpus 1), and more consideration is given to the concept of migration as a means of escaping from persecution, mentioned in Corpus 1 but much more so in Corpus 2.

(40) Some old reasons are: hunger, diseases, unemployment, no living perspectives, war, civil violence, political pursue, poverty... and many immigrants want to restart their lives in another country. [Spanish male]
(41) They are absconding from drought, from working on nearly slavery conditions or wars. [Spanish female]

In fact, we have noted that one of the biggest differences as regards terminology in quantitative terms is that in Corpus 1, the word *refugee* is not used at all whereas in Corpus 2, it is used 45 times, often making specific reference to Syrians escaping from the war in their homeland.

(42) The refugees are people run away of her countries because in them there are wars and conflicts. [Spanish female]
(43) The difference that I see between an immigrant and a refugee is that the second are escaping from their country because it is probable that there is a war. [Spanish female]

(44) Syrian's people are a refugee. In their country there is a war, and they run away of Syrian. [Spanish female]

The Spanish females in our 2017 data seem to be *more radical* in that they support "no border controls", and show a belief in world citizenship.

(45) I think that the countries should open their borders. [Spanish female]
(46) I honestly believe that a more open world with less barriers where people consider themselves citizens of the world and could easily move from a country to another would be a better place. [Spanish female]
(47) Of all I have to say that all of us are world citizens. [Spanish male]
(48) I still seek for a world citizenship. [Spanish female]

6 Conclusion

The aim of this chapter was to analyse, describe and compare the attitudes to the phenomenon of immigration of 150 Spanish and visiting Erasmus University students attending a Spanish technically oriented university. Two different corpora were analysed: Corpus 1 contained compositions which were gathered between 2008 and 2013 and were divided into Spanish females and males and Erasmus females and males. Corpus 2 involved only Spanish students, gathered in 2017, and was also divided into females and males. ATLAS.ti was used for the analysis which allowed the researchers to carry out a qualitative-descriptive analysis of the young people's attitudes classifying these into three broad categories: positive, negative and neutral points of view.

Of the 880 quotations in both Corpus 1 and 2, there were more negative than positive comments made about immigration. Although there is not a great difference between the two, 40 % are negative, 32 % are positive: it is, however, the strong nature of some of the negative comments that is more striking.

In Corpus 1, Erasmus students are more negative, especially the females. It is noted that highly stereotyped attitudes that *requote* much of the anti-immigration discourse found among certain politicians and the mass media are used – that is, immigration as a problem/threat; the (too) high number of immigrants; how the immigrant population pushes the crime rate up; immigration as a threat to the in-groups' culture and identity; how they take our jobs and so on.

Regarding Spanish Corpus 1 and 2, the males show more empathy in Corpus 1, much less in Corpus 2, whilst the opposite happens with Spanish females. Negative comments dropped from 77 in Corpus 1 to 63 in Corpus 2, whilst positive comments rose from 77 (Corpus 1) to 98 (Corpus 2).

Turning to our initial hypothesis, during the period 2013–2017, the focus of the mass media in Spain became more *sympathetic* to the plight of the refugees especially after the impact of the photograph of little Aylan Kurdi lying dead on a Mediterranean beach. As a result, it would seem that the Spanish female group, as observed in their attitudes in Corpus 2, seem more conscious of the plight of millions who have to leave their homes in order to seek a safer and/or more dignified life in Europe. As we noted, there is now a specific reference made to refugees (mentioned 45 times), whereas in Corpus 1 there is no mention at all. This would seem to mirror the news coverage especially from 2015, as the students show that they are much more conscious of what being a refugee involves – that is, dangerous journeys in order to flee from wars, the so-called mafias who demand huge payments and then do not fulfill their promises of taking the refugees to safer shores; and perhaps more importantly, the empathy shown with the reflections they make referring to "how would you feel if you were in their shoes".

The results of our research indicate that there is a need to investigate gender differences and also societal, individual and media influences on attitudes to immigration especially among young people. There are many questions to be answered, perhaps starting with, where do young people get their news input from nowadays – that is, automatic news feeds, social networks, and so on since so few watch television.

Although no claim is made that our results are representative and can be extrapolated to other contexts, some of our findings are comparable to other studies in the field. López-Maestre/Scheu Lottgen (2003: 229) carried out a similar study and found that a "naturalized problematic view of immigration" prevailed in their students' compositions. These negative attitudes were expressed using different linguistic resources such as metaphors (Immigration as a war, Immigration as an enemy), lexical choice and modality, among others. They also concluded that the attitudes would appear to stem from what the writers have been exposed to in other discourses. Little attention is given to proposing solutions. However, in our study, it was found that some attitudes had changed over the years, and more empathy was shown, and possible solutions presented which were based on the idea of equality, social justice and a more critical analysis of the reasons people have for migrating.

As a follow-up to the present study, it would be interesting to be able to add to Corpus 2 more recent Erasmus exchange students' compositions in order to collate results with the Spanish group in Corpus 2 and also to see if these attitudes have also changed over time. Other aspects related to the corpus analysis that could provide interesting information would be to look in detail at modality, presuppositions, legitimization and metaphors, and lastly, the question of author's voice. Finally, we recommend addressing social issues such as immigration in language classrooms through critical discourse awareness (Prieto Ramos 2001), and through the development of the capabilities approach (like cosmopolitan citizenship, and so on) in foreign language classrooms (Rascón Moreno et al. 2013; Crosbie 2014).

References

Andreu Andres, Mª Ángeles/Astor Guardiola, Aurora/Boquera Matarredonda, María/MacDonald, Penny/Montero Fleta, Begoña/Pérez Sabater, Carmen 2010. Analysing EFL Learner Output in the MiLC Project: An Error *It's, But Which Tag? In Campoy, Mari Carmen/Bellés-Fortuño, Begoña/Gea-Valor, Maria Lluisa (eds.) *Corpus-Based Approaches to English Language Teaching*. London: Continuum, 167–180.

Arikan, Gizem/Bloom, Pazit Ben-Nun 2012. The Influence of Societal Values on Attitudes towards Immigration. *International Political Science Review* 34/2, 210–226.

Bergamaschi, Alessandro 2013. Adolescents and Prejudice: A Comparative Study of the Attitudes of Two European Adolescent Populations Regarding the Issues That Are Raised by Increasing Cultural and Religious Pluralism. *International Journal of Intercultural Relations* 37/3, 102–112.

Boomgaarden, Hajo G./Vliegenthart, Rens 2009. How News Content Influences Anti-Immigration Attitudes: Germany, 1993–2005. *European Journal of Political Research* 48/4 516–542.

Bridges, Sarah/Mateut, Simona 2014. Should They Stay or Should They Go? Attitudes towards Immigration in Europe. *Scottish Journal of Political Economy* 61/4, 397–429.

Buades Fuster, Josep/Díe Olmos, Luis/Melero Valdés, Luisa 2010. *Actitudes de los Valencianos y Valencianas ante la Población Inmigrante. Encuesta a Residentes en la Comunitat Valenciana con Nacionalidad Española*. Valencia: Fundación CeiMigra. <https://ec.europa.eu/migrant-integration/index.cfm?action=media.download&uuid=2A131C48-C1D8-1C56-E30EA53464009D01>.

Cachón Rodríguez, Lorenzo 2012. Marco Institucional de la Discriminación y Tipos de Inmigrantes en el Mercado de Trabajo en España. *Reis* 69/95, 105–124.

Centro de Investigaciones Sociales (CIS) 2018. *Estudio nº 3223. Barómetro de opinión*. Septiembre, 2018. <http://datos.cis.es/pdf/Es3223mar_A.pdf>.

Crosbie, Veronica 2014. Cosmopolitan Capabilities in the HE Language Classroom. *Journal of Social Science Education* 13/2, 24–38.

Davidov, Eldad/Cieciuch, Jan/Meuleman, Bart/Schmidt, Peter/Algesheimer, René/Hausherr, Mirjam 2015. The Comparability of Measurements of Attitudes toward Immigration in the European Social Survey: Exact versus Approximate Measurement Equivalence. *Public Opinion Quarterly* 79/S1, 244–266.

Domke, David/McCoy, Kelley/Torres, Marcos 1999. News Media, Racial Perceptions and Political Cognition. *Communication Research* 26/5, 570–607.

Duriez, Bart/Soenens, Bart 2009. The Intergenerational Transmission of Racism: The Role of Right-Wing Authoritarianism and Social Dominance Orientation. *Journal of Research in Personality* 43/5, 906–909.

El País 2007. *Los Valencianos Consideran La Inmigración Positiva y Al Mismo Tiempo Su Mayor Problema*. 7 October 2007, 34–35. <https://elpais.com/diario/2007/10/07/cvalenciana/1191784678_850215.html>.

Green, Eva G.T. 2007. Guarding the Gates of Europe: A Typological Analysis of Immigration Attitudes across 21 Countries. *International Journal of Psychology* 42/6, 365–379.

Hainmueller, Jens/Hiscox, Michel J. 2007. Educated Preferences: Explaining Attitudes toward Immigration in Europe. *International Organization* 61/2, 399–442.

Hooghe, Marc 2004. Political Socialization and the Future of Politics. *Acta Politica* 39/4, 331–341.

Hooghe, Marc/Wilkenfeld, Britt 2008. The Stability of Political Attitudes and Behaviors across Adolescence and Early Adulthood: A Comparison of Survey Data on Adolescents and Young Adults in Eight Countries. *Journal of Youth and Adolescence* 37/2, 155–167.

Igartua, Juan José/Humanes, Maria Luisa/Muñiz, Carlos/Cheng, Lifen/Mellado, Claudia/Medina, Eudomary/Erazo, Maria de los Ángeles 2004. La Información sobre Inmigración e Inmigrantes en la Prensa Española. ¿Barreras Mediáticas a la Integración o Imágenes que Generan Xenofobia? Paper presented at *Diálogo Comunicación y Diversidad Cultural. Forum 2004*, Barcelona, 24–27 May. <http://www.portalcomunicacion.com/dialeg/paper/pdf/110_igartua.pdf>.

Igartua, Juan José/Muñiz, Carlos/Cheng, Lifen 2005. La Inmigración en la Prensa Española. Aportaciones Empíricas y Metodológicas desde la Teoría del Encuadre Noticioso. *Migraciones* 17, 143–181.

Lippmann, Walter 1922. *Public Opinion*. New York: Harcourt, Brace and Co.

López-Maestre, María D./Scheu Lottgen, Dagmar 2003. Students' Discourse on Immigration. Attitudes and Ideological Values: A Critical View. *International Journal of English Studies* 3/1, 209–233.

Markaki, Yvonni/Longhi, Simonetta 2013. What Determines Attitudes to Immigration in European Countries? An Analysis at the Regional Level. *Migration studies* 1/27, 311–337.

Migration Observatory 2011. *Thinking behind the Numbers: Understanding Public Opinion on Immigration in Britain*. University of Oxford. URL: www.migrationobservatory.ox.ac.uk

Muñiz-Muriel, Carlos/Igartua Perosanz, Juan José/Otero Parra, José Antonio/Sánchez Hernández, Citlali 2008. El Tratamiento Informativo de la Inmigración en los Medios Españoles: Un Estudio Comparativo de la Prensa y Televisión. *Perspectivas de la Comunicación* 1/1, 97–112.
Oliver, Mary Beth 1999. Caucasian Viewers' Memory of Black and White Criminal Suspects in the News. *Journal of Communication* 49/3, 46–60.
Peffley, Mark/Shields, Todd/Williams, Bruce 1996. The Intersection of Race and Crime in Television News Stories: An Experimental Study. *Political Communication* 13/3, 309–327.
Prieto Ramos, Fernando 2001. Why Do *they* Hit the Headlines? Critical Media Literacy in the Foreign Language Class. *Journal of Intercultural Studies* 22/1, 33–49.
Rascón Moreno, Diego/Díaz Perez, Francisco Javier/Díez Bedmar, María Belén./García Ramírez, Paola 2013. *Developing Global Citizenship Competence in English Studies: A Proposal of Activities*. Muenchen: Lincom.
Reindes, Heinz 2003. Politische Sozialisation in der Adoleszenz. Eine Re-Interpretation quantitativer Längsschnittuntersuchungen in Deutschland. *Zeitschrift für Entwicklungspsychologie und Pädagogische Psychologie* 35/2, 98–110.
Sonck, Nathalie/Loosveldt, Geert 2010. Impact of Poll Results on Personal Opinions and Perceptions of Collective Opinion. *International Journal of Public Opinion Research* 22/2, 230–255.
Stephan, Walter G./Lausanne, C. Renfro/Esses, Victoria/Stephan, Cookie White/Martin, Tim 2005. The Effects of Feeling Threatened on Attitudes towards Immigrants. *International Journal of Intercultural Relations* 29/1, 1–19.
Van Dijk, Teun 1993. *Elite Discourse and Racism*. Newbury Park, CA: Sage.
Vergeer, Maurice/Lubbers, Marcel/Scheepers, Peer 2000. Exposure to Newspapers and Attitudes towards Ethnic Minorities: A Longitudinal Analysis. *Howard Journal of Communication* 11/2, 127–143.
Zapata-Barrero, Ricard 2009. Policies and Public Opinion Towards Immigrants: The Spanish Case. *Ethnic and Racial Studies* 32/7, 1101–1120.

Silvia Molina-Plaza/Samira Allani

Multimodal Women Engineers' Identity Construction

1 Introduction

The link between multimodality, social semiotics and social concerns forms the nexus of this chapter. In what follows, we intend to explore the ways in which linguistic and visual semiotic resources are deployed for the representation of women engineers in their professional identities. Different studies suggest that women are under-represented in Science, Technology, Engineering and Mathematics (STEM) fields as in the workforce (McIlwee/Robinson 1992; Hill/Corbett/St. Rose 2010). According to the International Labor Organization (ILO) report *The gender gap in employment: What's holding women back* published in December 2017 and updated in March 2018, there are different barriers holding women back from finding a decent job. The current global labor force participation rate for women is close to 49 % whereas it is 75 % for men (International Labor Organization 2019).

This difference of percentage points becomes even more striking in the context of engineering. Although the number of women in engineering has grown in the past thirty years all over the world, it is still unclear why there are not as many women as men working in engineering. The current situation in the UK is that the number of women in engineering is just 11 %, one of the lowest rates in Europe. Several studies, colleges, universities and organizations want to redress this imbalance and foster gender diversity and inclusion in the engineering field (Faulkner 2000; Cameron 2006; Hatmaker 2012). One of the pioneering organizations is *The Women's Engineering Society* (WES) in the United Kingdom, a professional network of women engineers, scientists and technologists offering inspiration, support and professional development almost for one hundred years.

WES is an attempt to overcome different levels of barriers women face in engineering: system, institutional and interpersonal barriers (Wyer 2003) by building a social support network that aims to create a diverse engineering community. This network functions as a meaning-making social practice as well, a means of controlling the selection of certain structural possibilities and the retention of this over time, a type of *marketization* of women as engineers. The medium used for supporting women to achieve their potential as professional engineers and technical leaders is through its website. We analyze this issue in sections 3.1 and 3.2 below.

Several studies (Perry/Bodkin 2000; Askehave/Nielsen 2005) have paid attention to the features of web genres that can be used to specific communicative purposes. These include marketing, reputation management and legitimizing stance. WES website is an internet-based multimedia genre that women engineers have designed to communicate with one another and with the public. Its multimodal rhetorical strategy is based on a simultaneous interplay between two systems: *conceptual* or verbal, and *perceptual* or visual (see Rinn 2014), which interrelate with sound (videos) and web design. The overall aim is that women engineers identify with WES ethos and spirit. This website promotes *performing identities* – that is, actions successful women engineers do to perform their public selves, which may also help other women to increase their visibility (Lemke 2013).

Against this general framework, we will investigate the different multimodal communicative strategies used by WES to present women engineers and, in particular, we will focus on data from several webpages devoted to the home page and role models section. By introducing multimodal analysis, this chapter shows how WES tries to persuade the engineering community by co-deploying different modes of communication of professional engineering – verbal and visual semiotic resources – in order to make women more salient both in the conceptual (linguistic) and perceptual (imagistic and aural) systems. Both systems interact on the meaning-making practices of this activist and networking website.

2 Multimodality as a framework of analysis

Multimodality has become an established research area for linguistically informed discourse analysis for the last decade (Unsworth 2001, Unsworth/Cleirigh 2009; O'Halloran 2004; Baldry/Thibault 2006; Kress/van Leeuwen 2006; Bateman 2008; Lemke 2013; Scollon/Scollon 2014). It seems clear that messages using different modes are more persuasive than monomodal texts (Bateman 2008).

This study adopts a socio-semiotic perspective. In particular, we use Halliday's (2004) meta-functions and Kress and van Leeuwen's (2006) notions of visual grammar to examine visual and textual resources. For the ideational metafunction, Kress and van Leeuwen differentiate between narrational and conceptual visuals. The former visually depict some action whereas the latter show a kind of classification or analysis. The interpersonal metafunction deals with the construal of social relationships, whereby language creates our social collective as well as personal being (Halliday/Matthiessen 1999). For the textual metafunction, attention will be paid to salience and framing. Salience is determined as based on the identification of visual cues that enhance verbal language (Machin 2007). Framing starts from a decision to mark and/or delimit a *space* (material or conceptual) which establishes a concern at a particular socio-political level. Both framing and salience help to explain the multimodal representation of women engineers as active social actors and their social action (van Leeuwen 2008).

Finally yet importantly, two key areas in website creation are explored following Baldry and Thibault's (2006) multimodal analysis and Djonov's (2007) website study from a systemic perspective. Baldry and Thibault (2006: 104) describe the webpage as a "*visual-spatial unit* displayed in a computer screen" with a dynamic and interactive interface between the computer user and the possibilities of the website as a whole. They put forward two relevant concepts for our investigation:

(i) the *Resource Integration Principle,* a tight integration of the verbal, the visual and the spatial, which enhances communicative impact; and
(ii) *cluster analysis*, local groupings of information in a webpage that contribute to multimodal meaning-making at a micro and macro-level.

Baldry and Thibault (2006) also pay attention to *contrasts* between meaning-making modes. These contrasts require us to analyze these layers of meaning as separate and yet connected elements. Consideration of these layers requires epistemological and ideological understanding as activated by the content (professional engineering in this case) and context (the role of women engineers in engineering). Both context and content are co-constitutive processes, each making and reinforcing one another.

Djonov's (2007) study claims that not all webpages and navigation options within a website enjoy the same status. This understanding underpins the notion of *website hierarchy*, a concept highly discussed in professional hypermedia design and usability literature, and also a central concept in the analysis of websites. There are two dominant perspectives to this concept:

(i) the *segmental perspective*, that focuses on individual pages and their distance from the homepage; and
(ii) the *holistic perspective,* whereby the highest level in a website hierarchy is the website as a whole, followed by its sections and subsections.

Because of the seemingly irreconcilable nature of these two perspectives, this scholar proposes a reconceptualization of website hierarchy by adducing the notion of *hierarchy of Themes* as based on the tenets of Systemic Functional Linguistics (SFL). As a central notion in SFL, the hierarchy of Themes represents a key point in the interpretation of textual meaning. Theme is regarded as crucial in the organization of text and the coherence of its message. Indeed, according to Martin (1992) the hierarchy of themes can account for the levels of textual structure of complex texts; it can hence be considered a valuable tool for the analysis of websites and their expandability (Djonov 2007).

3 Study aims and analysis of the home page and role models sections

Our research aims are to examine how multimodal semiotic resources are integrated in the website and how these features interact as a complex discourse strategy for representing women engineers as competent professionals.

We therefore draw upon the hierarchy of Themes in our analysis of the WES homepage (<https://www.wes.org.uk/>) and explore its construction of meaning and its structuring of information. In our analysis, we consider the homepage first as the highest-level macro-Theme for the WES website and then as the multimodal unit in focus. Next we examine its most salient elements which act as macro-Themes. We also focus on the role models section, which encourages other women to find out what it is like to be a woman in engineering, science and technology.

To ensure a correct understanding of what follows, this section provides information on the data we work with. First, we briefly summarize how a homepage works and discuss the main features of the WES homepage. Second, we analyze two cases of role model women represented within the Role Models section of the WES website. We have focused on the general layout and the distribution of visual and textual elements (pictures, narratives and videos that characterize the global structure of these webpages). More specifically, we pay attention to rhetorical values attached to visual elements, such as colors, layout, pictures and main tabs, and textual elements. We also pay attention to the communicative purpose – that is, storytelling (when texts include the stories of "real women engineers"), addresses to the reader and keywords used.

3.1 Homepage

As a user's point of entry to the website and its meanings (Baldry/Thibault 2006), homepages play an essential role in conveying the aims and functions of websites. Their elements and arrangement carry more than mere information. They establish the *interpersonal appeal* and its *indexing of social values* (Baldry/Thibault 2006: 119).

Since a homepage is the point of departure in the users' orientation within the website (see fig. 13-1), its appraisal is highly determined by the interaction between content organization, design and navigation options. These elements pinpoint the path aimed for users to take and the meaning they should construct. Their arrangement reflects a certain

Multi-level Masthead: Two clusters of navigation bars	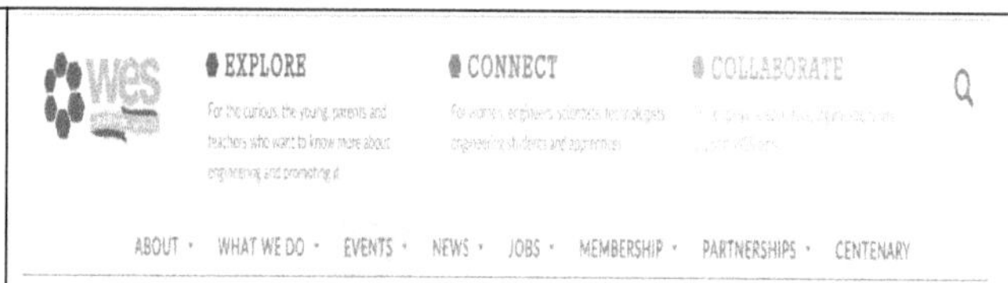
Central area: Image Slider with automatic scrolling	
Whitespace devoted to highlighting a higher-level theme: Role Models for the community of women engineers	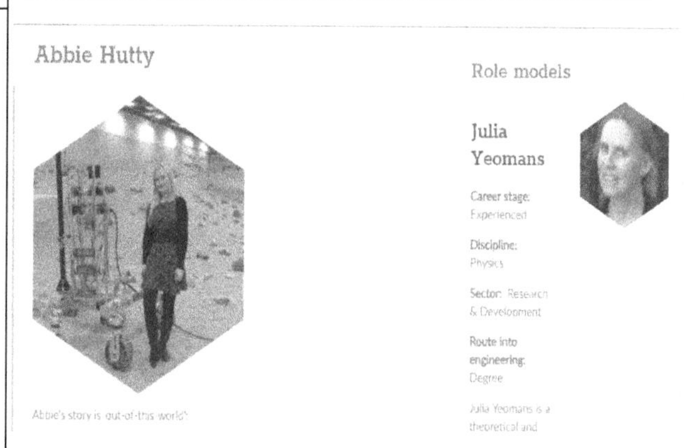
Multiple footers	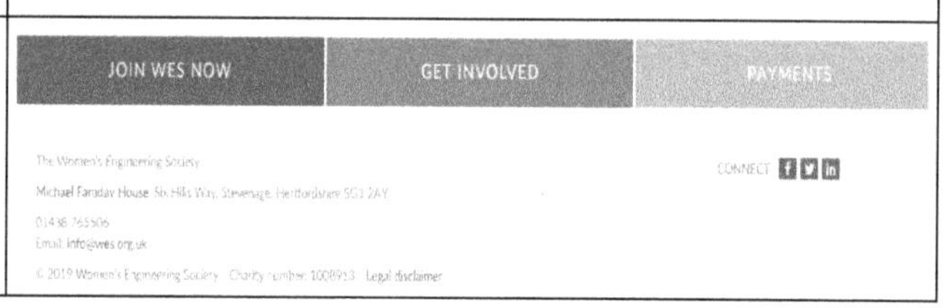

Fig. 13-1: WES page homepage analysis.

hierarchy of Themes, as in SFL textual meaning analysis (Djonov 2007). This notion refers to the scaffolding of information flow in written texts.

In our analysis of the multimodal meaning enacted within the WES homepage, we have focused on two areas. The first area is concerned with the design features contributing to the creation of the web message(s) through visual and linguistic elements. The second area investigates the hierarchy of themes signaled by these features and its potential in revealing not only how content is structured and made coherent in the website but, more importantly, what elements are chosen as ideational points of departure for its message.

3.2 The design of the WES homepage

The main features signaling the organization of the content of the WES homepage are the multi-level header, or what is referred to as masthead, the central area that features an image-slider and the multi-level footers. In the masthead, there are two navigation bars divided into two clusters, one at the top and the other one right below. In the top cluster, the logo of the WES organization is placed on the left side, three hyperlink anchors are in the middle and a website search icon is on the right side. The second cluster is a navigational dropdown menu that leads to seven main multi-layered sections.

The top cluster comes across as more salient than the one below, thanks to its marked typography with the use of all-caps and the colors of WES. The cluster brings together a landmark (the logo) and fully fledged call to action hyperlink anchors, which read as follows: EXPLORE, CONNECT, and COLLABORATE in big capital letters creating salience. The choice of the Call to Action, a well-known strategy in marketing, is probably intended to prompt the users' immediate response, first by guiding them in their website navigation and then by encouraging them to engage with the WES projects and mission. The design and word choice of these anchors help to shape an identity filled with energy and action. Indeed, the imperative mood in the three hypertext anchors makes up an upfront message or even perhaps a straightforward request to action which fulfills the website highest interpersonal meta-function: that of changing the social reality of women engineers.

As for the vibrant color scheme embodying the WES identity, the choice is not arbitrary. The selection of violet, green and white is a revealing indication of activism. Indeed, these colors were the colors of the women's suffrages movements in the USA and Britain. The colors represent liberty and dignity and evoke women's struggle for equal rights. Some graphic designers classify these colors if combined as clashing colors, as they come opposite to each other on the color wheel. Clashing colors tend to have a positive effect, however, thanks to their high visibility pairings, which demand attention and create salience. The choice of colors in WES and their use in hyperlink anchors create a powerful marker of identity, as they rely on a prevailing resource for constructing textuality through cohesion and contrast (van Leeuwen 2011). The design choices in color and typography are used ideationally to represent both actions and values. The hyperlink anchors not only prompt users to action, but also transmit the values and attributes of the women engineers who attempt to build better positions for their community with their struggle for social recognition and equality.

3.3 The hierarchy of Themes in WES homepage

WES homepage is examined using the hierarchy of Themes as an analytic tool (Djonov 2007; Knox 2014). Indeed, the structure of a website is modeled as a hierarchy of Themes where coherence is created by packaging information into unified wholes (website sections). Accordingly, the homepage is considered the highest-level macro-Theme (Djonov 2007), since it is the entry point for the website and determines what and how content is accessible.

The hierarchy of Themes is determined by closely examining the homepage main elements, technically referred to as *anchors*, which are the visible and clickable words in the webpage. As a tool for orientation, the homepage reveals the kinds of strategies used to walk users through the content of the WES website. Figure 13-2 shows the hierarchy of Themes enacted in the WES website, signaled by the position allotted to each subsection and its degree of salience in the homepage.

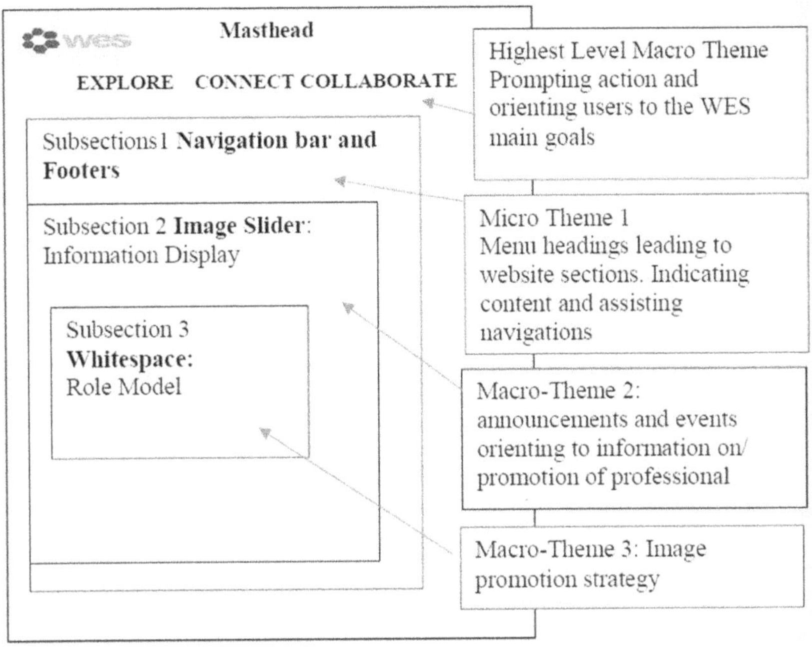

Fig. 13-2: WES website hierarchy of themes signaled in the homepage.

The analysis reveals four main clusters in the homepage acting as the macro-Themes for the WES homepage and equally pointing to the hierarchy of Themes in the whole website. The first cluster consists of hyperlink anchors appearing both at the top and at the bottom of the page and is identified as the highest-level Macro-Theme. This cluster seems to bind the website sections together and to reveal its main mission. The three remaining macro-Theme-clusters also show how information, projects and values are organized in the website and the best ways that users should follow to grasp and engage with them.

The highest-level macro-Theme appears in the masthead (top page) and in the bottom page and consists of hyperlink anchors verbalized in the imperative mood. Three of these anchors are located at the top: EXPLORE, CONNECT, COLLABORATE, and each one is mirrored by an equivalent hyperlink anchor at the bottom of the page: JOIN WES, GET INVOLVED, DONNATE. Bolding and size of these anchors produce emphasis on the screen. Thus, they invite different website users to delve into the resources put forward by WES and get involved with its enterprise. Apparently, each hyperlink anchor is devoted to a specific kind of audience, as it goes along with a small print line indicating the target group of people in each section. The first anchor EXPLORE, for instance, leads to the subsection devoted to informing the general public about engineering and the opportunities opened up through this profession: "Engineers work together to create solutions that help others. An important part of being an engineer is caring about the world around you and wanting to change it for the better". The use of the imperative tense in this macro-Theme signals an interpersonal meta-function that seeks to engage web users in the pursuit of gender equality among engineers. This highest-level macro-Theme with three anchors, voiced through a call-to action approach, underscores the urge to campaign for women engineers and to upgrade their social and professional positions.

Macro-Theme 1 corresponds to both the navigation bar below the masthead and the web links located in the footer. The drop-down navigation bar outlines the website sections and subsections. Macro-Theme 2 is located in the center of the homepage and consists of an image slider, which is a design feature allowing multiple messages to be displayed in the same space. The slider offers eight visual features, each combining image with words (writing) to publicize professional events. The first slide placed at the top enacts as Theme to the ones embedded. This slide uses multimodal resources to announce a campaign called *WE50* aiming at raising awareness of the discrepancy between the number of men *versus* women in engineering professions. The interaction of these multimodal choices in the image slider area allows WES to promote professional events while bringing the users' attention to its role as a reliable information and networking source for women engineers.

Interestingly, macro-Theme 3 comes underneath the slider, combines image and words and takes a highly visible position in the homepage. Located in an unmarked portion of the homepage, technically referred to as *whitespace*, this macro-theme serves to signal an important section in the website named *Role Models*. The section aims to inspire the website visitors with biographical information on successful women engineers and is thematically signaled in the homepage via a hypertext icon. This hypertext, verbalized in an imperative statement

("Browse through our inspiring role model pages") invites users to learn from success stories, hence realizes an interpersonal function of the message. Nonetheless, *Role Models* as a macro-theme does not only point to the aforementioned subsection, but it also displays a powerful preview of a successful woman engineer, named Abbie Hutty. An aerospace engineer involved in a mission to Mars, and a selected ambassador for women in STEM fields, Ms. Hutty acts as an introductory element and contributes to predicting a set of hyper-themes (Martin 1992) located in the Role model section. By foregrounding a role model example in the homepage, its high level position in the hierarchy of Themes and the importance of its visibility for WES are signaled. This strategic choice serves the values and highest mission of WES and plays a valuable role in the image promotion of women engineers in general.

The WES homepage fulfills the fundamental aims of a homepage, by successfully establishing the mission of the website, guiding visitors to its main parts and clearly revealing its options for navigation. The analysis shows that, undeniably, the homepage offers an optimum orientation to the users of the WES website.

3.4 Role Models section

Following on from the previous section, we further explore the topic of role models for women engineers and examine how their social identities, roles and relationships are constructed and represented through the multimodal interplay of (i) static photos and recorded videos; and (ii) textual and visual displays of engineers in their settings. We seek to establish who is represented in which mode; whether women engineers are endowed with active or passive discourse roles and their discursive practices. Indeed, when clicking on the Role Models section, the user sees a vivid short paragraph describing the active role of engineers in society with adjectives of positive axiology:

> Engineering is all around us, and so are engineers – **practical, imaginative, sociable and innovative** people who design, make and improve hidden components like electronic circuits through to large scale complexes like the Hong Kong

> airport. What is it like to be a woman in engineering, science and technology? Find out by exploring some of our inspiring role models here. [Bold added]

The data in this study comes from a sample of the ten analyzed testimonies. This section shows with practical examples what it is like to be a woman in engineering, science and technology. Each testimony has an average of 700–1,000 words and the typical structure consists of a biodata, motivation and finally advice to other women.

The information in this webpage is neatly organized into three sections and targets specific audiences: career stage (student, early career, mid-career, experienced, retired, legend, other); sector (communications, mining, etc.) and engineering discipline. The central role of identity in workplace interactions – that is, how people perceive themselves and their colleagues at work – has been the subject of several studies (e.g. Angouri/Marra 2011; Schnurr 2013; Schnurr/Zayts 2017). This is also the case for women engineers, who need to construct and negotiate their own professional identities in everyday interactions as they position themselves in relation to their male colleagues. While constructing their identities as engineers, women try to become insiders and gain a sense of belonging among their male colleagues (Hatmaker 2012).

This view of identity as "something people do and not just what they are" (Widdicombe 1998: 191) will be explored in two examples: Julie Yeomans and Abbie Hutty. Both will try to capture the complexities involved in the multimodal and discursive processes of identity construction and negotiation. In this role models section, the most straightforward way of organizing information is to put old information in theme position and new information towards the end of the theme. Besides, the thematic development, which follows the notion of stack structure introduced by Nash (1980), lists facts that are piled up, as it were, to support a position.

Three features stand out in these webpages; first, the layout is vertical, with hyperlinks included alongside long chunks of texts, which conveys a certain static impression; second, the fairly limited number of sentences, triggering non-linear reading (Askehave/Nielsen 2005) and third, there are very few pictures, which only focus on women engineers at the forefront of technological innovation.

Fig. 13-3: Julia Yeomans' public image in the Role Models section.

3.5 Julia Yeomans

This page is centered on Professor Yeomans, a leading physicist (see Fig. 13-3). Her photo and its positioning in the center of the page make her the most salient object within the visual field of this page. She stands out markedly against the predominantly white background. Her smiling face attracts the viewer's attention. There is a bio note beside her photo, informing that Julia is an expert Physics Professor researching in the fields of soft condensed matter and biophysics (ideational function).

The interplay of the written text and the visual is conservative, following the conventions for the production of an academic curriculum vitae (cv). In fact, it reminds of the traditional printed version of a cv. The cv informs the viewer about her achievements and leading discoveries in Physics. The white background is an unmarked modal selection (Kress/van Leeuwen 2006), characteristic of scientific journals for experts.

From a discourse point of view, two ideational categories are worthy of mention in her bio note: a) the analysis of keywords and material process verbs and clauses. The former is used in this bio in order to zoom into areas of interest for engineers: (apprenticeship, research, direct, organize, expertise, etc.) and give cohesion to Yeomans' cv; the latter are material process verbs ("runs a research group") and relational clauses ("She is a member of the Advisory Panel"). Both material and relational processes represent her as relatively powerful and responsible for research actions. As a senior scholar, she includes her research interests, publications and committee memberships. This finding is consistent with Hyland and Tse's (2012) study. Interestingly, a rhetorical strategy is the recourse to impersonal references to Julia Yeomans through the use of third person. It is a formal communication strategy, more focused on information rather than on interaction with the viewer.

In addition to this bio note, two hyperlinks are located at the bottom of her role model's webpage, enabling the user to act upon the webpage. These links combine the visual and the textual mode by showing her expertise as a top physicist, giving a lecture at University and at the same time the viewer can access her professional biodata posted on the prestigious Royal Society website.

Her lecture, titled *Nature's engines: powering life* (34' 52"), illustrates how she constructs and negotiates her identity as Physics Professor (interpersonal function). The textual function orders the interconnected flow of both *ideational and interpersonal* meanings to compose a coherent lecture in this video. She portrays herself as a recognized expert and active participant in her field with a technical-scientific semantic register. In addition, her short, analytical sentences focused on processes and graphs to support her explanation demonstrate her linguistic self-confidence. As Julia is oriented to her students, she frequently uses "okay" at the end of utterances, checking understanding in an informal way. This salient use of a transition device facilitates communication, as a standard positive politeness discourse strategy used in the context of lecturing.

From a multimodal perspective, the meaning of the participant is established by de-emphasizing detail. Julia is gazing at her students and the blackboard. Her body posture and facial expression are relaxed and concentrated; Julia is portrayed as a woman in control, focusing on her teaching and her engagement with students. Her close proxemics to the blackboard reveals that she is well aware of being recorded; she is shown as a social actor acting in the world.

Textually, the hyperlinks for social media sharing in the bottom cluster take on visual salience. They are separated off to some extent from the video, thereby encouraging the user to share this information in different social networks.

Interpersonally, Yeomans' role model page has potential for dialogic engagement with the reader, as it evokes a positive response from the viewer. Professor Yeomans is a reassuring and welcoming professional figure, member of one of the most prestigious universities in the world, Oxford University. The meanings and values of her social practice are negotiated and hybridized. The communicative aim is to create public interest and recruiting young women for STEM disciplines.

3.6 Abbie Hutty

Ms. Abbie Hutty is a mechanical engineer who is building a Mars Rover to be launched in 2020 (see Fig. 13-4). She is also a STEM ambassador to address the lack of understanding about engineering careers.

Fig. 13-4: Abbie Hutty's public image in the Role Models section.

Her webpage is structured as a mini-narrative: it explains her background, how she got into engineering and what she does. As Kress and Van Leeuwen (2006) put it, this is a composite multimodal website comprising text-image combinations, the latter being photos and videos. These parts are interacting and affecting one another, as we will try to explain below.

She is presented in the webpage as a heroine, regarded by WES as worthy of emulation. The upper section containing Huttie's photo is presented as *the ideal* (Holsanova/Holmberg/Holmqvist 2006; Kress/ van Leeuwen 2006), whereas the lower section text is perceived as specific, informative and practical, and presented as *the real*. The picture on top is taken at the lab, next to her Mars Rover prototype. The image is salient because it attracts the viewer's attention to this robot created by a young engineer. The framing distinguishes her from the outer world. Her photograph is in a relationship of intersemiotic repetition (Royce 2007) with the text describing her Mars Rover project, and engages the reader with the rest of her narrative. The general belief that STEM careers are difficult is challenged with this image of a successful female engineer involved in an exciting Mars Mission to be launched in 2020.

Multimodality implies the multi-tiered complexity of this webpage. The analysis of Halliday's (2004) three meta-functions provides a useful dimension to organize the meaning in this webpage. The ideational function of Hutty's role model text corresponds to what this text is and does: it is a first-hand account of how she decided to become a mechanical engineer and her narrative is adapted to the lay public. This popularization of engineering knowledge to adapt this communicative event and the constraints of the webpage is referred to as "recontextualization" by Calsamiglia and van Dijk (2004: 370). Abbie Hutty carries out a creative narrative, which implies more than terminological adjustments. She considers the public prior's knowledge on mechanical engineering and tries to arouse her audience interest by creating a scenario which might engage with other young students, in order to attract them to this engineering discipline. The interpersonal function corresponds to the professional identity projected by her own account in written mode and hyperlinks. The viewer gets to know she is the youngest ever Fellow of the Institution of Mechanical Engineers. Finally, the textual function corresponds to how the other two are presented in the webpage. Abbie uses the first person to recount her personal experience and trajectory and also the pronoun "you", coupled with connotative lexis (highlighted in bold in the verbatim quotation below) in the final part of her written account so as to relate to her personal feelings:

> To anyone who is thinking about a career in engineering I'd say find something that **inspires** you, and go for it. There are so many **exciting** fields that you can get into- and all of them are keen to recruit **passionate**, able new staff. [Bold added]

This choice of first person and second person pronouns stand in sharp contrast with the use of third person or impersonal constructions in other role model accounts. It seems that younger engineers prefer less neutral communication strategies, focused on interaction rather than just neutral information.

4 Concluding remarks

WES webpages are flexible tools and their analysis cannot be dissociated from the cultural context in which they are embedded. This context is neatly summarized by WES as follows:

> Since its inception, WES has worked to try to ensure that women have the opportunities to work and to be educated, campaigning for equal rights, equal education and equal pay in a sector which remains heavily male dominated. Today, only 11 % of the British engineering workforce is female, yet women have played and continue to play a significant role in the field. The upsurge of interest in women's history in 2018 with the celebration of the centenary of the achievement of partial female suffrage makes the case that women's part in changing society is of great interest and inspiration and must not be allowed to be forgotten.

Turning now to our research aims, this study has identified and critically discussed how women engineers present themselves in the UK. With regard to the integration of multimodal resources, we have found that the information provided by each mode (verbal, visual and aural) is combined skillfully at different given points in the webpages. Their conceptual system revolves on three sections of the website that make WES discourse persuasive, according to the rhetorical strategy of the EXPLORE-CONNECT-COLLABORATE model. The EXPLORE link tries to attract students to STEM careers by explaining what engineers do. The CONNECT section aims at the networking and adherence of the audience to active involvement and lastly, the COLLABORATE hyperlink tries to encourage work in partnership with other women. All these sections try to engage the addressee both visually (using big capital letters with bolding) and conceptually (including relevant information).

WES website tries to link women engineers as members of a wider social network because the website re-contextualizes the participant roles and activities that engineers do. Besides, it builds connections with other texts and media, using hyperlinks and different modes or channels. This integration of channels serves to provide coherence to the different sections of the website, enabling the viewer to establish relations between them to construct a global meaning of what it means for women to work in different engineering fields. Regarding our second claim that multimodal cues (verbal, visual and aural) act as a complex discourse strategy, we have observed that this website uses all the resources (verbal and non-verbal) consciously. This builds and interprets the discourses about women engineers in a positive light, within the appropriate context, and creates a persuasive message within the engineering community and companies.

No doubt, the study of websites is a complex task, as many factors are to be taken into account in their construction by discourse participants – in this case, WES members. The study of this website has enabled a fine-grained analysis of some of the multimodal tools used on this new emerging genre, which is professional websites. However, it is obvious that further research could focus on other corporate websites of engineering companies in order to better understand how they construct women engineers' identities and enhance to the modeling of multimodal websites analysis.

Acknowledgments

We gratefully acknowledge Elizabeth Donnelly's and Professor Julia Yeomans' permission to reproduce images from the Women's Engineering Society website.

References

Angouri, Jo/Marra, Meredith (eds.) 2011. *Constructing Identities at Work*. Basingstoke, Hampshire: Palgrave McMillan.

Askehave, Inger/Nielsen, Anne E. 2005. Digital Genres: A Challenge to Traditional Genre Theory. *Information Technology & People* 18/2, 120–141.

Baldry, Anthony/Thibault, Peter, P. 2006. *Multimodal Transcription and Text Analysis*. London: Equinox.

Bateman, John 2008. *Multimodality and Genre: A Foundation for the Systematic Analysis of Multimodal Documents*. New York: Palgrave Macmillan.

Calsamiglia, Helena/van Dijk, Teun A. 2004. Popularization Discourse and Knowledge about the Genome. *Discourse and Society* 15/4, 369–389.

Cameron, Deborah 2006. Theorising the Female Voice in Public Contexts. In Baxter, Judith (ed.) *Speaking Out: The Female Voice in Public Contexts*. Basingstoke: Palgrave Macmillan, 3–20.

Djonov, Emilia 2007. Website Hierarchy and the Interaction between Content Organization, Webpage and Navigation Design: A Systemic Functional Hypermedia Discourse Analysis Perspective. *Information Design Journal* 15/2, 144–162.

Faulkner, Wendy 2000. The Power and the Pleasure? A Research Agenda for "Making Gender Stick" to Engineers. *Science, Technology & Human Values* 25/1, 87–119.

Halliday, Michael A. K. 2004. *An Introduction to Functional Grammar*. London: Arnold.

Halliday, Michael A. K./Matthiessen, Christian 1999. *Construing Experience through Meaning: A Language Based Approach to Cognition*. London: Casell.

Hatmaker, Deneen M. 2012. Engineering Identity: Gender and Professional Identity Negotiation among Women Engineers. *Gender, Work & Organization* 20/4, 382–396.

Hill, Catherine/Corbett, Christianne/St. Rose, Andresse 2010. *Why so Few? Women in Science, Technology, Engineering, and*

Mathematics. American Association of University Women. <https://files.eric.ed.gov/fulltext/ED509653.pdf>.

Holsanova, Jana/Holmberg, Nils/Holmqvist, Kenneth 2006. Tracing Integration of Text and Information Graphics in Newspaper Reading. *Lund University Cognitive Studies* 125, 1–19.

Hyland, Ken/Tse, Polly 2012. 'She has Received Many Honours': Identity Construction in Article Bio Statements. *Journal of English for Academic Purposes* 11/2, 155–165.

International Labor Organization 2019. *The Gender Gap in Employment: What's Holding Women Back?* < https://www.ilo.org/infostories/en-GB/Stories/Employment/barriers-women>.

Knox, John S. 2014. Online Newspapers: Structure and Layout. In Jewitt, Carey (ed.) *The Routledge Handbook of Multimodal Analysis* (2nd ed.). London: Routledge, 440–449.

Kress, Gunther/Van Leeuwen, Theo 2006. *Reading Images: The Grammar of Visual Design*. London: Routledge.

Lemke, Jay 2013. Multimedia and Discourse Analysis. In Gee, J. Paul/Handford, Michael (eds.) *Routledge Handbook of Discourse Analysis*. London: Routledge, 79–89.

Machin, David 2007. *Introduction to Multimodal Analysis*. London: Hodder Arnold.

Martin, James R. 1992. *English Text: System and Structure*. Amsterdam: John Benjamins.

McIlwee, Judith S./Robinson, J. Gregg 1992. *Women in Engineering: Gender, Power, and Workplace Culture*. New York: State University of New York Press.

Nash, Walter 1980. *Designs in Prose*. London: Longman.

O'Halloran, Kay L. 2004. *Multimodal Discourse Analysis*. London: Continuum.

Perry, Monica/Bodkin, Charles 2000. Content Analysis of Fortune 100 Company Web Sites. *Corporate Communications: An International Journal* 5/2, 87–97.

Rinn, M. 2014. Argumentation, Persuasion and Manipulation on Revisionist Websites: A Multimodal Rhetorical Analysis. In Maiorani, Arianna/Christie, Christine (eds.) *Multimodal Epistemologies*. London: Routledge, 145–158.

Royce, Terry D. 2007. Intersemiotic Complementarity: A Framework for Multimodal Discourse Analysis. In Royce, Terry D./Bowcher, Wendy (eds.) *New Directions in the Analysis of Multimodal Discourse*. New Jersey: Lawrence Erlbaum, 63–109.

Schnurr, Stephanie 2013. *Exploring Professional Communication. Language in Action*. Abingdon: Routledge.

Schnurr, Stephanie/Zayts, Olga 2017. *Language and Culture at Work*. Abingdon: Routledge.

Scollon, Ron/Scollon, Suzie Wong 2014. Multimodality and Language: A Retrospective and Prospective View. In Jewitt, Carey (ed.) *The Routledge Handbook of Multimodal Analysis* (2nd ed.). London: Routledge, 205–216.

Unsworth, Len 2001. *Teaching Multiliteracies Across the Curriculum: Changing Contexts of Text and Image in Classroom Practice*. Buckingham: Open University Press.

Unsworth, Len/Cleirigh, Chris 2009. Multimodality and Reading: The Construction of Meaning through Image-Text Interaction. In Jewitt, Carey (ed.) *The Routledge Handbook of Multimodal Analysis* (2nd ed.). London: Routledge, 151–164.

van Leeuwen, Theo 2008. New Forms of Writing, New Visual Competencies. *Visual Studies* 23/2, 130–135.

van Leeuwen, Theo 2011. *The Language of Colour: An Introduction*. London: Routledge.

Widdicombe, Sue 1998. Identity as an Analysts' and a Participants' Resource. In Antaki, Charles/Widdicombe, Sue (eds.) *Identities in Talk*. Thousand Oaks, CA: Sage Publications, 191–206.

Wyer, Mary 2003. Intending to Stay: Images of Scientists, Attitudes Toward Women, and Gender as Influences on Persistence Among Science and Engineering Majors. *Journal of Women and Minorities in Science and Engineering* 9, 1–16.

List of Figures

List of Tables

Notes on Contributors

Samira Allani (PhD) is an adjunct lecturer at the Department of Applied linguistics at the Technical University of Madrid (UPM). Her primary area of research is discourse analysis, which she approaches from a multidisciplinary perspective at the interface of critical discourse studies, cognitive linguistics, argumentation theory and pragmatics. She is an expert in foreign language theory and practice and has a long and rich experience in both teaching English for specific purposes and teacher training.

Ana Bocanegra-Valle is Senior Lecturer at the University of Cadiz (Spain). Her main research interests include Maritime English, ESP/EAP methodology and education (mainly needs analysis and materials design), English for research publication purposes and ESP/EAP discourse. She has been Editor-in-chief of the LSP journal *Ibérica* for eight years and is at present Book Review editor for *ESP Today* and *RESLA*. She has published articles and book chapters in prestigious journals and publishing houses and has served as peer reviewer for journals both in Spain and abroad. She is the head of the research group LaCAP (*Languages applied to communication in academic and professional settings*) and is at present participating in a national R&D project ("Ecologies of genres and ecologies of languages: An analysis of the dynamics of local, cross-border and international scientific communication") and an international Erasmus+ project ("TRAILs: LSP teacher training Summer School").

Llum Bracho is Doctor in Translation and Interpretation from the Universitat Jaume I in Castellón, Spain, and Associate Professor in the Department of Applied Linguistics at the Universitat Politècnica de València where she teaches Catalan for Specific Purposes. She has several publications in the field of translation including the book *Environmental Translation in Catalan: Culture, Ideology and the Environment* (Lambert Academic Publishing, 2010).

Oana Maria Carciu is Lecturer in English in the degrees of Primary and Early Childhood Education at the University of Zaragoza (Spain), The Faculty of Social Sciences and Education (Huesca Campus). Her main research largely concentrates on the written academic discourse of English for Specific Purposes, particularly focusing on medical language. Other research interests include corpus linguistics, genre analysis of academic discourse, mixed-methods approaches to research in academic settings, academic literacies, and multilingual scholars' language practices for research and teaching in the context of the internationalization of higher education.

Carmen Carracelas-Juncal is Associate Professor of Spanish in the School of Social Science and Global Studies at The University of Southern Mississippi (USA). She teaches linguistics and literature both at the undergraduate and graduate level in the World Languages program. She incorporates service-learning into her teaching and has directed several study abroad programs in Spain. Her current research interests include study abroad, service-learning, teaching and learning, heritage speakers, and early language learning.

Mária Czellér is Associate Professor and head of the Institute of Business Communication and Professional Language Studies at the University of Debrecen, Hungary. Prior to this present position, she worked in France on a six-year bilateral contract as a visiting lecturer at the University of Strasbourg. Her academic interests include teaching and research in languages for specific purposes.

Pamela Faber is Full Professor in the Department of Translation and Interpreting at the University of Granada, where she lectures on Terminology and Specialized Translation. She holds degrees from the University of North Carolina at Chapel Hill, the University of Paris IV, and the University of Granada. She is the director of the LexiCon research group, with whom she has carried out various national and international research projects that focus on applications of Frame-based Terminology to knowledge representation and the design of specialized knowledge bases. She is the author of over a hundred articles, chapters, and books on terminology, specialized lexicography, and lexical semantics.

Jonás Fouz-González is a lecturer and researcher at the University of Murcia. His research interests include computer-assisted pronunciation training, second language acquisition (in particular, pronunciation acquisition), and English phonetics and phonology. So far most of his research has dealt with the different ways in which technology can facilitate pronunciation training, with a focus on aspects that tend to be fossilized in the interlanguage of Spanish EFL learners. His recent publications include "Trends and Directions in Computer Assisted Pronunciation Training" (Palgrave Macmillan, 2015), "Twitter-based EFL pronunciation instruction" (*Language Learning & Technology,* 2016), "Pronunciation instruction through Twitter: the case of commonly mispronounced words" (*Computer Assisted Language Learning*, 2017) or "Podcast-based pronunciation training: Enhancing FL learners' perception and production of fossilised segmental features" (*ReCALL*, 2019).

Elspeth Jones is Emerita Professor of the Internationalisation of Higher Education, Leeds Beckett University and Honorary Visiting Fellow, Centre for Higher Education Internationalisation (CHEI), Università Cattolica del Sacro Cuore, Milan. With over 35 years in international education, her specialisms include personal, professional and employability outcomes from international mobility, strategic leadership, internationalisation of the curriculum at home and abroad, global citizenship, and intercultural competence development. She is series editor for *Internationalization in Higher Education* (Routledge), winner of the European Association for International Education's (EAIE) Award for Excellence in Research, and former Chair of the EAIE's Expert Community on Internationalisation at Home. She has published widely, including the edited and co-edited collections *Internationalising Higher Education* (Routledge, 2007); *Internationalisation and the Student Voice* (Routledge, 2009); *Global and Local Internationalisation* (Sense Publishers, 2016); and *The Globalization of Internationalization: Emerging Voices and Perspectives* (Routledge, 2017).

Enric Llurda is Professor of Applied Linguistics at Universitat de Lleida. He has edited and co-authored five books, and has extensively published in international journals and edited volumes. His research interests include non-native language teachers, English as a lingua franca, language attitudes, multilingualism, translanguaging, internationalisation and language education and policy in higher education institutions. He is the coordinator of the research group *Cercle de Lingüística Aplicada*, and is currently leading the research project "Towards a plurilingual approach in teaching English as a lingua franca at university".

Ricardo Mairal-Usón is Full Professor of Linguistics and Rector at the *Universidad Nacional de Educación a Distancia* (Spain). He has also been Vicerrector for Academic Staff and Planning (2016–2018), Vicerrector for Research and Transference (2013–2016) and has been President of the Spanish Association of Applied Linguistics (2011–2017). He has been working on linguistic engineering and natural language processing. He has also lectured extensively as keynote speaker at national and international conferences of Linguistics and has participated as an invited Professor in several doctoral programmes at other universities. He has been the co-founder of the research group LEXICOM (www.lexicom.es) and worked on the design of FunGramKB (www.fungramkb.com), a multifunctional and multilingual lexical conceptual knowledge base for the development of natural language processing applications. He has also been responsible for the research project SECONDS (http://www.seconds.edu.es), which is concerned with neuroscience and clinical applications.

Penny MacDonald is a member of the Department of Applied Linguistics and Associate Professor in English for Specific Purposes at the Universitat Politècnica de València, Spain. She has a PhD in English Philology from the University of Valencia and has taught English in Spain for the last 30 years. She is a member of the DIAAL research group (<http://www.upv.es/diaal/>). Her research interest lies mainly in the field of (critical) discourse analysis, CLIL, interlanguage error analysis and corpus linguistics. Recent publications include: Computer learner corpora: analysing interlanguage errors in synchronous and asynchronous communication (2013); Linguistic needs in virtual communication and labour mobility: The CoMoViWo Project (2015); "We All Make Mistakes!". Analysing an Error-coded Corpus of Spanish University Students' Written English (2016); The invisibility of the translator in environmental translation (2017); The use of pragmatic strategies for CLIL scaffolding (2018).

Vasi Mocanu is currently a Lecturer in Catalan Language and Culture at the University of Salamanca. She graduated with honors in English Studies in 2013, in 2014 she obtained her MA in English Language Teaching, and in 2019 she completed her PhD. She has been a member of the *Cercle de Lingüística Aplicada* research group at the University of Lleida since 2014. Her research is concerned with multilingualism, identity, and diversity in the era of globalization, with an emphasis on language learning processes in situations of mobility. Her thesis investigated the implications for language and identity in study abroad programmes in Northern, Eastern, and Southern Europe.

Silvia Molina-Plaza obtained a position as tenured Senior Lecturer (Associate Professor) at the University of Castilla-La Mancha. She obtained another tenured Senior Lecturer position at the Technical University of Madrid where she is currently teaching at the Department of Applied Linguistics to Science and Technology. She has gained recognition for eighteen years of quality research. Her research has focused on the translation from English to Spanish, contrastive analysis (modality and collocations), Pragmatics and Discourse Analysis applied to ESP in numerous book chapters, articles, papers and she has attended several national and international conferences.

Laura-Mihaela Muresan is Professor of English at The Bucharest University of Economic Studies (Romania), where she co-ordinates an English-medium, Academic Development masters'. She teaches Genre Analysis, EAP and English for Economics. Her research interests include English for Research Publication Purposes, and pedagogical interventions for improving the scholars' academic literacies and language competences. Her publications include "English for research publication and dissemination in bi-/multiliterate environments: the case of Romanian academics" (2014, with C. Pérez-Llantada), "Changing research writing practices in Romania: Perceptions and attitudes" (2014, with M. Bardi), or "New roles for language teachers in higher education. A collaborative perspective of language and content teachers' views" (2018, with V. Robu). She has recently published the volume *Pedagogies and Policies for Publishing Research in English: Local Initiatives Supporting International Scholars* (Routledge, 2019), co-edited with James N. Corcoran and Karen Englander.

Martha C. Pennington (Ph.D. Linguistics, University of Pennsylvania) is an internationally known English language and teacher education scholar who has held teaching and administrative positions in the US, the UK, and Hong Kong. She is affiliated with the University of London at the School for Oriental and African Studies as a Professorial Research Associate in Linguistics and at Birkbeck College as a Research Fellow in Applied Linguistics and Communication. Her pronunciation books include an edited collection, *Phonology in Context* (Palgrave Macmillan, 2007) and a co-authored work (with Pamela Rogerson Revell), *Pronunciation Teaching and Research* (Palgrave Macmillan, 2019). Prof. Pennington has also recently published (with Robert P. Waxler), *Why Reading Books Still Matters: The Power of Literature in Digital Times* (Routledge, 2018), and is currently completing *Teacher-Student Relationship: Key to Effective Teaching and Learning in Contexts of Diversity* (Routledge) and *Introduction to Bilingualism and Multilingualism: People and Languages in Contact* (Wiley-Blackwell).

Carmen Sancho Guinda is Senior Lecturer in the Department of Applied Linguistics at the Universidad Politécnica de Madrid, where she teaches English for Academic and Professional Communication at the School of Aerospace Engineering and in-service seminars for engineering teachers undertaking English-medium instruction. Her research interests are the interdisciplinary study of academic and professional discourses/genres, innovation in the learning of academic competencies, and the study of emotion in professional settings. Her most recent publications are *Stance and Voice in Written Academic Genres* (Palgrave, 2012), co-edited with Ken Hyland, *Narratives in Academic and Professional Genres* (Peter Lang, 2013), co-edited with Maurizio Gotti, *Interpersonality in Legal Genres* (Peter Lang, 2014), co-edited with Ruth Breeze and Maurizio Gotti, *Essential Competencies for English-medium University Teaching* (Springer, 2017), co-edited with

Ruth Breeze, and *Engagement in Professional Genres* (John Benjamins, 2019). She is editor-in-chief of *Ibérica*, co-editor of the online journal *Language Value* and a member of the editorial boards of high-impact international journals.

Sven Tarp is Head of the Centre for Lexicography at the Aarhus University (Denmark). He is also Extraordinary Professor at the University of Stellenbosch (South Africa), Extraordinary Board Member of the International Centre for Lexicography at the University of Valladolid (Spain) and Yuh Shan Professor at the Center for Lexicographical Studies at Guangdong University of Foreign Studies (China). With a PhD in specialised lexicography (1993) and a Senior Doctor's Degree in learners' lexicography (2006), he is the editor or co-editor of several specialised dictionaries and has published a big number of contributions in journals and well-known series. He is the author of *Lexicography in the Borderland Between Knowledge and Non-knowledge* (2008), co-author of *Theory and Practice of Specialised Online Dictionaries* (2014) and co-editor of *Manual of Specialised Lexicography* (1995). He is one of the founders of the Function Theory of Lexicography.

Troy Wiwczaroski began his career as Teaching Assistant at the prestigious Washington University in St. Louis, where he did his Masters and Doctorate. He has lived and worked in The Netherlands, Germany and Switzerland, and has been living and working in Debrecen, Hungary, since 1995. He is currently an Associate Professor at Debrecen University, Faculty of Economic Sciences, and his research focuses on the development of business relevant skills and competencies in higher education students. He has extensive experience in developing and holding workshops in presentation skills, customer communication, international negotiations and leader development for companies across Europe.

Linguistic Insights

Studies in Language and Communication

This series aims to promote specialist language studies in the fields of linguistic theory and applied linguistics, by publishing volumes that focus on specific aspects of language use in one or several languages and provide valuable insights into language and communication research. A cross-disciplinary approach is favoured and most European languages are accepted.

The series includes two types of books:

- Monographs – featuring in-depth studies on special aspects of language theory, language analysis or language teaching.
- Collected papers – assembling papers from workshops, conferences or symposia.

Each volume of the series is subjected to a double peer-reviewing process.

Vol. 1 Maurizio Gotti & Marina Dossena (eds)
Modality in Specialized Texts. Selected Papers of the 1st CERLIS Conference.
421 pages. 2001. ISBN 3-906767-10-8 · US-ISBN 0-8204-5340-4

Vol. 2 Giuseppina Cortese & Philip Riley (eds)
Domain-specific English. Textual Practices across Communities and Classrooms.
420 pages. 2002. ISBN 3-906768-98-8 · US-ISBN 0-8204-5884-8

Vol. 3 Maurizio Gotti, Dorothee Heller & Marina Dossena (eds)
Conflict and Negotiation in Specialized Texts. Selected Papers of the 2nd CERLIS Conference.
470 pages. 2002. ISBN 3-906769-12-7 · US-ISBN 0-8204-5887-2

Vol. 4 Maurizio Gotti, Marina Dossena, Richard Dury, Roberta Facchinetti & Maria Lima
Variation in Central Modals. A Repertoire of Forms and Types of Usage in Middle English and Early Modern English.
364 pages. 2002. ISBN 3-906769-84-4 · US-ISBN 0-8204-5898-8

Editorial address:

Prof. Maurizio Gotti Università di Bergamo, Dipartimento di Lingue, Letterature e Culture Straniere Piazza Rosate 2, 24129 Bergamo, Italy
Fax: +39 035 2052789, E-Mail: m.gotti@unibg.it

Vol. 5 Stefania Nuccorini (ed.)
Phrases and Phraseology. Data and Descriptions.
187 pages. 2002. ISBN 3-906770-08-7 · US-ISBN 0-8204-5933-X

Vol. 6 Vijay Bhatia, Christopher N. Candlin & Maurizio Gotti (eds)
Legal Discourse in Multilingual and Multicultural Contexts.
Arbitration Texts in Europe.
385 pages. 2003. ISBN 3-906770-85-0 · US-ISBN 0-8204-6254-3

Vol. 7 Marina Dossena & Charles Jones (eds)
Insights into Late Modern English. 2nd edition.
378 pages. 2003, 2007.
ISBN 978-3-03911-257-9 · US-ISBN 978-0-8204-8927-8

Vol. 8 Maurizio Gotti
Specialized Discourse. Linguistic Features and Changing Conventions.
351 pages. 2003, 2005.
ISBN 3-03910-606-6 · US-ISBN 0-8204-7000-7

Vol. 9 Alan Partington, John Morley & Louann Haarman (eds)
Corpora and Discourse.
420 pages. 2004. ISBN 3-03910-026-2 · US-ISBN 0-8204-6262-4

Vol. 10 Martina Möllering
The Acquisition of German Modal Particles. A Corpus-Based Approach.
290 pages. 2004. ISBN 3-03910-043-2 · US-ISBN 0-8204-6273-X

Vol. 11 David Hart (ed.)
English Modality in Context. Diachronic Perspectives.
261 pages. 2003. ISBN 3-03910-046-7 · US-ISBN 0-8204-6852-5

Vol. 12 Wendy Swanson
Modes of Co-reference as an Indicator of Genre.
430 pages. 2003. ISBN 3-03910-052-1 · US-ISBN 0-8204-6855-X

Vol. 13 Gina Poncini
Discursive Strategies in Multicultural Business Meetings.
2nd edition. 338 pages. 2004, 2007.
ISBN 978-3-03911-296-8 · US-ISBN 978-0-8204-8937-7

Vol. 14 Christopher N. Candlin & Maurizio Gotti (eds)
Intercultural Aspects of Specialized Communication.
2nd edition. 369 pages. 2004, 2007.
ISBN 978-3-03911-258-6 · US-ISBN 978-0-8204-8926-1

Vol. 15 Gabriella Del Lungo Camiciotti & Elena Tognini Bonelli (eds)
Academic Discourse. New Insights into Evaluation.
234 pages. 2004. ISBN 3-03910-353-9 · US-ISBN 0-8204-7016-3

Vol. 16 Marina Dossena & Roger Lass (eds)
Methods and Data in English Historical Dialectology.
405 pages. 2004. ISBN 3-03910-362-8 · US-ISBN 0-8204-7018-X

Vol. 17 Judy Noguchi
The Science Review Article. An Opportune Genre in
the Construction of Science.
274 pages. 2006. ISBN 3-03910-426-8 · US-ISBN 0-8204-7034-1

Vol. 18 Giuseppina Cortese & Anna Duszak (eds)
Identity, Community, Discourse. English in Intercultural Settings.
495 pages. 2005. ISBN 3-03910-632-5 · US-ISBN 0-8204-7163-1

Vol. 19 Anna Trosborg & Poul Erik Flyvholm Jørgensen (eds)
Business Discourse. Texts and Contexts.
250 pages. 2005. ISBN 3-03910-606-6 · US-ISBN 0-8204-7000-7

Vol. 20 Christopher Williams
Tradition and Change in Legal English. Verbal Constructions in Prescriptive Texts.
2nd revised edition. 216 pages. 2005, 2007. ISBN 978-3-03911-444-3.

Vol. 21 Katarzyna Dziubalska-Kolaczyk & Joanna Przedlacka (eds)
English Pronunciation Models: A Changing Scene.
2nd edition. 476 pages. 2005, 2008. ISBN 978-3-03911-682-9.

Vol. 22 Christián Abello-Contesse, Rubén Chacón-Beltrán, M. Dolores López-Jiménez & M. Mar Torreblanca-López (eds)
Age in L2 Acquisition and Teaching.
214 pages. 2006. ISBN 3-03910-668-6 · US-ISBN 0-8204-7174-7

Vol. 23 Vijay K. Bhatia, Maurizio Gotti, Jan Engberg & Dorothee Heller (eds)
Vagueness in Normative Texts.
474 pages. 2005. ISBN 3-03910-653-8 · US-ISBN 0-8204-7169-0

Vol. 24 Paul Gillaerts & Maurizio Gotti (eds)
Genre Variation in Business Letters. 2nd printing.
407 pages. 2008. ISBN 978-3-03911-681-2.

Vol. 25 Ana María Hornero, María José Luzón & Silvia Murillo (eds)
Corpus Linguistics. Applications for the Study of English.
2nd printing. 526 pages. 2006, 2008. ISBN 978-3-03911-726-0

Vol. 26 J. Lachlan Mackenzie & María de los Ángeles Gómez-González (eds)
Studies in Functional Discourse Grammar.
259 pages. 2005. ISBN 3-03910-696-1 · US-ISBN 0-8204-7558-0

Vol. 27 Debbie G. E. Ho
Classroom Talk. Exploring the Sociocultural Structure of Formal ESL Learning.
2nd edition. 254 pages. 2006, 2007. ISBN 978-3-03911-434-4

Vol. 28 Javier Pérez-Guerra, Dolores González-Álvarez, Jorge L. Bueno-Alonso & Esperanza Rama-Martínez (eds)
'Of Varying Language and Opposing Creed'. New Insights into Late Modern English.
455 pages. 2007. ISBN 978-3-03910-788-9

Vol. 29 Francesca Bargiela-Chiappini & Maurizio Gotti (eds)
Asian Business Discourse(s).
350 pages. 2005. ISBN 3-03910-804-2 · US-ISBN 0-8204-7574-2

Vol. 30 Nicholas Brownlees (ed.)
News Discourse in Early Modern Britain. Selected Papers of CHINED 2004.
300 pages. 2006. ISBN 3-03910-805-0 · US-ISBN 0-8204-8025-8

Vol. 31 Roberta Facchinetti & Matti Rissanen (eds)
Corpus-based Studies of Diachronic English.
300 pages. 2006. ISBN 3-03910-851-4 · US-ISBN 0-8204-8040-1

Vol. 32 Marina Dossena & Susan M. Fitzmaurice (eds)
Business and Official Correspondence. Historical Investigations.
209 pages. 2006. ISBN 3-03910-880-8 · US-ISBN 0-8204-8352-4

Vol. 33 Giuliana Garzone & Srikant Sarangi (eds)
Discourse, Ideology and Specialized Communication.
494 pages. 2007. ISBN 978-3-03910-888-6

Vol. 34 Giuliana Garzone & Cornelia Ilie (eds)
The Use of English in Institutional and Business Settings.
An Intercultural Perspective.
372 pages. 2007. ISBN 978-3-03910-889-3

Vol. 35 Vijay K. Bhatia & Maurizio Gotti (eds)
Explorations in Specialized Genres.
316 pages. 2006. ISBN 3-03910-995-2 · US-ISBN 0-8204-8372-9

Vol. 36 Heribert Picht (ed.)
Modern Approaches to Terminological Theories and Applications.
432 pages. 2006. ISBN 3-03911-156-6 · US-ISBN 0-8204-8380-X

Vol. 37 Anne Wagner & Sophie Cacciaguidi-Fahy (eds)
Legal Language and the Search for Clarity / Le langage juridique et la quête de clarté. Practice and Tools / Pratiques et instruments.
487 pages. 2006. ISBN 3-03911-169-8 · US-ISBN 0-8204-8388-5

Vol. 38 Juan Carlos Palmer-Silveira, Miguel F. Ruiz-Garrido & Inmaculada Fortanet-Gómez (eds)
Intercultural and International Business Communication.
Theory, Research and Teaching.
2nd edition. 343 pages. 2006, 2008. ISBN 978-3-03911-680-5

Vol. 39 Christiane Dalton-Puffer, Dieter Kastovsky, Nikolaus Ritt & Herbert Schendl (eds)
Syntax, Style and Grammatical Norms. English from 1500–2000.
250 pages. 2006. ISBN 3-03911-181-7 · US-ISBN 0-8204-8394-X

Vol. 40 Marina Dossena & Irma Taavitsainen (eds)
Diachronic Perspectives on Domain-Specific English.
280 pages. 2006. ISBN 3-03910-176-0 · US-ISBN 0-8204-8391-5

Vol. 41 John Flowerdew & Maurizio Gotti (eds)
Studies in Specialized Discourse.
293 pages. 2006. ISBN 3-03911-178-7

Vol. 42 Ken Hyland & Marina Bondi (eds)
Academic Discourse Across Disciplines.
320 pages. 2006. ISBN 3-03911-183-3 · US-ISBN 0-8204-8396-6

Vol. 43 Paul Gillaerts & Philip Shaw (eds)
The Map and the Landscape. Norms and Practices in Genre.
256 pages. 2006. ISBN 3-03911-182-5 · US-ISBN 0-8204-8395-4

Vol. 44 Maurizio Gotti & Davide Giannoni (eds)
New Trends in Specialized Discourse Analysis.
301 pages. 2006. ISBN 3-03911-184-1 · US-ISBN 0-8204-8381-8

Vol. 45 Maurizio Gotti & Françoise Salager-Meyer (eds)
Advances in Medical Discourse Analysis. Oral and Written Contexts.
492 pages. 2006. ISBN 3-03911-185-X · US-ISBN 0-8204-8382-6

Vol. 46 Maurizio Gotti & Susan Šarcević (eds)
Insights into Specialized Translation.
396 pages. 2006. ISBN 3-03911-186-8 · US-ISBN 0-8204-8383-4

Vol. 47 Khurshid Ahmad & Margaret Rogers (eds)
Evidence-based LSP. Translation, Text and Terminology.
584 pages. 2007. ISBN 978-3-03911-187-9

Vol. 48 Hao Sun & Dániel Z. Kádár (eds)
It's the Dragon's Turn. Chinese Institutional Discourses.
262 pages. 2008. ISBN 978-3-03911-175-6

Vol. 49 Cristina Suárez-Gómez
Relativization in Early English (950-1250). the Position of Relative Clauses.
149 pages. 2006. ISBN 3-03911-203-1 · US-ISBN 0-8204-8904-2

Vol. 50 Maria Vittoria Calvi & Luisa Chierichetti (eds)
Nuevas tendencias en el discurso de especialidad.
319 pages. 2006. ISBN 978-3-03911-261-6

Vol. 51 Mari Carmen Campoy & María José Luzón (eds)
Spoken Corpora in Applied Linguistics.
274 pages. 2008. ISBN 978-3-03911-275-3

Vol. 52 Konrad Ehlich & Dorothee Heller (Hrsg.)
Die Wissenschaft und ihre Sprachen.
323 pages. 2006. ISBN 978-3-03911-272-2

Vol. 53 Jingyu Zhang
The Semantic Salience Hierarchy Model. The L2 Acquisition of Psych Predicates
273 pages. 2007. ISBN 978-3-03911-300-2

Vol. 54 Norman Fairclough, Giuseppina Cortese & Patrizia Ardizzone (eds)
Discourse and Contemporary Social Change.
555 pages. 2007. ISBN 978-3-03911-276-0

Vol. 55 Jan Engberg, Marianne Grove Ditlevsen, Peter Kastberg & Martin Stegu (eds)
New Directions in LSP Teaching.
331 pages. 2007. ISBN 978-3-03911-433-7

Vol. 56 Dorothee Heller & Konrad Ehlich (Hrsg.)
Studien zur Rechtskommunikation.
322 pages. 2007. ISBN 978-3-03911-436-8

Vol. 57 Teruhiro Ishiguro & Kang-kwong Luke (eds)
Grammar in Cross-Linguistic Perspective.
The Syntax, Semantics, and Pragmatics of Japanese and Chinese.
304 pages. 2012. ISBN 978-3-03911-445-0

Vol. 58 Carmen Frehner
Email – SMS – MMS
294 pages. 2008. ISBN 978-3-03911-451-1

Vol. 59 Isabel Balteiro
The Directionality of Conversion in English. A Dia-Synchronic Study.
276 pages. 2007. ISBN 978-3-03911-241-8

Vol. 60 Maria Milagros Del Saz Rubio
English Discourse Markers of Reformulation.
237 pages. 2007. ISBN 978-3-03911-196-1

Vol. 61 Sally Burgess & Pedro Martín-Martín (eds)
English as an Additional Language in Research Publication and Communication.
259 pages. 2008. ISBN 978-3-03911-462-7

Vol. 62 Sandrine Onillon
Pratiques et représentations de l'écrit.
458 pages. 2008. ISBN 978-3-03911-464-1

Vol. 63 Hugo Bowles & Paul Seedhouse (eds)
Conversation Analysis and Language for Specific Purposes.
2nd edition. 337 pages. 2007, 2009. ISBN 978-3-0343-0045-2

Vol. 64 Vijay K. Bhatia, Christopher N. Candlin & Paola Evangelisti Allori (eds)
Language, Culture and the Law.
The Formulation of Legal Concepts across Systems and Cultures.
342 pages. 2008. ISBN 978-3-03911-470-2

Vol. 65 Jonathan Culpeper & Dániel Z. Kádár (eds)
Historical (Im)politeness.
300 pages. 2010. ISBN 978-3-03911-496-2

Vol. 66 Linda Lombardo (ed.)
Using Corpora to Learn about Language and Discourse.
237 pages. 2009. ISBN 978-3-03911-522-8

Vol. 67 Natsumi Wakamoto
Extroversion/Introversion in Foreign Language Learning.
Interactions with Learner Strategy Use.
159 pages. 2009. ISBN 978-3-03911-596-9

Vol. 68 Eva Alcón-Soler (ed.)
Learning How to Request in an Instructed Language Learning Context.
260 pages. 2008. ISBN 978-3-03911-601-0

Vol. 69 Domenico Pezzini
The Translation of Religious Texts in the Middle Ages.
428 pages. 2008. ISBN 978-3-03911-600-3

Vol. 70 Tomoko Tode
Effects of Frequency in Classroom Second Language Learning.
Quasi-experiment and stimulated-recall analysis.
195 pages. 2008. ISBN 978-3-03911-602-7

Vol. 71 Egor Tsedryk
Fusion symétrique et alternances ditransitives.
211 pages. 2009. ISBN 978-3-03911-609-6

Vol. 72 Cynthia J. Kellett Bidoli & Elana Ochse (eds)
English in International Deaf Communication.
444 pages. 2008. ISBN 978-3-03911-610-2

Vol. 73 Joan C. Beal, Carmela Nocera & Massimo Sturiale (eds)
Perspectives on Prescriptivism.
269 pages. 2008. ISBN 978-3-03911-632-4

Vol. 74 Carol Taylor Torsello, Katherine Ackerley & Erik Castello (eds)
Corpora for University Language Teachers.
308 pages. 2008. ISBN 978-3-03911-639-3

Vol. 75 María Luisa Pérez Cañado (ed.)
English Language Teaching in the European Credit Transfer System. Facing the Challenge.
251 pages. 2009. ISBN 978-3-03911-654-6

Vol. 76 Marina Dossena & Ingrid Tieken-Boon van Ostade (eds)
Studies in Late Modern English Correspondence. Methodology and Data.
291 pages. 2008. ISBN 978-3-03911-658-4

Vol. 77 Ingrid Tieken-Boon van Ostade & Wim van der Wurff (eds)
Current Issues in Late Modern English.
436 pages. 2009. ISBN 978-3-03911-660-7

Vol. 78 Marta Navarro Coy (ed.)
Practical Approaches to Foreign Language Teaching and Learning.
297 pages. 2009. ISBN 978-3-03911-661-4

Vol. 79 Qing Ma
Second Language Vocabulary Acquisition.
333 pages. 2009. ISBN 978-3-03911-666-9

Vol. 80 Martin Solly, Michelangelo Conoscenti & Sandra Campagna (eds)
Verbal/Visual Narrative Texts in Higher Education.
384 pages. 2008. ISBN 978-3-03911-672-0

Vol. 81 Meiko Matsumoto
From Simple Verbs to Periphrastic Expressions: The Historical Development of Composite Predicates, Phrasal Verbs, and Related Constructions in English.
235 pages. 2008. ISBN 978-3-03911-675-1

Vol. 82 Melinda Dooly
Doing Diversity. Teachers' Construction of Their Classroom Reality.
180 pages. 2009. ISBN 978-3-03911-687-4

Vol. 83 Victoria Guillén-Nieto, Carmen Marimón-Llorca & Chelo Vargas-Sierra (eds)
Intercultural Business Communication and Simulation and Gaming Methodology.
392 pages. 2009. ISBN 978-3-03911-688-1

Vol. 84 Maria Grazia Guido
English as a Lingua Franca in Cross-cultural Immigration Domains.
285 pages. 2008. ISBN 978-3-03911-689-8

Vol. 85 Erik Castello
Text Complexity and Reading Comprehension Tests.
352 pages. 2008. ISBN 978-3-03911-717-8

Vol. 86 Maria-Lluisa Gea-Valor, Isabel García-Izquierdo & Maria-José Esteve (eds)
Linguistic and Translation Studies in Scientific Communication.
317 pages. 2010. ISBN 978-3-0343-0069-8

Vol. 87 Carmen Navarro, Rosa Mª Rodríguez Abella, Francesca Dalle Pezze & Renzo Miotti (eds)
La comunicación especializada.
355 pages. 2008. ISBN 978-3-03911-733-8

Vol. 88 Kiriko Sato
The Development from Case-Forms to Prepositional Constructions in Old English Prose.
231 pages. 2009. ISBN 978-3-03911-763-5

Vol. 89 Dorothee Heller (Hrsg.)
Formulierungsmuster in deutscher und italienischer Fachkommunikation. Intra- und interlinguale Perspektiven.
315 pages. 2008. ISBN 978-3-03911-778-9

Vol. 90 Henning Bergenholtz, Sandro Nielsen & Sven Tarp (eds)
Lexicography at a Crossroads. Dictionaries and Encyclopedias Today, Lexicographical Tools Tomorrow.
372 pages. 2009. ISBN 978-3-03911-799-4

Vol. 91 Manouchehr Moshtagh Khorasani
The Development of Controversies. From the Early Modern Period to Online Discussion Forums.
317 pages. 2009. ISBN 978-3-3911-711-6

Vol. 92 María Luisa Carrió-Pastor (ed.)
Content and Language Integrated Learning. Cultural Diversity.
178 pages. 2009. ISBN 978-3-3911-818-2

Vol. 93 Roger Berry
Terminology in English Language Teaching. Nature and Use.
262 pages. 2010. ISBN 978-3-0343-0013-1

Vol. 94 Roberto Cagliero & Jennifer Jenkins (eds)
Discourses, Communities, and Global Englishes
240 pages. 2010. ISBN 978-3-0343-0012-4

Vol. 95 Facchinetti Roberta, Crystal David, Seidlhofer Barbara (eds)
From International to Local English – And Back Again.
268 pages. 2010. ISBN 978-3-0343-0011-7

Vol. 96 Cesare Gagliardi & Alan Maley (eds)
EIL, ELF, Global English. Teaching and Learning Issues
376 pages. 2010. ISBN 978-3-0343-0010-0

Vol. 97 Sylvie Hancil (ed.)
The Role of Prosody in Affective Speech.
403 pages. 2009. ISBN 978-3-03911-696-6

Vol. 98 Marina Dossena & Roger Lass (eds)
Studies in English and European Historical Dialectology.
257 pages. 2009. ISBN 978-3-0343-0024-7

Vol. 99 Christine Béal
Les interactions quotidiennes en français et en anglais. De l'approche comparative à l'analyse des situations interculturelles.
424 pages. 2010. ISBN 978-3-0343-0027-8

Vol. 100 Maurizio Gotti (ed.)
Commonality and Individuality in Academic Discourse.
398 pages. 2009. ISBN 978-3-0343-0023-0

Vol. 101 Javier E. Díaz Vera & Rosario Caballero (eds)
Textual Healing. Studies in Medieval English Medical, Scientific and Technical Texts.
213 pages. 2009. ISBN 978-3-03911-822-9

Vol. 102 Nuria Edo Marzá
The Specialised Lexicographical Approach. A Step further in Dictionary-making.
316 pages. 2009. ISBN 978-3-0343-0043-8

Vol. 103 Carlos Prado-Alonso, Lidia Gómez-García, Iria Pastor-Gómez &
David Tizón-Couto (eds)
New Trends and Methodologies in Applied English Language Research.
Diachronic, Diatopic and Contrastive Studies.
348 pages. 2009. ISBN 978-3-0343-0046-9

Vol. 104 Françoise Salager-Meyer & Beverly A. Lewin
Crossed Words. Criticism in Scholarly Writing?
371 pages. 2011. ISBN 978-3-0343-0049-0.

Vol. 105 Javier Ruano-García
Early Modern Northern English Lexis. A Literary Corpus-Based Study.
611 pages. 2010. ISBN 978-3-0343-0058-2

Vol. 106 Rafael Monroy-Casas
Systems for the Phonetic Transcription of English. Theory and Texts.
280 pages. 2011. ISBN 978-3-0343-0059-9

Vol. 107 Nicola T. Owtram
The Pragmatics of Academic Writing.
A Relevance Approach to the Analysis of Research Article Introductions.
311 pages. 2009. ISBN 978-3-0343-0060-5

Vol. 108 Yolanda Ruiz de Zarobe, Juan Manuel Sierra &
Francisco Gallardo del Puerto (eds)
Content and Foreign Language Integrated Learning.
Contributions to Multilingualism in European Contexts
343 pages. 2011. ISBN 978-3-0343-0074-2

Vol. 109 Ángeles Linde López & Rosalía Crespo Jiménez (eds)
Professional English in the European context. The EHEA challenge.
374 pages. 2010. ISBN 978-3-0343-0088-9

Vol. 110 Rosalía Rodríguez-Vázquez
The Rhythm of Speech, Verse and Vocal Music. A New Theory.
394 pages. 2010. ISBN 978-3-0343-0309-5

Vol. 111 Anastasios Tsangalidis & Roberta Facchinetti (eds)
Studies on English Modality. In Honour of Frank Palmer.
392 pages. 2009. ISBN 978-3-0343-0310-1

Vol. 112 Jing Huang
Autonomy, Agency and Identity in Foreign Language Learning and Teaching.
400 pages. 2013. ISBN 978-3-0343-0370-5

Vol. 113 Mihhail Lotman & Maria-Kristiina Lotman (eds)
Frontiers in Comparative Prosody. In memoriam: Mikhail Gasparov.
426 pages. 2011. ISBN 978-3-0343-0373-6

Vol. 114 Merja Kytö, John Scahill & Harumi Tanabe (eds)
Language Change and Variation from Old English to Late Modern English.
A Festschrift for Minoji Akimoto
422 pages. 2010. ISBN 978-3-0343-0372-9

Vol. 115 Giuliana Garzone & Paola Catenaccio (eds)
Identities across Media and Modes. Discursive Perspectives.
379 pages. 2009. ISBN 978-3-0343-0386-6

Vol. 116 Elena Landone
Los marcadores del discurso y cortesía verbal en español.
390 pages. 2010. ISBN 978-3-0343-0413-9

Vol. 117 Maurizio Gotti & Christopher Williams (eds)
Legal Discourse across Languages and Cultures.
339 pages. 2010. ISBN 978-3-0343-0425-2

Vol. 118 David Hirsh
Academic Vocabulary in Context.
217 pages. 2010. ISBN 978-3-0343-0426-9

Vol. 119 Yvonne Dröschel
Lingua Franca English. The Role of Simplification and Transfer.
358 pages. 2011. ISBN 978-3-0343-0432-0

Vol. 120 Tengku Sepora Tengku Mahadi, Helia Vaezian & Mahmoud Akbari
Corpora in Translation. A Practical Guide.
135 pages. 2010. ISBN 978-3-0343-0434-4

Vol. 121 Davide Simone Giannoni & Celina Frade (eds)
Researching Language and the Law. Textual Features and Translation Issues.
278 pages. 2010. ISBN 978-3-0343-0443-6

Vol. 122 Daniel Madrid & Stephen Hughes (eds)
Studies in Bilingual Education.
472 pages. 2011. ISBN 978-3-0343-0474-0

Vol. 123 Vijay K. Bhatia, Christopher N. Candlin & Maurizio Gotti (eds)
The Discourses of Dispute Resolution.
290 pages. 2010. ISBN 978-3-0343-0476-4

Vol. 124 Davide Simone Giannoni
Mapping Academic Values in the Disciplines. A Corpus-Based Approach.
288 pages. 2010. ISBN 978-3-0343-0488-7

Vol. 125 Giuliana Garzone & James Archibald (eds)
Discourse, Identities and Roles in Specialized Communication.
419 pages. 2010. ISBN 978-3-0343-0494-8

Vol. 126 Iria Pastor-Gómez
The Status and Development of N+N Sequences in
Contemporary English Noun Phrases.
216 pages. 2011. ISBN 978-3-0343-0534-1

Vol. 127 Carlos Prado-Alonso
Full-verb Inversion in Written and Spoken English.
261 pages. 2011. ISBN 978-3-0343-0535-8

Vol. 128 Tony Harris & María Moreno Jaén (eds)
Corpus Linguistics in Language Teaching.
214 pages. 2010. ISBN 978-3-0343-0524-2

Vol. 129 Tetsuji Oda & Hiroyuki Eto (eds)
Multiple Perspectives on English Philology and History of Linguistics.
A Festschrift for Shoichi Watanabe on his 80th Birthday.
378 pages. 2010. ISBN 978-3-0343-0480-1

Vol. 130 Luisa Chierichetti & Giovanni Garofalo (eds)
Lengua y Derecho. líneas de investigación interdisciplinaria.
283 pages. 2010. 978-3-0343-0463-4

Vol. 131 Paola Evangelisti Allori & Giuliana Garzone (eds)
Discourse, Identities and Genres in Corporate Communication.
Sponsorship, Advertising and Organizational Communication.
324 pages. 2011. 978-3-0343-0591-4

Vol. 132 Leyre Ruiz de Zarobe & Yolanda Ruiz de Zarobe (eds)
Speech Acts and Politeness across Languages and Cultures.
402 pages. 2012. 978-3-0343-0611-9

Vol. 133 Thomas Christiansen
Cohesion. A Discourse Perspective.
387 pages. 2011. 978-3-0343-0619-5

Vol. 134 Giuliana Garzone & Maurizio Gotti
Discourse, Communication and the Enterprise. Genres and Trends.
451 pages. 2011. ISBN 978-3-0343-0620-1

Vol. 135 Zsuzsa Hoffmann
Ways of the World's Words.
Language Contact in the Age of Globalization.
334 pages 2011. ISBN 978-3-0343-0673-7

Vol. 136 Cecilia Varcasia (ed.)
Becoming Multilingual.
Language Learning and Language Policy between Attitudes and Identities.
213 pages. 2011. ISBN 978-3-0343-0687-5

Vol. 137 Susy Macqueen
The Emergence of Patterns in Second Language Writing.
A Sociocognitive Exploration of Lexical Trails.
325 pages. 2012. ISBN 978-3-0343-1010-9

Vol. 138 Maria Vittoria Calvi & Giovanna Mapelli (eds)
La lengua del turismo. Géneros discursivos y terminología.
365 pages. 2011. ISBN 978-3-0343-1011-6

Vol. 139 Ken Lau
Learning to Become a Professional in a Textually-Mediated World.
A Text-Oriented Study of Placement Practices.
261 pages. 2012. ISBN 978-3-0343-1016-1

Vol. 140 Sandra Campagna, Giuliana Garzone, Cornelia Ilie & Elizabeth Rowley-Jolivet (eds)
Evolving Genres in Web-mediated Communication.
337 pages. 2012. ISBN 978-3-0343-1013-0

Vol. 141 Edith Esch & Martin Solly (eds)
The Sociolinguistics of Language Education in International Contexts.
263 pages. 2012. ISBN 978-3-0343-1009-3

Vol. 142 Forthcoming.

Vol. 143 David Tizón-Couto
Left Dislocation in English. A Functional-Discoursal Approach.
416 pages. 2012. ISBN 978-3-0343-1037-6

Vol. 144 Margrethe Petersen & Jan Engberg (eds)
Current Trends in LSP Research. Aims and Methods.
323 pages. 2011. ISBN 978-3-0343-1054-3

Vol. 145 David Tizón-Couto, Beatriz Tizón-Couto, Iria Pastor-Gómez & Paula Rodríguez-Puente (eds)
New Trends and Methodologies in Applied English Language Research II.
Studies in Language Variation, Meaning and Learning.
283 pages. 2012. ISBN 978-3-0343-1061-1

Vol. 146 Rita Salvi & Hiromasa Tanaka (eds)
Intercultural Interactions in Business and Management.
306 pages. 2011. ISBN 978-3-0343-1039-0

Vol. 147 Francesco Straniero Sergio & Caterina Falbo (eds)
Breaking Ground in Corpus-based Interpreting Studies.
254 pages. 2012. ISBN 978-3-0343-1071-0

Vol. 148 Forthcoming.

Vol. 149 Vijay K. Bhatia & Paola Evangelisti Allori (eds)
Discourse and Identity in the Professions. Legal, Corporate and Institutional Citizenship.
352 pages. 2011. ISBN 978-3-0343-1079-6

Vol. 150 Maurizio Gotti (ed.)
Academic Identity Traits. A Corpus-Based Investigation.
363 pages. 2012. ISBN 978-3-0343-1141-0

Vol. 151 Priscilla Heynderickx, Sylvain Dieltjens, Geert Jacobs, Paul Gillaerts & Elizabeth de Groot (eds)
The Language Factor in International Business.
New Perspectives on Research, Teaching and Practice.
320 pages. 2012. ISBN 978-3-0343-1090-1

Vol. 152 Paul Gillaerts, Elizabeth de Groot, Sylvain Dieltjens, Priscilla Heynderickx & Geert Jacobs (eds)
Researching Discourse in Business Genres. Cases and Corpora.
215 pages. 2012. ISBN 978-3-0343-1092-5

Vol. 153 Yongyan Zheng
Dynamic Vocabulary Development in a Foreign Language.
262 pages. 2012. ISBN 978-3-0343-1106-9

Vol. 154 Carmen Argondizzo (ed.)
Creativity and Innovation in Language Education.
357 pages. 2012. ISBN 978-3-0343-1080-2

Vol. 155 David Hirsh (ed.)
Current Perspectives in Second Language Vocabulary Research.
180 pages. 2012. ISBN 978-3-0343-1108-3

Vol. 156 Seiji Shinkawa
Unhistorical Gender Assignment in Lahamon's *Brut*. A Case Study of a Late Stage in the Development of Grammatical Gender toward its Ultimate Loss.
186 pages. 2012. ISBN 978-3-0343-1124-3

Vol. 157 Yeonkwon Jung
Basics of Organizational Writing: A Critical Reading Approach.
151 pages. 2014. ISBN 978-3-0343-1137-3.

Vol. 158 Bárbara Eizaga Rebollar (ed.)
Studies in Linguistics and Cognition.
301 pages. 2012. ISBN 978-3-0343-1138-0

Vol. 159 Giuliana Garzone, Paola Catenaccio, Chiara Degano (eds)
Genre Change in the Contemporary World. Short-term Diachronic Perspectives.
329 pages. 2012. ISBN 978-3-0343-1214-1

Vol. 160 Carol Berkenkotter, Vijay K. Bhatia & Maurizio Gotti (eds)
Insights into Academic Genres.
468 pages. 2012. ISBN 978-3-0343-1211-0

Vol. 161 Beatriz Tizón-Couto
Clausal Complements in Native and Learner Spoken English. A corpus-based study with Lindsei and Vicolse. 357 pages. 2013. ISBN 978-3-0343-1184-7

Vol. 162 Patrizia Anesa
Jury Trials and the Popularization of Legal Language. A Discourse Analytical Approach.
247 pages. 2012. ISBN 978-3-0343-1231-8

Vol. 163 David Hirsh
Endangered Languages, Knowledge Systems and Belief Systems.
153 pages. 2013. ISBN 978-3-0343-1232-5

Vol. 164 Eugenia Sainz (ed.)
De la estructura de la frase al tejido del discurso. Estudios contrastivos español/italiano.
305 pages. 2014. ISBN 978-3-0343-1253-0

Vol. 165 Julia Bamford, Franca Poppi & Davide Mazzi (eds)
Space, Place and the Discursive Construction of Identity.
367 pages. 2014. ISBN 978-3-0343-1249-3

Vol. 166 Rita Salvi & Janet Bowker (eds)
Space, Time and the Construction of Identity.
Discursive Indexicality in Cultural, Institutional and Professional Fields.
324 pages. 2013. ISBN 978-3-0343-1254-7

Vol. 167 Shunji Yamazaki & Robert Sigley (eds)
Approaching Language Variation through Corpora. A Festschrift in Honour of Toshio Saito.
421 pages. 2013. ISBN 978-3-0343-1264-6

Vol. 168 Franca Poppi
Global Interactions in English as a Lingua Franca. How written communication is changing under the influence of electronic media and new contexts of use.
249 pages. 2012. ISBN 978-3-0343-1276-9

Vol. 169 Miguel A. Aijón Oliva & María José Serrano
Style in syntax. Investigating variation in Spanish pronoun subjects.
239 pages. 2013. ISBN 978-3-0343-1244-8

Vol. 170 Inés Olza, Óscar Loureda & Manuel Casado-Velarde (eds)
Language Use in the Public Sphere. Methodological Perspectives and Empirical Applications
564 pages. 2014. ISBN 978-3-0343-1286-8

Vol. 171 Aleksandra Matulewska
Legilinguistic Translatology. A Parametric Approach to Legal Translation.
279 pages. 2013. ISBN 978-3-0343-1287-5

Vol. 172 Maurizio Gotti & Carmen Sancho Guinda (eds)
Narratives in Academic and Professional Genres.
513 pages. 2013. ISBN 978-3-0343-1371-1

Vol. 173 Madalina Chitez
Learner corpus profiles. The case of Romanian Learner English.
244 pages. 2014. ISBN 978-3-0343-1410-7

Vol. 174 Chihiro Inoue
Task Equivalence in Speaking Tests.
251 pages. 2013. ISBN 978-3-0343-1417-6

Vol. 175 Gabriel Quiroz & Pedro Patiño (eds.)
LSP in Colombia: advances and challenges.
339 pages. 2014. ISBN 978-3-0343-1434-3

Vol. 176 Catherine Resche
Economic Terms and Beyond: Capitalising on the Wealth of Notions.
How Researchers in Specialised Varieties of English Can Benefit from Focusing on Terms.
332 pages. 2013. ISBN 978-3-0343-1435-0

Vol. 177 Forthcoming.

Vol. 178 Cécile Desoutter & Caroline Mellet (dir.)
Le discours rapporté: approches linguistiques et perspectives didactiques.
270 pages. 2013. ISBN 978-3-0343-1292-9

Vol. 179 Ana Díaz-Negrillo & Francisco Javier Díaz-Pérez (eds)
Specialisation and Variation in Language Corpora.
341 pages. 2014. ISBN 978-3-0343-1316-2

Vol. 180 Pilar Alonso
A Multi-dimensional Approach to Discourse Coherence. From Standardness to Creativity.
247 pages. 2014. ISBN 978-3-0343-1325-4

Vol. 181 Alejandro Alcaraz-Sintes & Salvador Valera-Hernández (eds)
Diachrony and Synchrony in English Corpus Linguistics.
393 pages. 2014. ISBN 978-3-0343-1326-1

Vol. 182 Runhan Zhang
Investigating Linguistic Knowledge of a Second Language.
207 pages. 2015. ISBN 978-3-0343-1330-8

Vol. 183 Hajar Abdul Rahim & Shakila Abdul Manan (eds.)
English in Malaysia. Postcolonial and Beyond.
267 pages. 2014. ISBN 978-3-0343-1341-4

Vol. 184 Virginie Fasel Lauzon
Comprendre et apprendre dans l'interaction. Les séquences d'explication en classe de français langue seconde.
292 pages. 2014. ISBN 978-3-0343-1451-0

Vol. 185 Forthcoming.

Vol. 186 Wei Ren
L2 Pragmatic Development in Study Abroad Contexts
256 pages. 2015. ISBN 978-3-0343-1358-2

Vol. 187 Marina Bondi & Rosa Lorés Sanz (eds)
Abstracts in Academic Discourse. Variation and Change.
361 pages. 2014. ISBN 978-3-0343-1483-1

Vol. 188 Giuditta Caliendo
Rethinking Community. Discourse, Identity and Citizenship in the European Union.
240 pages. 2017. ISBN 978-3-0343-1561-6

Vol. 189 Paola Evangelisti Allori (ed.)
Identities in and across Cultures.
315 pages. 2014. ISBN 978-3-0343-1458-9

Vol. 190 Erik Castello, Katherine Ackerley & Francesca Coccetta (eds).
Studies in Learner Corpus Linguistics. Research and Applications for Foreign Language Teaching and Assessment.
358 pages. 2015. ISBN 978-3-0343-1506-7

Vol. 191 Ruth Breeze, Maurizio Gotti & Carmen Sancho Guinda (eds)
Interpersonality in Legal Genres.
389 pages. 2014. ISBN 978-3-0343-1524-1

Vol. 192 Paola Evangelisti Allori, John Bateman & Vijay K. Bhatia (eds)
Evolution in Genre. Emergence, Variation, Multimodality.
364 pages. 2014. ISBN 978-3-0343-1533-3

Vol. 193 Jiyeon Kook
Agency in Arzt-Patient-Gesprächen. Zur interaktionistischen Konzeptualisierung von Agency
271 pages. 2015. ISBN 978-3-0343-1666-8

Vol. 194 Susana Nicolás Román & Juan José Torres Núñez (eds)
Drama and CLIL. A new challenge for the teaching approaches in bilingual education.
170 pages. 2015. ISBN 978-3-0343-1629-3

Vol. 195 Alessandra Molino & Serenella Zanotti (eds)
Observing Norm, Observing Usage. Lexis in Dictionaries and in the Media.
430 pages. 2015. ISBN 978-3-0343-1584-5

Vol. 196 Begoña Soneira
A Lexical Description of English for Architecture. A Corpus-based Approach.
267 pages. 2015. ISBN 978-3-0343-1602-6

Vol. 197 M Luisa Roca-Varela
False Friends in Learner Corpora. A corpus-based study of English false friends in the written and spoken production of Spanish learners.
348 pages. 2015. ISBN 978-3-0343-1620-0

Vol. 198 Rahma Al-Mahrooqi & Christopher Denman
Bridging the Gap between Education and Employment. English Language Instruction in EFL Contexts.
416 pages. 2015. ISBN 978-3-0343-1681-1

Vol. 199 Rita Salvi & Janet Bowker (eds)
The Dissemination of Contemporary Knowledge in English. Genres, discourse strategies and professional practices.
171 pages. 2015. ISBN 978-3-0343-1679-8

Vol. 200 Maurizio Gotti & Davide S. Giannoni (eds)
Corpus Analysis for Descriptive and Pedagogical Purposes. ESP Perspectives.
432 pages. 2014. ISBN 978-3-0343-1516-6

Vol. 201 Ida Ruffolo
The Perception of Nature in Travel Promotion Texts. A Corpus-based Discourse Analysis.
148 pages. 2015. ISBN 978-3-0343-1521-0

Vol. 202 Ives Trevian
English suffixes. Stress-assignment properties, productivity, selection and combinatorial processes.
471 pages. 2015. ISBN 978-3-0343-1576-0

Vol. 203 Maurizio Gotti, Stefania Maci & Michele Sala (eds)
Insights into Medical Communication.
422 pages. 2015. ISBN 978-3-0343-1694-1

Vol. 204 Carmen Argondizzo (ed.)
European Projects in University Language Centres. Creativity, Dynamics, Best Practice.
371 pages. 2015. ISBN 978-3-0343-1696-5

Vol. 205 Aura Luz Duffé Montalván (ed.)
Estudios sobre el léxico. Puntos y contrapuntos.
502 pages. 2016. ISBN 978-3-0343-2011-5

Vol. 206 Maria Pavesi, Maicol Formentelli & Elisa Ghia (eds)
The Languages of Dubbing. Mainstream Audiovisual Translation in Italy.
275 pages. 2014. ISBN 978-3-0343-1646-0

Vol. 207 Ruth Breeze & Inés Olza (eds)
Evaluation in media discourse. European perspectives.
268 pages. 2017. ISBN 978-3-0343-2014-6

Vol. 208 Vijay K. Bhatia & Maurizio Gotti (eds)
Arbitration Discourse in Asia.
331 pages. 2015. ISBN 978-3-0343-2032-0

Vol. 209 Sofía Bemposta-Rivas, Carla Bouzada-Jabois, Yolanda Fernández-Pena, Tamara Bouso, Yolanda J. Calvo-Benzies, Iván Tamaredo (eds)
New trends and methodologies in applied English language research III. Synchronic and diachronic studies on discourse, lexis and grammar processing.
280 pages. 2017. ISBN 978-3-0343-2039-9

Vol. 210 Francisco Alonso Almeida, Laura Cruz García & Víctor González Ruiz (eds)
Corpus-based studies on language varieties.
285 pages. 2016. ISBN 978-3-0343-2044-3

Vol. 211 Juan Pedro Rica Peromingo
Aspectos lingüísticos y técnicos de la traducción audiovisual (TAV).
177 pages. 2016. ISBN 978-3-0343-2055-9

Vol. 212 Maria Vender
Disentangling Dyslexia. VenderPhonological and Processing Deficit in Developmental Dyslexia.
338 pages. 2017. ISBN 978-3-0343-2064-1

Vol. 213 Zhilong Xie
Bilingual Advantages. Contributions of Different Bilingual Experiences to Cognitive Control Differences Among Young-adult Bilinguals.
221 pages. 2016. ISBN 978-3-0343-2081-8

Vol. 214 Larissa D'Angelo
Academic posters. A textual and visual metadiscourse analysis.
367 pages. 2016. ISBN 978-3-0343-2083-2

Vol. 215 Evelyne Berger
Prendre la parole en L2. Regard sur la compétence d'interaction en classe de langue.
246 pages. 2016. ISBN 978-3-0343-2084-9

Vol. 216 David Lasagabaster and Aintzane Doiz (eds)
CLIL experiences in secondary and tertiary education: In search of good practices.
262 pages. 2016. ISBN 978-3-0343-2104-4

Vol. 217 Elena Kkese
Identifying Plosives in L2 English: The Case of L1 Cypriot Greek Speakers.
317 pages. 2016. ISBN 978-3-0343-2060-3

Vol. 218 Sandra Campagna, Elana Ochse, Virginia Pulcini & Martin Solly (eds)
Languaging in and across Communities: New Voices, New Identities. Studies in Honour of Giuseppina Cortese.
507 pages. 2016. ISBN 978-3-0343-2073-3

Vol. 219 Adriana Orlandi & Laura Giacomini (ed.)
Defining collocation for lexicographic purposes. From linguistic theory to lexicographic practice.
328 pages. 2016. ISBN 978-3-0343-2054-2

Vol. 220 Pietro Luigi Iaia
Analysing English as a Lingua Franca in Video Games. Linguistic Features, Experiential and Functional Dimensions of Online and Scripted Interactions.
139 pages. 2016. ISBN 978-3-0343-2138-9

Vol. 221 Dimitrinka G. Níkleva (ed.)
La formación de los docentes de español para inmigrantes en distintos contextos educativos.
390 pages. 2017. ISBN 978-3-0343-2135-8

Vol. 222 Katherine Ackerley, Marta Guarda & Francesca Helm (eds)
Sharing Perspectives on English-Medium Instruction.
308 pages. 2017. ISBN 978-3-0343-2537-0

Vol. 223 Juana I. Marín-Arrese, Julia Lavid-López, Marta Carretero, Elena Domínguez Romero, Mª Victoria Martín de la Rosa & María Pérez Blanco (eds)
Evidentiality and Modality in European Languages. Discourse-pragmatic perspectives.
427 pages. 2017. ISBN 978-3-0343-2437-3

Vol. 224 Gilles Col
Construction du sens : un modèle instructionnel pour la sémantique.
292 pages. 2017. ISBN 978-3-0343-2572-1

Vol. 225 Ana Chiquito & Gabriel Quiroz (eds)
Pobreza, Lenguaje y Medios en América Latina.
362 pages. 2017. ISBN 978-3-0343-2142-6

Vol. 226 Xu Zhang
English Quasi-Numeral Classifiers. A Corpus-Based Cognitive-Typological Study.
360 pages. 2017. ISBN 978-3-0343-2818-0

Vol. 227 María Ángeles Orts, Ruth Breeze & Maurizio Gotti (eds)
Power, Persuasion and Manipulation in Specialised Genres. Providing Keys to the Rhetoric of Professional Communities.
368 pages. 2017. ISBN 978-3-0343-3010-7

Vol. 228 Maurizio Gotti, Stefania Maci & Michele Sala (eds)
Ways of Seeing, Ways of Being: Representing the Voices of Tourism.
453 pages. 2017. ISBN 978-3-0343-3031-2

Vol. 229 Dino Selvaggi
Plurilingual Code-Switching between Standard and Local Varieties.
A Socio-Psycholinguistic Approach
371 pages. 2018. ISBN 978-3-0343-2663-6

Vol. 230 Anca-Cristina Sterie
Interprofessional interactions at the hospital. Nurses' requests and reports of problems in calls with physicians.
371 pages. 2017. ISBN 978-3-0343-2734-3

Vol. 231 Xiaodong Zhang
Understanding Chinese EFL Teachers' Beliefs and Practices in the Textbook-Based Classroom.
189 pages. 2017. ISBN 978-3-0343-3053-4

Vol. 232 Manuela Caterina Moroni & Federica Ricci Garotti (Hrsg.)
Brücken schlagen zwischen Sprachwissenschaft und DaF-Didaktik.
345 pages. 2017. ISBN 978-3-0343-2667-4

Vol. 233 Dimitrinka Georgieva Níkleva
Necesidades y tendencias en la formación del profesorado de español como lengua extranjera
401 pages. 2017. ISBN 978-3-0343-2946-0

Vol. 234 Juan Santana-Lario & Salvador Valera (Hrsg.)
Competing patterns in English affixation.
272 pages. 2017. ISBN 978-3-0343-2701-5

Vol. 235 Francisco Salgado-Robles
Desarrollo de la competencia sociolingüística por aprendices de español en un contexto de inmersión en el extranjero
241 pages. 2018. ISBN 978-3-0343-2323-9

Vol. 236 Maria Chiara Janner
Sguardi linguistici sulla marca. Analisi morfosintattica dei nomi commerciali in italiano
345 pages. 2017. ISBN 978-3-0343-2667-4

Vol. 237 Bárbara Herrero Muñoz-Cobo & Otman El Azami Zalachi
La primavera del árabe marroquí.
192 pages. 2017. ISBN 978-3-0343-3104-3

Vol. 238 Consuelo Pascual Escagedo
El papel del oyente en la construcción de la conversación espontánea de estudiantes italianos en su interlengua y en su lengua materna
295 pages. 2017. ISBN 978-3-0343-3186-9

Vol. 239 Stefania M. Maci
The MS Digby 133 *Mary Magdalene*. Beyond scribal practices: language, discourse, values and attitudes.
336 pages. 2017. ISBN 978-3-0343-3256-9

Vol. 240 Eliecer Crespo-Fernández
Taboo in Discourse. Studies on Attenuation and Offence in Communication.
326 pages. 2018. ISBN 978-3-0343-3018-3

Vol. 241 Jana Altmanova, Maria Centrella, Katherine E. Russo (eds)
Terminology & Discourse / Terminologie et discours.
424 pages. 2018. ISBN 978-3-0343-2417-5

Vol. 242 Xavier Blanco et Inès Sfar (dir.)
Lexicologie(s) : approches croisées en sémantique lexicale.
442 pages. 2018. ISBN 978-3-0343-3056-5

Vol. 243 Yunfeng Ge
Resolution of Conflict of Interest in Chinese Civil Court Hearings. A Perspective of Discourse Information Theory.
302 pages. 2018. ISBN 978-3-0343-3313-9

Vol. 244 Carla Vergaro
Illocutionary Shell Nouns in English
322 pages. 2018. ISBN 978-3-0343-3069-5

Vol. 245 Paolo Frassi
L'adjectif en français et sa définition lexicographique.
270 pages. 2018. ISBN 978-3-0343-3394-8

Vol. 246 Suwilai Premsrirat and David Hirsh (eds)
Language Revitalization. Insights from Thailand
328 pages. 2018. ISBN 978-3-0343-3497-6

Vol. 247 Wei Wang
Researching Learning and Learners in Genre-based Academic Writing Instruction
282 pages. 2018. ISBN 978-3-0343-3297-2

Vol. 248 Isusi Alabarte, Alberto & Lahuerta Martínez, Ana Cristina (eds)
La comprensión lectora de lengua extranjera
Estudio de los factores de familiaridad, interés, género y métodos de evaluación
336 pages. 2018. ISBN 978-3-0343-3493-8

Vol. 249 Mercedes Eurrutia Cavero
Approche didactique du langage techno-scientifique
Terminologie et discours
374 pages. 2018. ISBN 978-3-0343-3512-6

Vol. 250 Aurora Ruiz Mezcua (ed.)
Approaches to Telephone Interpretation
Research, Innovation, Teaching and Transference
268 pages. 2018. ISBN 978-3-0343-3330-6

Vol. 251 Morini Massimiliano
A Day in the News
A Stylistic Analysis of Newsspeak
188 pages. 2018. ISBN 978-3-0343-3507-2

Vol. 252 Ignacio Guillén-Galve & Ignacio Vázquez-Orta (eds.)
English as a Lingua Franca and Intercultural Communication
Implications and Applications in the Field of English Language Teaching
414 pages. 2018. ISBN 978-3-0343-2763-3

Vol. 253 Bianca Del Villano
Using the Devil with Courtesy
Shakespeare and the Language of (Im)Politeness
216 pages. 2018. ISBN 978-3-0343-2315-4

Vol. 254 David Hirsh (ed.)
Explorations in Second Language Vocabulary Research
252 pages. 2018. ISBN 978-3-0343-2940-8

Vol. 255 Tania Baumann (ed.)
Reiseführer - Sprach- und Kulturmittlung im Tourismus / Le guide turistiche - mediazione linguistica e culturale in ambito turistico
270 pages. 2018. ISBN 978-3-0343-3402-0

Vol. 256 Ariadna Sánchez-Hernández & Ana Herraiz-Martínez (eds)
Learning second language pragmatics beyond traditional contexts
376 pages. 2018. ISBN 978-3-0343-3437-2

Vol. 257 Albert Bastardas-Boada, Emili Boix-Fuster, Rosa Maria Torrens (eds)
Family Multilingualism in Medium-Sized Linguistic Communities
336 pages. 2019. ISBN 978-3-0343-2536-3

Vol. 258 Forthcoming

Vol. 259 Catia Nannoni
Participe présent et gérondif dans la presse française contemporaine
176 pages. 2019. ISBN 978-3-0343-3631-4

Vol. 260 Nieves Rodríguez Pérez & Bárbara Heinsch (eds.)
Contextos multilingües. Mediadores interculturales, formación del profesorado de lenguas extranjeras
289 pages. 2019. ISBN 978-3-0343-3768-7

Vol. 261 Forthcoming

Vol. 262 Laura Nadal
Lingüística experimental y contraargumentación
233 pages. 2019. ISBN 978-3-0343-3791-5

Vol. 263 Claudia Claridge & Merja Kytö (eds.)
Punctuation in Context – Past and Present Perspectives
288 pages. 2019. ISBN 978-3-0343-3790-8

Vol. 264 Maurizio Gotti, Stefania Maci, Michele Sala (eds.)
Scholarly Pathways
530 pages. 2020. ISBN 978-3-0343-3860-8

Vol. 265 Ruth Breeze, Ana M. Fernández Vallejo (eds.)
Politics and populism across modes and media
350 pages. 2020. ISBN 978-3-0343-3707-6

Vol. 266 Jean Marguerite Jimenez
Understanding the Effects of Immediate Electronic Corrective Feedback on Second Language Development
252 pages. 2020. ISBN 978-3-0343-3815-8

Vol. 267 Sergio Rodríguez-Tapia, Adela González-Fernández (eds)
Lenguas y turismo: estudios en torno al discurso, la didáctica y la divulgación
380 pages. 2020. ISBN 978-3-0343-3881-3

Vol. 268 Ana Bocanegra-Valle (ed.)
Applied Linguistics and Knowledge Transfer. Employability, Internationalisation and Social Challenges
344 pages. 2020. ISBN 978-3-0343-3714-4

www.ingramcontent.com/pod-product-compliance
Ingram Content Group UK Ltd.
Pitfield, Milton Keynes, MK11 3LW, UK
UKHW021836100926
8556IPUK00004B/371

9 783034 337144